Understanding Sustainability

Richard Adrian Reese

Also by Richard Adrian Reese:

What Is Sustainable

Sustainable or Bust

Printed by CreateSpace
Charleston, South Carolina
ISBN-13: 978-1530284870
ISBN-10: 1530284872

http://wildancestors.blogspot.com

Cover photo title: "A smoky day at the Sugar Bowl — Hupa"
Photograph by Edward S. Curtis, 1923.
Library of Congress
Prints and Photographs Division
Washington, D.C.
Reproduction Number: LC-USZ62-47020

Table of Contents

Introduction

Welcome to *Understanding Sustainability!* On the following pages you will find reviews of books that explore many facets of ecological sustainability, an extremely important subject that is poorly understood in our society. You will meet authors with gifts for thinking outside the box, writers who tell fascinating stories. It's sad to wreck the ecosystem for no good reason — or any reason at all. It's especially sad that those on the frontlines of the great demolition are among the world's "best-educated" people. We can do better.

In its original meaning, a sustainable way of life is one that can continue for millennia without causing permanent degradation to the ecosystem. All animals have succeeded at living in this manner, and they have done so for millions of years. They can satisfy their essential needs (food and shelter) without damaging the community of life, a vital skill.

But one species has spawned several billion smarty-pants renegades who have stumbled far from the path of balance, violating the laws of nature. This outlaw society is zooming into deep trouble, and it barely understands why. If we understood why, there is a fair chance that we would behave in a manner that was less destructive, less insane. There is a better chance that we would abandon myths that hobble our ability to think clearly and live responsibly.

Outlaw society is heavily addicted to extracting nonrenewable resources, like coal, oil, gas, metals, phosphates, potash, and on and on. The reserves of these resources are diminishing every day, while the cost of extracting them increases. Obviously, this approach can only operate temporarily. It has an expiration date, a point at which the goodies are depleted, the bubble bursts, and the machine shuts down. No other animals suffer from addiction to nonrenewable resources, because they continue to live in their traditional manner. They did not get lost.

Outlaw society is also heavily addicted to depleting renewable resources at rates faster than nature can replenish them. We're exterminating forests, mass murdering fish, destroying topsoil, draining aquifers, and pumping rivers dry. This is also a dead end. Other animals don't mutilate the ecosystem.

Outlaw society generates many wastes and emissions at levels far beyond the ecosystem's ability to harmlessly absorb them, and this is causing serious irreparable damage — melting icecaps, acidic seawater, coastal dead zones. No wild animal has basic needs that require high impact amusements like automobiles, computers, or electricity — these are "wants" not "needs," and we don't need wants. Needs are basic and simple, wants include everything money can buy. Living to hoard wants and appear prosperous is a bad path.

Most of humankind is in overshoot, because our population and way of life far exceeds the long-term carrying capacity of Earth's ecosystem. Every day, the planet's carrying capacity shrinks, as resources are further depleted, and the ongoing ecological wreckage accumulates. This worsens the overshoot. Nature has a low tolerance for overshoot, and outlaw society is too lost to comprehend why it's circling the drain. Luckily, there are effective cures for ignorance, and they are most often found outside the walls of the outlaw culture.

In the following pages, you will not find The Solution. Only problems have solutions — sleepiness is a problem that can be solved by taking a nap. Predicaments, on the other hand, cannot be effectively eliminated by solutions. There are no rituals, medicines, or gizmos for undoing climate change, or inspiring educators to abandon their diabolical obsession with perpetual growth. We are way over our heads in predicaments.

Every civilization collapses, and ours will too, one way or another, suddenly or gradually. This is perfectly normal. Industrial civilization was designed to grow like crazy, flame out, and collapse. And we were thoroughly trained to devote our lives to it, so don't be embarrassed. The consumer way of life has been a surreal adventure in soul-killing foolishness. The squirrels in the tree outside my window are so much healthier and happier. They live in the here and now, satisfying their needs, playing with great enthusiasm, celebrating the perfection of creation, like our ancestors did.

Now, if these yucky ideas make you twitch and squirm, there is an effective distraction — magical thinking! The well-educated wizards of outlaw society have a thrilling answer for everything — sustainable growth, sustainable fish mining, sustainable soil mining, sustainable forest mining, and on and on. I call this ersatz sustainability, a murky

2

elixir of snake oil loaded with mind-numbing intoxicants. We see and hear the word sustainable many times each day, and this is what it usually refers to. Sustainability can be anything we want it to be! If we call something "sustainable" enough times, then it is! Whee!

The devious wizards are giddy with joy, because humankind has finally completed the long and difficult journey to Utopia. This is it! We are the luckiest generation of all! Wild predators no longer devour our friends and relatives. Pandemic disease and world wars are ancient history. More and more babies survive to maturity and reproduce. Natural selection no longer weeds out the weaklings and mutants, because science has rendered evolution obsolete. We're working hard on a cure for death.

A growing population is wonderful, because it allows more and more to enjoy the Utopian delights. Feeding ten billion will be no problem, thanks to science and technology. Eliminating climate change will be a piece of cake. The transition from fossil energy to renewable energy will be smooth and painless. Ingenious innovation will make all the bad stuff go away, and we'll all be able to continue enjoying a wondrous high tech lifestyle without any major sacrifices. Electric cars, green energy, and all the latest gadgets can now be made from sustainable fairy dust and good vibes. Utopia is awesome!

The Sustainable Development cult has billions of radicalized believers. Its holy mission is to keep industrial civilization on life support for as long as possible, at any cost, and leave the bills for the kids. It's about enduring jobs you don't like, to buy stuff you don't need, to impress people you don't respect. It's about living as if we are the last generation, without a thought for those who come after us.

Nobody reading these pages in the twenty-first century will experience humankind's return to genuine sustainability. Healing will take centuries, and success is not guaranteed. Luck is fickle. Our closest living relatives, chimps and bonobos, share about 99 percent of our genes. Their ancestors have lived in the same place for two million years without trashing it. They did not get lost.

Humans strayed onto a very different path, and the way that most of us now live is the opposite of sustainable. Yet every day we are bombarded by grand proclamations of ersatz sustainability, thundering geysers of bull excrement. My mission here is to provide intelligent pilgrims with tools that increase their ability to recognize the difference between ecological sustainability and ersatz sustainability — before the lights go out.

It is deeply troubling to contemplate the staggering implications of ecological sustainability, because they blow the fundamental illusions of our culture to smithereens. Where we belong is so far from where we are, and widespread ignorance is not our friend. Well-fed minds and clear thinking are vital.

The reviews in *Understanding Sustainability* will introduce you to dozens of books that might be of interest. Reviews provide only a limited overview of the contents, as I interpret them. They are never a substitute for reading the full work. Authors that intrigue you may have written other books or essays. They may be the stars of online videos. I do not agree with every idea in every book reviewed here. Authors frequently present information that is controversial. Critical thinking is essential for any adventure in learning. Do your best.

Understanding Sustainability is a companion to my previous book, *Sustainable or Bust*, another collection of book reviews. Both supplement my first book, *What is Sustainable*, an introduction to environmental history and good old fashioned fundamentalist sustainability. If you like one, you'll like them all.

Enjoy!

Locust

Early white settlers on the high plains of the western U.S. were always bummed out when colossal swarms of locusts dropped by for lunch. The sky would darken, and the land would be filled with the roaring buzz of millions of fluttering wings. Within an hour or so, everything was covered with them, including the settlers, who frantically tried to brush off the hundreds of hungry insects that were chewing apart their clothing.

They were Rocky Mountain locusts, a North American species that lived west of the Mississippi — and the stars of Jeffrey Lockwood's book, *Locust*. When swarming, these insects were a horror show. A swarm could devour 50 tons of greenery in a day. Trains couldn't move because the tracks were too greasy. Swarms were like tornadoes, wiping out one area while leaving other neighbors in the region untouched.

In June of 1875, folks in Nebraska observed a swarm that was 1,800 miles long (2,900 km), 110 miles wide (177 km), and between a quarter and a half mile deep (0.4 to 0.8 km). It devoured 198,000 square miles (512,000 km^2), an area almost as large as Colorado and Wyoming. The swarm took five days to pass. Lockwood estimated that it might have been 10 billion locusts — possibly the biggest assemblage of animals ever experienced by human beings.

Normally, maybe 80 percent of the time, locusts stayed in their home base, in the river valleys of the northern Rockies, a habitat that may have consisted of a mere 2,000 acres (809 ha). They ate, reproduced, and enjoyed life.

Periodic droughts would reduce the available food supply, causing locusts to crowd into pockets of surviving greenery. Dry weather eliminated the population control provided by fungal diseases. Drought also concentrated the nutritional value of vegetation. Warmer temperatures meant that locusts grew to maturity more quickly, so they spent less time in the nymph stage, when predators took a heavy toll on the helpless youngsters. The swarming process was triggered by crowding. They could either starve or see the world.

A hungry swarm of two million American settlers moved into the high plains in the 1870s, and ravaged the short grass prairie with cows and plows. They planted lots of wheat, and then discovered that locusts preferred wheat to everything else on the menu.

The settlers exterminated the bison that were perfectly adapted to the ecosystem, and brought in cattle that were unsuited for the arid climate, did not fancy the native vegetation, and died like flies during frigid winters. They exterminated the wolves, and other wild predators, because they enjoyed owning and exploiting dimwitted domesticated herbivores.

Settlers attempted to import their Western European way of life to an ecosystem where it could not possibly thrive. Instead of trying to adapt to the ecosystem, they expected the ecosystem to adapt to their exotic fantasies — a traditional recipe for failure. In their dream world, locusts were pests, wolves were pests, bison were pests — death to all pests!

The Indians perceived locusts, wolves, and bison as being sacred relatives, not pests. The Indians enjoyed a time-proven culture that was well adapted to the ecosystem. Can you guess who the Indians considered to be pests?

Long ago, in the wilderness of Judea, there was a holy roller named John. One day, he baptized a lad called Jesus. The heavens opened up, a spirit appeared, and led Jesus away to the wilderness for a life changing 40 day vision quest. The Baptist had a wild diet: "And the same John had his raiment of camel's hair, and a leathern girdle about his loins; and his meat was locusts and wild honey." (Matthew 3:4)

To the Indians, locusts were a sacred source of nutritious food. Their tasty flesh was rich with calories and 60 percent protein. In the aftermath of a swarm, in just an hour, they could forage 200 pounds (90 kg) of dried insects, storing away 273,000 calories. It was faster, easier, and safer than hunting large, strong, speedy herbivores with sharp horns that took great pleasure in trampling and disemboweling hunters.

At the Great Salt Lake, Mormons discovered that locusts couldn't swim. Millions would drown, and then the winds would push their bodies to the shore, in piles six feet high (1.8 m) and two miles long (3.2 km). As the corpses rotted, memorable fragrances wafted on the air. While a tremendous source of excellent food rotted away, the settlers complained about the stink.

White settlers loathed the locusts. Comically, every effort made to exterminate the swarms failed — flooding, rollers, dynamite, trawlers, poisons, flamethrowers. During the swarming phase, resistance was futile, the insects were impossible to control.

Eventually, entomologists were summoned to combat the insects with science. Several chapters shine spotlights on famous entomologists who strove to understand locusts, and render them harmless to the devastating swarms of white settlers.

As more settlers moved into the high plains, the locust numbers declined. There were fewer swarms. Attention shifted to other challenges. Eventually, entomologists realized that nobody had seen a locust in a long time. The last Rocky Mountain locust died in Manitoba in 1902. They went extinct, but folks didn't notice for quite a while. It was unimaginable that critters that existed in such enormous numbers could completely disappear within a few decades.

A number of half-baked theories attempted to explain the spooky extinction, but Lockwood was the one who finally solved the mystery. He visited several "grasshopper glaciers" where layers of dead locusts could be observed, and found locusts that died 800 years ago. Swarming was not caused by settlers.

One day, he had an insight. Monarch butterflies are vulnerable to extinction because the forests where they spend the winter are being eliminated, and this is a bottleneck. The bottleneck for the locusts was their home base along northern river valleys — arable lands, exactly where whites preferred to settle. Irrigation, tilling, and cattle grazing hammered the locusts where they were most vulnerable, home sweet home.

Entomologists around the world work tirelessly to discover new methods for exterminating agricultural pest species, and the insects always succeed in outwitting the wizards. The Rocky Mountain locust is the one and only major insect pest to be completely wiped out, and they were driven to extinction unintentionally.

They were "pests" only in the eyes of the civilized. Prior to white settlement, there were no plowmen, ranchers, pests, or entomologists, just a wild ecosystem living in its traditional manner. Maybe entomologists should help us exorcize the pests in our nightmare worldview, teach us how to live in balance, and call an end to the futile poisonous war on our insect relatives.

Lockwood mused that crowding also inspires bizarre behavior in humans. We have powerful urges to escape from the neurotic mob, and fly away to places of refuge, to pure unspoiled suburban utopias.

He noted that while locust populations sometimes soared to enormous peaks, vast numbers did not guarantee long-term survival. He noted that the human population is currently at an enormous peak. Both humans and locusts are generalists that can migrate and adapt. Locusts dined on at least 50 varieties of plants. Humans, on the other hand, largely depend on three plants: rice, wheat, and corn. Will climate change be our bottleneck?

Make Prayers to the Raven

In 1976 and 1977, anthropologist Richard Nelson lived with the Koyukon people of northwestern Alaska. Their vast forested homeland is in the region where the Koyukuk River feeds into the Yukon River. They are Athapaskan people, and they live inland from the Inupiaq Eskimos, who inhabit the coastal region to the west.

When Russian explorers found the Koyukon in 1838, they already had tobacco, iron pots, and other stuff, acquired via trade with Eskimos. They had already been hammered by smallpox. In 1898, they experienced a sudden infestation of gold prospectors; luckily, their streams were gold-free. Unluckily, the gold rush ended their isolation from white society. Swarms of missionaries and educators buzzed around the forest, determined to help the ignorant heathens rise out of barbarism, and discover the wonders of civilization, sin, and eternal damnation.

When Nelson arrived in 1976, they were no longer nomadic. About 2,000 Koyukon lived in eleven villages. They travelled by snowmobile, hunted with rifles, and worshipped a Jewish guru. Most of those under 30 spoke only English, and some were not fond of anthropologists. Nelson spent a lot of time with the elders, who had been raised in the old ways. Then he wrote an important book, *Make Prayers to the Raven.* (In their stories, the creator was Raven.)

The Koyukon were the opposite of vegans. About 90 percent of their diet was animal foods. The bears, moose, geese, and salmon they ate came from the surrounding area, and were killed, butchered, and cooked by close friends and family. Their survival depended on the wildlife. They were extremely careful to take only what they needed, and to waste nothing.

Their wilderness was the opposite of big box grocery outlets that have an endless supply of fizzy sugar drinks, frozen pizza, and corn chips. A year of abundant salmon might be followed by a meager year. During Nelson's visit, there were plenty moose and caribou, animals that had been scarce 30 years earlier. The Koyukon had to pay close attention to the land, and continually fine-tune their relationship to it. When times were lean, people starved — prior to the adaptation of rifles. Now, they also had dependable access to the mysterious industrial substances that white folks referred to as "food."

8

Traditional Koyukon society needed nothing from the outside world. Their relationship to the ecosystem was one of absolute reverence and respect. They were not masters or managers, they were simply members of the family of life. The humble status of humans is evident in a frequently quoted phrase: "Every animal knows way more than you do."

Nelson said it like this: "Traditional Koyukon people live in a world that watches, in a forest of eyes. A person moving through nature — however wild, remote, even desolate the place may be — is never truly alone. The surroundings are aware, sensate, personified. They feel. They can be offended. And they must, at every moment, be treated with proper respect. All things in nature have a special kind of life, something unknown to contemporary Euro-Americans, something powerful."

The Koyukon were not exotic freaks. Their worldview and spirituality had much in common with all other cultures that thrived in the long era before the domestication fad. They were perfectly wild and free — healthy, happy, intelligent, normal human beings. Most modern people go to their graves without ever experiencing the magnificent beauty and power of the living world, the joy and wonder of the gift of life, the awe of being fully present in a sacred reality. Most of them live and die in monotonous manmade habitats, having established no spiritual connection to life.

Nelson was born in Madison, Wisconsin. His father was employed by the state. Their middle class life provided food, clothing, and shelter. A large portion of his childhood was spent in institutions of education — indoors — digesting, memorizing, and regurgitating words and numbers. At that time, Madison was a disaster of concrete, traffic, and hordes of strangers. Decades earlier, the forest and wildlife had been devoured by the metastasizing city. So, as a young animal, Nelson was raised in devastating poverty, like most modern kids, isolated from wildness and freedom.

Anyway, something cool happened. In 1973, Nelson hooked up with the University of Alaska and began spending time with Native Americans. He arrived with his Euro-American cultural programming, and its wacky anthropocentric model of the natural world. He had zero doubt that his perception of reality was correct and proper; it was absolute truth.

Then, he hung out with the Koyukon, and this blew his belief system completely out of the water. They were intelligent people, and they saw the world in a very different way. This made his Ph.D. mind whirl and spin. "My Koyukon teachers had learned through their own traditions about dimensions in nature that I, as a Euro-American, had either not learned to perceive or had been explicitly taught do not exist."

In less than 200 years, the white wizards of Wisconsin have transformed a healthy wilderness into a hideous nightmare called Madison. It never occurred to them to adapt to the ecosystem, live with great respect and mindfulness, and preserve its health for future generations. The Koyukon, on the other hand, have inhabited their forest for thousands of years, and it doesn't look much different from how they found it. They know every place in their forest as well as you know your kitchen. Every location is rich with stories and spirits.

The Egyptians erected huge pyramids, enduring monuments to their civilized megalomania, built by legions of miserable slaves. The Koyukon have achieved something far more impressive. "This legacy is the vast land itself, enduring and essentially unchanged despite having supported human life for countless centuries."

Nelson's book is a reflection of their culture. He provided separate chapters to describe the physical realm and climate, insects and amphibians, fishes, birds, small mammals, predators, and large animals. Eighteen pages are devoted to their relationship with bears, and birds get 43 pages. The core of their culture is their relationships with the non-human relatives that share their land, and the need to nurture these relationships with absolute respect. Nature always punishes acts of disrespect with bad luck, illness, or death — to the offender, or to a family member.

The good news here is that it's not impossible for a highly educated adult to override their cultural programming and experience the beauty and power of creation. Most never do. The important message of this book is that we are absolutely lost, but there are paths that are not lost, healthy paths. Our cage is not locked, and it's so much nicer outside. It's alive!

The Mortal Sea

Until the twentieth century, it was commonly believed that the oceans — filled with vast quantities of fish — were immortal. It was impossible for mere humans to ever make a dent in the sea's enormous bounty. Similarly, iron miners once believed that the huge Lake Superior lodes could be mined for eternity. They believed that the white pines of the region were so numerous that it would be impossible to cut them all down. Incredible fantasies are common among folks who are blissfully ignorant of environmental history, and don't understand the reality of fish mining, mineral mining, forest mining, soil mining.

A society unaware of environmental history is like an elder lost in an Alzheimer's fog. He doesn't recognize his wife or children, and has no memory of who he is, where he is, or what he's done. Environmental history turns on floodlights, sharply illuminating the path of our journey, making the boo-boos stand out like sore thumbs. It's more than a little embarrassing, but if we can see the pitfalls, we're less likely to plunge into them. In theory, we're capable of learning from our mistakes.

Jeffrey Bolster is a history professor who once loved to fish. He realized that the Hall of History desperately needed more illumination on humankind's abusive relationship with the oceans, because it was a tragicomedy of endlessly repeated self-defeating mistakes. He wrote *The Mortal Sea*, which focused on the rape of the North Atlantic — and he quit fishing.

In prehistoric Western Europe, many folks congregated along the water's edge. They harvested shellfish from the sea, but most of their fish came from rivers and estuaries. Following the transition to agriculture and metal tools, their population grew and grew. Forests were cut, fields were plowed, and streams were loaded with eroded soil, livestock wastes, human sewage, and industrial discharges. Hungry mobs got too good at catching too many fish with too many traps. England passed the Salmon Preservation Act in 1285, but it was little enforced and generally ignored.

Meanwhile, Viking innovations resulted in boat designs that were excellent for travelling the open seas. They made it possible to aggressively pursue saltwater seafood, which was incredibly abundant. Vikings learned to air-dry cod, which could be stored for years, and provide sustenance for long voyages of walrus hunting, auk killing, raping, and pillaging. Before long, all coastal communities started building seaworthy boats, and hauling in the cod, mackerel, herring, and so on. The human population grew, and marine life diminished.

In the sixteenth century, when Europeans explored the American shoreline, they were astonished by the abundance of sea life. They observed hundreds of thousands of walruses, which could grow up to 2,600 pounds (1,180 kg), critters that were nearly extinct at home. In those days, the oil industry was based on whales, walruses, and seals.

Halibut could grow to 700 pounds (317 kg). There were sturgeons more than 600 pounds (272 kg), and cod five feet long (1.5 m). One lad caught 250 cod in an hour, with just four hooks. They killed seabirds like there was no tomorrow, often using them for fish bait. Lobsters were huge and plentiful, but their flesh spoiled quickly, so they were fed to hogs, used for bait, and spread on fields for fertilizer.

Maine and northward was home to the Mi'kmaqs and Malecites, who got 90 percent of their calories from sea life. Their population was not supersized by agriculture. They had no metal tools or high tech boats, nor a spirituality in which humans were the masters of the universe. For some reason, they had failed to destroy their ecosystem. Then, they were discovered, and the whites went crazy with astonishing greed. "By 1800 the northwest Atlantic was beginning to resemble European seas." Where's the fish?

Between America and Europe, the boreal North Atlantic had been among the world's most productive fishing grounds. The bulk of the book discusses how clever white folks skillfully transformed unimaginable abundance into an aquatic disaster area. In the waters off Maine, Peak Cod occurred around the Civil War (1861–1865), long before industrial-scale fish mining. By 1875, writers were speculating about the extinction of menhaden, lobster, halibut, eider, shad, salmon, mackerel, and cod.

The fish mining industry was driven by a desperate arms race. Hand-line fishing had been the norm since the Middle Ages. Each fisherman set four to twenty-eight baited hooks. Then, geniuses invented long-line fishing, which used 4,000 hooks. More fish were caught, and more money was made. By 1870, some fishers were setting 63 miles of lines with 96,000 baited hooks.

By 1880, geniuses were delighted to discover that gill nets could triple the haul — and they eliminated the need for bait, which was getting scarce and expensive. For mackerel mining, the new purse seines were fabulous. They used nets to surround an entire school of fish, and could land 150,000 per day. In 1905 came steam-powered otter trawls — huge nets dragged across the sea floor that caught everything. Only 45 percent of the fish landed were kept. Unmarketable fish were tossed back dead, including juveniles of marketable species. Obviously, these millions of dead juveniles did not grow into mature fish, reproduce, and maintain the viability of the species.

Throughout the long gang rape of the North Atlantic, there were always voices urging caution and conservation, but they never ran the show. As more and more capital poured into fish mining enterprises, resistance to regulation increased. The one and only objective for fat cats was maximizing short-term profits. Government bureaucrats who monitored the industry experimented with many interesting programs for increasing fish stocks — everything except for reducing fishing pressure.

New technology expanded the market for seafood. Salting and drying were replaced by keeping fish on ice, and shipping them to market by rail. Later, canneries created even bigger demand for fish. The first floating fish factory was launched in 1954, and was followed by many more. These boats had assembly lines for gutting, cleaning, and filleting the fish. The fillets were quick frozen, for indefinite storage. Waste was turned to fishmeal, another source of profit.

In 1992, the cod landings in Canada vanished, and the fishery was closed. The U.S. closed fishing on Georges Bank and the Gulf of Maine. "The impossible had occurred. People had killed most of the fish in the ocean." Folks had been overfishing since Viking days, but industrial fishing put the process into overdrive. The cod show no signs of recovery.

Bolster concluded that the way to avoid unsustainable harvests was to adopt the precautionary approach, which meant always selecting the least destructive option. This would be an excellent idea in a world ruled by pure reason. History reminds us that any enterprise that generates wealth and status tends to turn people into destructive maniacs.

Today, the fish mining industry is working hard to terminate itself — before oceanic acidification beats it.

One more thing before I go. Some folks have dreams of replacing today's maritime fleet with zero emission sailing ships, but they don't remember the downside. Bolster warns us, "Fishing made coal mining look safe. No other occupation in America came close to the deep-sea fisheries for workplace mortality." In just Gloucester, from 1866 to 1890, more than 380 schooners and 2,450 men were lost at sea. When powerful squalls race in, sailboats are hard to control, and very dangerous.

Sailing ships could also replace the motorized ships now used for hauling trade goods across seas. Imagine the mountains of raw materials needed to build hundreds of thousands of new ships. Never forget that long distance trade has a long history of unintended catastrophes, like the spread of bubonic plague, cholera, malaria, influenza, measles, smallpox, rinderpest, potato blight, chestnut blight, and on and on. It isn't necessary for a sustainable future.

Renewable Energy Cannot Sustain a Consumer Society

We live in a fantasy world. We have blind faith that we'll be able to sustainably feed nine or ten billion people in 2050, a wish-based belief. We have blind faith that technology will vaporize all challenges that appear in our path over the coming centuries. Economic growth will continue forever. We'll celebrate a glorious victory over climate change by switching to safe, clean renewable energy, in a smooth and painless manner. Our high standard of living will keep getting better and better as we zoom toward utopia. The best is yet to come!

Australian professor Ted Trainer is not entranced by blind faith, and he explained his heresy in *Renewable Energy Cannot Sustain a Consumer Society*. Attempting to transition to a future powered only by renewable energy, while maintaining our current mode of high waste living, would be the opposite of smooth and painless. Indeed, it's impossible, he says. Renewables simply can't produce as much energy as we currently get from burning enormous amounts of sequestered carbon (fossil fuel).

In modern societies, electric power is highly reliable for both households and industries. Power companies generate electricity, feed it into their distribution grid, and send it to consumers. Excess electricity cannot be easily stored, and insufficient electricity leads to brownouts. So, utilities must be very careful to generate electricity at levels that closely match the swings in demand. Today's centralized power systems are designed to do a good job of this, but they are not designed to reliably distribute electricity generated by decentralized sources, like wind farms or solar facilities.

Coal-powered plants can run at full capacity all the time, and they can be built anywhere. Solar and wind facilities can run at full capacity only during ideal conditions. For example, a solar thermal plant can run at peak on a hot summer day, but its average annual production is just 25 percent of peak. The capacity of solar and wind facilities is highly dependent on location. They cannot be built anywhere, and the ideal locations are chosen first. The potential for future expansion is limited.

Photovoltaic panels convert sunlight directly into electricity. They produce little or no energy at dawn, dusk, night, or during cloudy periods. For large-scale generation, solar thermal is better, because it generates heat, which can be stored for use during off-peak periods. Ideal locations for solar thermal are deserts, like the Sahara, or the U.S. southwest. The drawback is that ideal locations are typically distant from population centers, and significant energy is lost when power is sent thousands of kilometers away. Even in ideal locations, output during summer is five times higher than winter.

Wind power is even less consistent. Wind velocity varies from year to year, from season to season, and from minute to minute. For 54 days in 2002, a wind farm in Denmark had zero production. A farm in Australia was nearly windless for five straight days. Winds can suddenly go calm over a wide region. Ideal locations are on hills and ridges.

This hard-to-predict variability is a serious obstacle to a renewable energy future. Neither wind nor solar can produce electricity sufficient to meet current demand, in a dependable manner. To provide dependable power, backup capacity is needed. One mode of backup is to use the surplus power, generated during peak hours, to pump water uphill into reservoirs, where it can later be used to generate hydroelectric power. For most regions, this is not an option.

Surplus electricity can also be used to generate hydrogen, which can be stored for later use. Storing energy in hydrogen is highly inefficient, expensive, and problematic. Putting one unit of hydrogen energy into a fuel cell requires at least four units of wind or solar energy. Hydrogen atoms are tiny, which makes them especially prone to leakage. A big tanker truck can only carry 288 kilograms (634 pounds) of hydrogen. Hydrogen does not make economic sense.

Backup electricity can also be generated by burning sequestered carbon, but this would result in undesirable greenhouse gas emissions. In a renewable energy future, for each megawatt of wind or solar capacity, systems would also need almost a megawatt of backup. The backup systems would be expensive, and they would be idle much of the time. They cannot be quickly cranked up to respond to demand surges, or to supply shortfalls due to clouds or calms.

A number of well-paid respectable-looking experts are preaching that the cure for climate change is nuclear energy. But 80 percent of the energy used today is not electricity. Trainer concluded, "If all electricity was generated by nuclear reactors, carbon dioxide emissions might be reduced by thirty percent." Uranium is nonrenewable, the supply is finite, and the top quality ores are gone. All facets of the nuclear industry are designed and operated by accident-prone tropical primates. Meanwhile, spent fuel remains intensely toxic for more than a million years, and we have yet to discover how to safely store it. A more mature option would be to focus intense attention on how we live and think.

The variability of wind and solar production is a huge challenge to a renewable energy future. A far greater challenge — the death blow — is the issue of liquid fuels. Liquid fuels are used to power cars, trucks, trains, planes, ships, wars, and our food system. Under perfect conditions, renewable energy might be able to generate ten percent of the energy currently produced by petroleum. Options include ethanol, methanol, and hydrogen fuel cells. Trainer discusses the serious drawbacks for each.

Clearly, a smooth and painless transition to a renewable energy future that allows us to continue living like crazy is an intoxicating fantasy. In addition to being impossible, it's also unsustainable. The "clean," high-tech wonderland will continue extracting nonrenewable resources for wind turbines, solar panels, transmission lines, roads, tractors, fuel cells, air conditioners, cell phones, and so on. It will do nothing to wean us from soil mining, water mining, forest mining, and fish mining — or shift population growth into reverse.

The consumer way of life is a dead end path. While reading, I kept thinking about my four grandparents, all of whom were born into non-electric, car-free households. They lived good lives. Food is a genuine need, but unsustainable energy is a devastating addiction — lots of fun at first, but deadly in the long run.

Trainer thought along the same lines. The big problem is that the dominant culture programs us to be competitive, acquisitive, individualists. He presented a dreamy vision called *The Simpler Way*, a joyful utopia of voluntary frugality, stress-free lifestyles, lovely gardens, and small cooperative communities — and we don't even have to give up modern technology! Really?

Instead of struggling to continue living like crazy, for as long as possible, by any means necessary, the intelligent option would be to slow down — to really slow down! That's the message here.

In 2012, Trainer wrote an updated 22-page summary of his analysis of renewable energy, *Can Renewable Energy Sustain Consumer Societies*. In 2011, he helped write a 48-page description of his vision for a happy green future, *The Simpler Way Report*. They are available online.

Too Hot to Touch

Modern society provides a long menu of predicaments to inspire our nightmares. For a number of years, climate change has been hogging the spotlight. It's time to have more nightmares about radiation. Folks think that if we simply quit building new reactors, the nuclear boo-boo will go away, and we can forget about it — wrong! William and Rosemarie Alley have shed much light on the subject with their book, *Too Hot to Touch*. It reveals a deeply embarrassing chapter that has been omitted from the glorious epic of technology and progress.

Nuclear weapons were invented during World War II. Nagasaki and Hiroshima were turned into ashtrays, but the enormous unintended consequences of half-baked genius have dwarfed the destruction of two cities. We continue to create stuff that will remain extremely toxic for millions of years, and none of it is stored in secure permanent facilities, where it will cause no harm.

The war was followed by an arms race. A hundred new bombs were detonated at the Nevada Test Range between 1951 and 1962. Nuke tests became a tourist attraction. Families sat in folding chairs at open-air spectator sites to see the amazing mushroom clouds. A few minutes after the blast, they were sprinkled with fine dust. Several decades later, thyroid cancer became very popular in the region.

Lunatics became giddy with nuclear mania. Some wanted to blast a new canal across Panama. Others dreamed of a coast-to-coast waterway across the U.S. Others wanted to nuke Gibraltar, and turn the Mediterranean into a freshwater sea. In the Soviet Union, 120 bombs were used for earthmoving projects.

In 1954, construction began on the first U.S. nuclear power reactor at Shippingport, Pennsylvania. At that time, nuclear waste was not seen to be especially dangerous. Robert Oppenheimer, at the Atomic Energy Commission, referred to the issue of radioactive waste as "unimportant." Experts were possessed by a stupefying blind faith in scientific magic — there was a brilliant solution for everything!

They contemplated a variety of schemes for making high-level waste disappear. Some recommended shooting it into space, or burying it in sea floor clay beds. The Soviets disposed it via deep well injection, in a liquid form that may not sit still for millions of years. The U.S., U.K., France, and the U.S.S.R. have dumped a lot of waste in the oceans. The Irish have caught contaminated lobsters and fish.

There are a number of radioactive elements and isotopes. All of them are unstable and become less dangerous over time, degrading at varying rates of speed. Most forms of uranium are mildly radioactive. The atoms that are heavier than natural uranium are manmade, and some remain dangerous for millions of years. Some are water soluble and highly mobile. Some are picked up by plants and animals, and are biomagnified as they move up the food chain.

Experts eventually realized that high-level radioactive wastes were nastier than expected. They had to be stored underground, in geologic repositories that would remain stable for a million years. Serious research began at an old salt mine in Kansas. Then, a plutonium plant in Colorado burned, and high-level waste was shipped to Idaho, where cardboard boxes of it were dumped into open trenches. The media reported the story, and the nation soon realized that nutjobs were in charge of handling terrifically toxic dreck. This detonated high-level fear. Kansas promptly nuked the proposed repository.

The next hot prospect was Yucca Mountain, on the edge of the Nevada Test Site. The government invested $10 billion on 25 years of research. The objective was to prove that the site would be safe for a million years. No place on Earth would be a perfect site. Dr. Alley believed that Yucca Mountain was close enough to ideal. (He spent years on the project, working for the U.S. Geological Survey.)

The core problem was that there were no politically suitable sites in the entire U.S., because every state would fiercely oppose a repository within their borders. The public had a reasonable fear of high-level waste. They also had a reasonable lack of trust in anything the government told them, after years of lies and deceptions. Nevada was no exception. The government's nuclear testing had already turned much of the state into a radioactive wasteland.

Obama was elected in 2008. Steven Chu was his Secretary of Energy. In March 2009, Chu announced, "Yucca Mountain was not an option." He presented no explanations or alternatives. Why did Chu kill the project? "Virtually all observers attributed the decision to pull the plug on Yucca Mountain as political payoff to Senate Majority Leader Harry Reid, a Democrat from Nevada. Nevada was a swing state in the election, and Obama had pledged to kill Yucca Mountain, if elected."

So today, "there are some 440 nuclear power plants in 31 countries. More are on the way. Yet, no country on Earth has an operating high-level waste disposal facility." As of 2012, American taxpayers were responsible for storing a growing collection of high-level waste — 70,000 tons of spent fuel, and 20,000 canisters of military waste. It's being stored at 121 sites in 39 states. In 15 other nations, 60 nuclear reactors are being built.

Industrial civilization is doing a fabulous job of trashing the planet's atmosphere, forests, soils, oceans, aquifers, and biodiversity. This is simply business as usual, and most of humankind is staring at their

cell phones. The future is not a matter for concern. Someday someone will build nuclear waste repositories, maybe. Almost no study has
been devoted to the risks of doing nothing, and letting the crap remain
where it is forever. The Alleys steer around this red-hot issue, leaving
readers to conjure worst-case nightmares.

Let's take a side trip to Google. The average U.S. reactor is 32
years old. Reactors are licensed for 40 years. When a license is not
renewed, the reactor must be decommissioned, a process that often
takes 60 years. First, the reactor is turned off, and the fuel rods removed. Then, wait 50 years. This allows the radiation levels in the facility to cool off, making it much safer for the remaining work to pro-
ceed. The buildings and contaminated soils are removed, and the site is
restored to a harmless field.

Fuel rods have a working life of about six years. Then, the spent
fuel, which is still highly radioactive, is moved to cooling pools, where
it must remain for at least five years. Then, ideally, it is stored in dry
casks. If the pumps for the cooling pool quit, the water boils, the pool
evaporates, and the rods are exposed to air. If the uranium pellets in
the rods are exposed to air, they melt, and begin releasing radioactive
gasses.

The meltdowns at Three Mile Island, Chernobyl, and Fukushima
were triggered by overheated fuel rods. Cleanup efforts at Chernobyl
have been hampered by the Ukraine's wheezing economy. Around
Chernobyl, citizens were permanently evacuated from a Zone of Alienation, which is larger than the state of Rhode Island.

In the U.S., the planned geologic repository did not materialize by
the promised date, and no site has been approved, so spent fuel is pil-
ing up at reactor sites. The Alleys note that some U.S. pools have been
loaded with four times more rods than they were designed for, which
increases potential risks. Moving the rods to safer dry casks would cost
billions of dollars.

Are we feeling lucky? What will the world look like in 50 years?
Will effective geologic repositories be built in time? Fifty years from
now, will we have the oil, heavy equipment, transportation systems,
functional governments, work crews, and wisdom to safely decommission the existing 440 reactors, plus the new ones being planned? Will
all of the reactors safely avoid disasters resulting from earthquakes, vol-

canoes, plane crashes, warfare, equipment failures, human errors, and sabotage?

If we cared about the generations to come, and if we were rational, what would a sane plan look like? Today, orbiting spacecraft passing in the night can clearly see the city lights below. My grandparents, and all of their ancestors, were born in homes without electricity. They managed to survive without light bulbs, TVs, cell phones, or the internet. They were good people who had satisfying lives. The lights cannot stay on forever.

The Sixth Extinction

I didn't rush to read Elizabeth Kolbert's book, *The Sixth Extinction*, because I imagined it would be a gloomy exposé on the unfortunate consequences of way too much half-baked cleverness — and it was. But it's also a fascinating story about the long saga of life on Earth, and the unclever booboos of the latest primate species. It's an outstanding book.

We have soared away into a fantasy world, where godlike humans spend their lives creating brilliant miracles. But today, a new mass extinction is gathering momentum. When we gaze back over the events of the last 450 million years, the wonders of our great achievements lose their shine. Kolbert rips off our virtual reality headsets, and serves us powerful medicine, a feast of provocative news.

The frog people have lived on this sweet planet for 400 million years, but many are now dying, because of a fungus called Bd. This fungus can live happily in the forest on its own, without an amphibian host, so endangered frogs rescued by scientists cannot be returned to the wild. The crisis began when humans transported frogs that carried the fungus, but were immune to it. There was money to be made in the frog business, and so the fungus has spread around the globe.

This is similar to the chestnut blight of a century ago. Entrepreneurs profitably imported chestnut seedlings from Asia. The Asian species was immune to the fungus it carried. American chestnut trees were not immune, and four billion died, almost all of them. The fungus persists, so replanting is pointless.

North American bats are dying by the millions from white-nose, caused by fungus that is common in Europe, where bats are immune to it. It was likely carried across the Atlantic by a tourist who dropped some spores in Howe Caverns, in New York. By 2013, the die-off had spread to 22 U.S. states and five Canadian provinces.

Welcome to New Pangaea! Once upon a time, long before we were born, all seven continents were joined together in a single continent, Pangaea. Over time, it broke apart, and ecosystems on each continent evolved in a unique way. In recent centuries, highly mobile humans have moved countless organisms from one ecosystem to another, both deliberately and unintentionally. The seven continents no longer enjoy the long-term stability provided by isolation.

On another front, many colonies of humans have become obsessed with burning sequestered carbon on an enormous scale. This is overloading the atmosphere with carbon, which the oceans absorb and convert to carbonic acid. Carbonic acid is a huge threat to marine life, except for lucky critters, like jellyfish. The world's coral reefs are dying.

Tropical rainforests are treasure chests of biological diversity. Tropical oceans generally are not, because of low levels of nutrients like nitrogen and phosphorus. Coral reefs are the shining exception. They provide habitat for thriving ecosystems, home to more than 500,000 species. This reminded me of beaver ponds, which are also sanctuaries of abundant life.

Coral polyps and beavers give us excellent examples of reciprocity. They create relationships that are mutually beneficial for many species. Reciprocity is a vital idea that most human cultures have forgotten. Our dominant culture has no respect for the wellbeing of ecosystems. It has a tradition of displacing or exterminating the indigenous species on the land, and replacing them with unsustainable manmade systems.

Evolution is fascinating. Rabbits and mice have numerous offspring, because they are vulnerable to predators. Other species have deflected the predator challenge by evolving to great size, like mammoths, hippos, and rhinos. Big critters have long lifespans and low birth rates. This trick worked very well until heavily armed *Homo sapiens* invaded their neighborhoods.

Kolbert imagines that the megafauna extinctions were not the result of a reckless orgy of overhunting. It probably took centuries.

Hunters had no way of knowing how much the mammoth population had gradually dwindled over the generations. Because they reproduced so slowly, they could have been driven to extinction by nothing more than modest levels of hunting. An elephant does not reach sexual maturity until its teens, and each pregnancy takes 22 months. There are never twins. Deer are still with us, because they reproduce faster, and flee faster.

Sadly, Neanderthals are no longer with us. They lived in Europe for at least 100,000 years, and during that time, their tool collection barely changed. They probably never used projectiles. They have acquired a reputation for being notorious dimwits, because they lived in a stable manner for a very long time, and didn't rubbish the ecosystem. *Homo sapiens* moved into Europe 40,000 years ago. By 30,000 years ago, the Neanderthals were gone. The DNA of modern folks, except Africans, contains up to four percent Neanderthal genes.

Homo sapiens has lived in a far more intense manner. In the last 10,000 years, we've turned the planet inside out. Kolbert wonders if there was a slight shift in our DNA that made us so unstable — a "madness gene." I wonder if we're simply the victims of cultural evolution that hurled us down a terrible path. If we had been raised in Neanderthal clans, would we be stable, sane, and happy?

Kolbert laments, "The Neanderthals lived in Europe for more than a hundred thousand years and during that period they had no more impact on their surroundings than any other large vertebrate. There is every reason to believe that if humans had not arrived on the scene, the Neanderthals would be there still, along with the wild horses and wooly rhinos."

Cultures have an amazing ability to put locks and chains on our mental powers. Kolbert describes how scientists (and all humans) typically struggle with disruptive information, concepts that bounce off our sacred myths. Bizarre new ideas, like evolution, extinction, or climate change, are reflexively dismissed as nonsense. As evidence of reality accumulates, increasing levels of absurd rationalizations must be invented. Eventually, someone actually acknowledges reality, and a paradigm shift is born.

For most of my life, human extinction has not been on my radar. By the end of Kolbert's book, readers understand that our extinction is more than a remote, theoretical possibility. What is absolutely certain is that we are pounding the planet to pieces. Everything is connected, and when one type of tree goes extinct, so do the insects that depend on it, as well as the birds that depend on the insects. When the coral polyps die, the fantastic coral reef ecosystem disintegrates.

The sixth mass extinction is clearly the result of human activities. The driving forces include the things we consider to be our great achievements — agriculture, civilization, industry, transportation systems. This is highly disruptive information, and everyone is working like crazy to rationalize our nightmares out of existence. Luckily, a number of people, like Kolbert, are beginning to acknowledge reality. Will there be a paradigm shift? Will we walk away from our great achievements, and spend the next 100,000 years living in balance with the planet?

Topsoil and Civilization

Outside the entrance of the glorious Hall of Western History are the marble lions, colorful banners, and huge stone columns. Step inside, and the popular exhibits include ancient Egypt, classical Greece, the Roman Empire, the Renaissance, Gutenberg, Magellan, Columbus, Galileo, and so on. If we cut a hole in the fence, and sneak around to the rear of the building, we find the dumpsters, derelicts, mangy dogs, and environmental history.

The Darwin of environmental history was George Perkins Marsh, who published *Man and Nature* in 1864. Few educated people today have ever heard of this visionary. Inspired by Marsh, Walter Lowdermilk, of the Soil Conservation Service, grabbed his camera and visited the sites of old civilizations in 1938 and 1939. He created a provocative 44-page report, *Conquest of the Land Through Seven Thousand Years*. The government distributed over a million copies of it, and it's still available online.

Lowdermilk helped inspire Tom Dale of the Soil Conservation Service, and Vernon Gill Carter of the National Wildlife Federation, to write *Topsoil and Civilization*, published in 1955. Both organizations cooperated in the production of this book. Following the horror show of the Dust Bowl, they were on a mission from God to promote soil conservation.

The book's introduction gets directly to the point, "The very achievements of civilized man have been the most important factors in the downfall of civilizations." Civilized man had the tools and intelligence needed "to domesticate or destroy a great part of the plant and animal life around him." He excelled at exploiting nature. "His chief troubles came from his delusions that his temporary mastership was permanent. He thought of himself as 'master of the world,' while failing to understand fully the laws of nature."

Readers are taken on a thrilling tour of the civilizations of antiquity. We learn how they developed new and innovative strategies for self-destruction. Stops include Egypt, Mesopotamia, the Mediterranean basin, Greece, China, India, and others. No society collapses because of a single reason, but declining soil health is always prominent among the usual suspects — no food, no civ.

The civilization of Egypt was the oddball. It thrived longest because of the unique characteristics of the Nile Valley. Then, in the twentieth century, they strangled the golden goose by building dams, which ended the annual applications of fertile silt, led to soil destruction, and shifted the system into self-destruct mode.

Mesopotamia (Iraq) was home to a series of civilizations that depended on irrigation. Creating and maintaining irrigation canals required an immense amount of manual labor, which legions of slaves were unhappy to provide. At the headwaters of the Tigris and Euphrates rivers, deforestation and overgrazing led to growing soil erosion, which flowed downstream, regularly clogging the canals. Eroded soils have filled in 130 miles (209 km) of the Persian Gulf. In 1955, the population in this region was only a quarter of what it had been 4,000 years ago.

Over the centuries, the region of Mesopotamia was conquered and lost many, many times. For the most part, replenishing soil fertility with manure and other fertilizers was a fairly recent invention. In the old days, an effective solution to soil depletion was to expand into less spoiled lands, and kill anyone who objected. Throughout the book, the number of wars is stunning. The tradition of farming is a bloody one.

It always damages the soil, sooner or later, which makes long-term stability impossible, and guarantees conflict.

Rome, Greece, and other Mediterranean civilizations were all burnouts, trashed by a combination of heavy winter rains, sloping lands, overgrazing, deforestation, soil depletion, and malaria. The legendary cedars of Lebanon once covered more than a million acres (404,000 ha). Today, just four tiny groves survive. "Deforestation and the scavenger goats brought on most of the erosion which turned Lebanon into a well-rained-on desert." Much of once-lush Palestine, "land of milk and honey," has been reduced to a rocky desert.

Adria was an island in the Adriatic Sea, near the mouth of the Po River in Italy. Eroding soils from upstream eventually connected the island to the mainland. Today, Adria is a farm town, 15 miles (24 km) from the sea, and its ancient streets are buried under 15 feet (4.5 m) of eroded soil. In Syria, the palaces of Antioch are buried under 28 feet (8.5 m) of silt. In North Africa, the ruins of Utica are 30 feet (9 m) below.

Even now, in the twenty-first century, some continue to believe that China provides a glowing example of sustainable agriculture — 4,000 years of farmers living in perfect harmony with the land. Chapter 11 provides a silver bullet cure for these fantastic illusions. "Erosion continues to ruin much of the land, reducing China, as a whole, to the status of a poor country with poor and undernourished people, mainly because the land has been misused for so long."

The authors aim floodlights on the fundamental defects of civilization, and then heroically reveal the brilliant solution, soil conservation. Their kinky fantasy was *permanent agriculture*, which could feed a gradually growing crowd for the next 10,000 years — a billion well-fed Americans enjoying a continuously improving standard of living. Their vision went far beyond conservation, which merely slowed the destruction. Their vision was about harmless perpetual growth, fully developing all resources, bringing prosperity to one and all, forever. Oy!

At the same time, they were excruciatingly aware that humankind was ravaging the land. "The fact is that there has probably been more man-induced erosion over the world as a whole during the past century than during any preceding thousand-year period. There are many reasons for the recent rapid acceleration of erosion, but the principal reasons are that the world has more people and the people are more civilized and hence are capable of destroying the land faster." The book is more than a little bipolar.

Topsoil and Civilization is a great primer on soil mining. I also recommend its shadow, a discourse on forest mining, *A Forest Journey*, by John Perlin. Readers will discover that the saga of civilization has an enormous dark side which is rarely mentioned in classrooms — environmental history. Students are usually served nothing more than the fairy tale version of our wondrous caves-to-skyscrapers ascent.

The real story is one of thousands of years of accelerating population growth, ruthless greed, countless wars, enormous suffering, and catastrophic ecocide. Understanding this pushes aside the baffling contradictions. The world snaps into sharp focus, and the pain of being fully present in reality begins — useful pain that can inspire learning and change.

The Coming Famine

Consumers live like toddlers, in a comfortable crib surrounded by colorful toys, with others providing our needs. We can turn on our computer without blowing apart mountains to fetch coal. We don't have to murder indigenous people to put gas in our Prius. We don't have to destroy rainforests to plant soy for our veggie burgers. Someone else does it for us. The grocery store always has food, so we can spend hour after hour staring at glowing screens.

Our growing collection of magical technology is clever and fascinating, but the long-term costs are higher than the benefits. These innovations will eventually step off the stage as we move beyond the cheap energy bubble. For almost the entire human saga, folks survived without bicycles, solar panels, and smart phones. Food, on the other hand, is a genuine need. Those who attempt to quit their food addiction soon experience painful withdrawal symptoms, lose a lot of weight, and then die.

Experts predict that our population will bloat to nine billion by 2050, but reality is often full of surprises. Other experts tell us that we're beating the stuffing out of the planet right now, with a wee herd of just seven billion. And yet, there is tireless jabber, by serious experts, about what needs to be done to feed nine billion, a project as sensible as space colonies. They are narrowly focused specialists, and reality is enormously complex. They don't understand overshoot, what goes up must come down. In their dream world, there are no limits to growth, and Growth is the god word.

Obviously, we could reduce almost all of our serious problems by shifting our population into reverse, and flooring the gas pedal — a rational strategy that's theoretically possible, but the experts are not interested, nor is anyone else. It's traitorous heresy. God commanded us to breed like there's no tomorrow, so we must. Big Mama Nature laughs and laughs at our folly and, with a mischievous twinkle in her eyes, fetches her medicine bag.

Julian Cribb is an Australian science writer. He often gets severe headaches from the painful clash that results from living in an anthropocentric culture while comprehending ecocentric reality. He began to suffer from nightmares, in which humankind's amazing techno-magic failed to provide regular happy meals for nine billion, resulting in human suffering. To confront his bad dreams, he rolled up his sleeves and did a lot of research, trying to envision a way to regularly provide nine billion happy meals. Then he wrote *The Coming Famine*.

The path we're on today is in the fast lane to an era of serious famine, which is expected to peak by 2050. It will not be a single global catastrophe, but a series of regional famines scattered over time and place. Rapid economic growth in nations like India and China is accelerating the fast lane, because one of the first desires of the newly prosperous is to have a luxurious high protein diet. This diet requires raising far more animals, which requires raising far more grain, which requires far more cropland, water, oil, fertilizer, machinery, and so on.

This high protein trend implies that increasing the table settings from seven billion to nine billion will actually require *doubling* global food production. Is that possible? Maybe, says Cribb, but it won't be easy. His book provides a valuable catalog of the serious obstacles to success, and it optimistically points to a slim chance of temporarily feeding the projected mega-crowd. Success requires massive, radical, intelligent change, on a global scale, really soon — the biggest miracle ever.

Climate change alone could block success. It may make it impossible to feed anything close to the current population, let alone nine billion, and it's out of control. Runoff from the Himalayan snowpack enables the survival of 1.3 billion people. Today, the snow melts gradually, allowing rivers to flow year round. Warming temperatures are likely to change snowpack patterns, sending winter precipitation downstream without delay. Many other regions, like the U.S. southwest, are also at high risk.

Water shortages alone could make dinner for nine billion impossible. We're already having serious water issues, and growing urban populations will divert more and more water from the fields, while contributing more and more pollutants. Aquifers are being drained right now. Rivers are being pumped dry. Hot weather is speeding the evaporation of reservoirs.

Cropland destruction alone could spoil the big dinner party. Soils are being depleted of nutrients. They are being carried away by water and wind. They are being rendered infertile by salt buildup. They are being buried by urban sprawl — most cities have been built on the finest farmland in the world. Deserts are expanding.

The end of the cheap energy bubble alone seems certain to cancel the party. Even if population growth stopped forever today, the end of cheap and abundant energy will radically change the crazy way we've been living for the last 200 years. Imagine feeding seven billion without farm machinery, irrigation pumps, refrigerators, and transportation systems. By 2050, when nine billion are expected for dinner, the global fuel gauge will be much closer to empty.

All life requires nitrogen, phosphorus, and potassium — remove any one and life ends. It takes cheap and abundant energy to manufacture, distribute, and apply fertilizers. Phosphorus is likely to become the first essential nutrient to reach crisis stage, since phosphate production peaked in 1989, and what remains is of declining quality. As rising demand exceeds supply, prices will get uppity, tempers will rise, fists will fly, and crop yields will wheeze. Phosphorus is transferred from the soil to the corn, from the corn to the hog, from the hog to the human, flushed down the toilet and sent to the sea, lost forever. Nutrients flow into cities and are not returned to the fields. Poop is precious. Remember that.

Our disastrous experiment with fossil energy enabled the mass production of synthetic nitrogen fertilizer, an enormous expansion of cropland and irrigation, and the tragic success of the Green Revolution. There were 2.5 billion people in 1950, and more than 7 billion today. The techno-miracle that could double food production by 2050 has yet to be imagined. Half of the fertilizer we apply never reaches the target plants, and neither does half of the irrigation water. Half of the food we grow is never eaten. It's really hard to reduce this costly waste. We've tried.

Cribb doesn't reveal the brilliant silver bullet solution for avoiding the coming famine, but he's bursting with smart suggestions. It's so hard being a smart person living in a society that has lost its mind. It drives him bonkers. He is focused on better management, tighter controls, and smarter processes. Other species have managed to do quite well without controlling their ecosystem, by simply adapting to it, and enjoying their lives. Could there be a lesson here?

Cribb has created an excellent book. It clobbers a generous number of dangerous illusions and lunatic fantasies, and it shines a floodlight on the monsters beneath the bed. It's well researched, easy to read, and an essential contribution to the human knowledgebase. Read it to the kids at bedtime, and make it the standard gift for weddings, birthdays, graduations, baby showers, and gift-oriented holidays.

The End of Plenty

Nothing is more precious than balance, stability, and sustainability. Today, we're hanging by our fingernails to a skyrocket of intense change, and it's the only way of life we've ever known. Joel Bourne has spent his life riding the rocket. He grew up on a farm, and studied agronomy at college, but sharp changes were causing many farmers to go bankrupt. Taking over the family farm would have been extremely risky, so he became a writer for farm magazines. Later, he was hired by *National Geographic*, where he has spent most of his career.

In 2008, he was assigned to cover the global food crisis, and this project hurled him into full awareness of the big picture. The Green Revolution caused food production to skyrocket, and world population doubled in just 40 years. Then, the revolution's gains maxed out, whilst population continued to soar even higher. Demographers have told us to expect another two or three billion for dinner in 2050. Obviously, this had the makings of an excellent book, so Bourne sat down and wrote *The End of Plenty*.

The subtitle of his book is "The Race to Feed a Crowded World," not "The Race to Tackle Overpopulation." A growing population thrills the business community, and a diminishing herd does not. Overpopulation is a problem that can be solved, and will be, either by enlightened self-restraint, by compulsory restraint, or, most likely, by the vigorous housekeeping of Big Mama Nature. Feeding the current population is thrashing the planet, and feeding even more will worsen everything, but maximizing growth is our primary objective. We are, after all, civilized people, and enlightened self-restraint is for primitive naked savages who live sustainably in roadless paradises.

As incomes rise, the newly affluent are enjoying a more luxurious diet. To satisfy this growing demand, food production must double by 2050. "We'll have to learn to produce as much food in the next four decades as we have since the beginning of civilization." Meanwhile, agriculture experts are not bursting with brilliant ideas. "Producing food for more than nine billion people without destroying the soil, water, oceans, and climate will be by far the greatest challenge humanity has ever faced." Bourne's book describes a number of gigantic obstacles to doubling food production — or even maintaining current production.

Automobiles are more addictive than crystal meth. Europeans guzzle biodiesel made from palm oil. Americans are binging on corn ethanol. The 2005 Energy Tax Act mandated the addition of biofuels to gasoline. From 2001 to 2012, the ethanol gold rush drove corn prices from $1.60 to $8.28. Not coincidentally, in 2008 food riots erupted in twenty countries. The Arab Spring revolts began in 2011, a year of record harvests and record prices. Today, almost 40 percent of the U.S. corn crop is being fed to motor vehicles — enough corn to feed everyone in Africa. Experts predict that we'll need four times more land for biofuels by 2030.

Crops require cropland, and almost all places ideal for farming are already in use, buried under roads and cities, or have been reduced to wasteland. Every year, a million hectares (2.4 million acres) of cropland are taken out of production because of erosion, desertification, or development. So, 90 percent of the desired doubling in food production will have to come from current cropland. At the same time, the farm soils currently in production have all seen better days. Agriculture is an unsustainable activity that normally depletes soil quality over time.

Another obstacle is yield, the amount of food that can be produced on a hectare of land. Between 1961 and 1986, cereal yields rose 89 percent, due to the Green Revolution. But per capita grain production peaked in 1986. Since then, population has been growing faster than yields. Crop breeding experts are wringing their hands. A number of indicators suggest that we are heading for "agricultural Armageddon," but the experts remain silent, praying for miracles. The biotech industry is focused on making huge profits selling seeds and poisons, not boosting yields.

Agriculture guzzles 70 percent of the water used by humans. Irrigated fields have yields that are two to three times higher than rain fed fields. Demand for water is projected to increase 70 to 90 percent by 2050, but water consumption today is already unsustainable. "Over the next few decades, groundwater depletion could cripple agriculture around the world."

Crop production is already being affected by climate change. Research indicates that further warming will take a substantial toll on crop yields. If temperatures rise 4°C, maybe half the world's cropland will become unsuitable for agriculture. Rising sea levels will submerge large regions currently used for rice production.

Meanwhile, population continues to grow, and some hallucinate that it will grow until 2100. In a nutshell, our challenge is "to double grain, meat, and biofuel production on fewer acres with fewer farmers, less water, higher temperatures, and more frequent droughts, floods, and heat waves." This must be done "without destroying the forests, oceans, soils, pollinators, or climate on which all life depends."

Ladies and gentlemen, this is an outstanding book, and easy to read. Most people have blind faith that innovation will keep the supermarkets filled forever. Folks who are more cautious tend to focus on stuff like solar panels, wind turbines, and electric cars. But food is essential for survival, and it gets far less attention than it deserves. By the end of the book, it's impossible to conclude that everything is under control, and that our wise leaders will safely guide us through the storm. Surprisingly, a few additional super-threats were not discussed in the book.

Bourne mentions that insects and weeds are developing resistance to expensive GMO wonder products, but stops there. Big Mama Nature is the mother of resistance. She never tires of producing new forms of life that are resistant to every toxin produced by science: insecticides, herbicides, fungicides, rodenticides, antibiotics. Every brilliant weapon we invent will only work temporarily. In terms of breeding new varieties of plants that are resistant to the latest biological threats, there are only so many tricks available. The low-hanging fruit has already been used. Just three plants enable the production of 80 to 90 percent of the calories we consume: corn, rice, and wheat.

The global food system is heavily dependent on petroleum fuels, which are finite and nonrenewable. No combination of biofuels or alternative energy can come anywhere close to replacing oil in agriculture and transport. In the coming decades, we will be forced to return to a muscle-powered food system. We are entirely unprepared for this, and the consequences will be very exciting for people who eat food.

There is a similar issue with fertilizer. Of the three primary plant nutrients, reserves of mineral phosphorus will be depleted first, and this will blindside conventional agriculture — no phosphorus, no life. A hundred years ago, Chinese farmers used zero commercial fertilizer. Every morning, long caravans of handcarts hauled large jugs of sewage from the cities to the fields.

In the end, readers are presented with two paths to the future. One path looks like a whirlwind of big trouble, and this is not just a comic book doomer fantasy — it's already blowing and rumbling. The other path is happy and wonderful. Humans will discover their legendary big brains, turn them on, shift industrial civilization into reverse, speed down the fast lane to genuine sustainability, and live happily ever after. Place your bets.

The Other Side of Eden

Hugh Brody is an English anthropologist. His parents were Jewish, and a number of their relatives died in the holocaust. Brody spent three decades in Canada hanging out with natives who were raised in hunter-gatherer societies. He worked for the government, and made documentary films.

Brody was raised in a nutjob civilization. He found the hunter-gatherers to be fascinating, because they had many virtues that were missing in modern society. The natives were kind and generous people. They radiated a profound love for the land of their birth, the home of their ancient ancestors. They deliberately had small families. Nobody gave orders to others. Everyone made their own decisions. Children were never disciplined.

He described his experiences in *The Other Side of Eden*, an excellent book. It examined the vast gulf between farming societies and hunter-gatherers — the broken and the free. In many ways, it was a predator-prey game. Wild people were useless obstacles to the insatiable hunger of the empire builders and soil miners.

Conquered hunters had to be broken — turned into educated, Christian, English-speaking wageworkers. They had to be made dependent on a farm-based civilization, and this required turning their lives and minds inside out. It was different in India, where the British colonized people who were already farmers. These folks were allowed to keep their language, religion, and culture. The empire simply skimmed off a portion of the cash flow and became a morbidly obese parasite.

Brody's family was Orthodox and Zionist. Later in life, his mind-altering experience with hunter-gatherers compelled him to reexamine his cultural programming. Genesis was essentially the creation story of western civilization. Eden was paradise, and Adam and Eve were provided with everything they needed. There was just one very simple rule to follow, and they promptly disobeyed it. God threw them out.

They had two sons. Cain was a farmer, and Abel was a herder. God was not a vegetarian, and he loved Abel's offerings of meat. Cain got jealous, and killed his brother. God condemned him to a life of endless toil. Eventually, God came to loath the troublesome humans, and decided to drown them all. Only a few were decent — Noah and his family were spared. God instructed the survivors to spread across the world, multiply, and subdue wildness.

So, the descendants of Noah were cursed to be wanderers, with no permanent home. Soil depletion, overbreeding, and belligerent neighbors forced them to keep moving. We think of hunters as being nomads, and farmers as sedentary, but the opposite is closer to the truth. Hunters tend to remain in the same territory for ages. Farmers commonly pack up and move when greener pastures become available.

Yes, hunters did eventually migrate to every corner of the planet, but the diaspora took more than 100,000 years. The new farming game grew explosively, and spread everywhere in a few thousand years. It was a huge and tragic change in the human journey, because it was thoroughly unsustainable, ravaged everything in its path, and created mobs of rootless broken people.

Over 200 years ago, Sir William Jones noticed that Sanskrit had similarities to languages, like Latin, Greek, and German. Other linguists pursued this notion, and discovered many related languages. These are now known as the Indo-European family of languages, and they are spoken by half of humankind. They likely originated in the Fertile Crescent, and spread in all directions, as agriculture expanded.

Brody noted that Genesis made no mention of hunter-gatherers, it was a story told by the victors. This Hebrew creation myth was especially peculiar in that it described two-legs as being superior to all the other animals. In the stories of wild people, two-legs were often portrayed as the newbies — clumsy, comical, childlike critters who had much to learn from the older, wiser species.

The natives of northern Canada believed that they lived in the most beautiful place in the world. It gave them everything they needed. They treated their home with great reverence and respect. They were extremely lucky that their chilly Eden wasn't prime real estate for agriculture. With the exception of horrific epidemics, they were relatively unmolested until the twentieth century.

But then, hell rumbled into Eden. Obnoxious missionaries told them they were wicked devil worshippers. The government built permanent settlements for them, with churches, schools, and stores. Their ancestral land became the property of the state. Loggers, ranchers, and miners moved in. A large region of Eden became a training ground for supersonic low altitude NATO bombers. By and by, the natives became fond of the pain-killing magic of oblivion drinking. The good old days were over.

The residential schools were sadistically cruel. Children were taken from their families and sent far away. The kids were beaten for speaking their language. Many were malnourished or sexually abused. Many died. The primary goal of school was ethnocide — eliminating wild culture. They weren't really creating improved people; they were breaking them, like ranchers break wild horses. The children were taught that they were primitive, and that everything they knew was wrong and stupid. After a year of English-only, they forgot their native tongue. It took years to relearn it, and many never did.

Control is the foundation of the farming mindset. Settlers ravage ancient forests with sharp axes and plows. They exterminate the wildlife and build sturdy fences. When Brody brought an Inuit elder to England, they took a drive in the country. Anaviapik was stunned, "It's all built!" The original ecosystem was gone. It was unbelievable.

On one project, Brody hung out with alcoholic natives in an urban skid row. He noted that white drinkers took great pride in holding their liquor while drinking heavily. It was uncool to stumble around or slur words. Respectable boozers remained in control. Natives, on the other hand, let go. "There is a welcome loss of self, a flight into another state of being, another kind of person" — a spirit journey.

Control is impossible in the hunting world. Fish, birds, and game go where they wish, and do as they please. Weather happens and patterns change suddenly without warning. Hunter-gatherers must continually pay close attention to the land and its creatures. A living ecosystem is not a predictable machine. Intuition and improvisation are essential for survival. Folks must be open to many states of mind. Dreams provided important information. "If there is a trail to be discovered, the dreamer must find it."

"It is artists, speculative scientists, and those whose journeys in life depend on not quite knowing the destination who are close to hunter-gatherers, who rely upon a hunter-gatherer mind." The civilized life is more like a painted pony on a merry-go-round, running in endless loops — a precise and repetitious pattern of work hours, schedules, destinations, and daily rituals. We march in deep ruts, unlike any other animal.

Techno-Fix

Welcome to our all-you-can-eat buffet of eco-predicaments, a remarkable achievement brought to you by our old friend, technological innovation. Our friend isn't evil. He's a hilarious charismatic trickster who excels at making comical mistakes. Every brilliant idea blows up in his face, flattens him with a boulder, or rockets him over a cliff. He never gives up. He never learns from his mistakes. He never succeeds.

Like the trickster, Americans are famous for our manic techno-optimism. Economic growth and material progress make us giddy with delight, and 72 percent of us believe that the benefits far outweigh the harms. The planet doesn't matter. Technology will certainly enable the kids to have a somewhat life-like experience, riveted to their glowing screens. A sane person can only conclude that we live in a world of illusions.

Techno-Fix, by Michael and Joyce Huesemann, takes us on a voyage through the hall of illusions. It provides readers with magic x-ray glasses that allow us to see right through heavy layers of encrusted bull excrement and clearly observe our way of life in its bare-naked essence. It delivers a super-sized serving of precious common sense that should be a central part of every youngster's rite of passage, but isn't.

The human species invented techno-addiction, a dangerous habit that seems impossible to quit; we always need bigger doses. This addiction has put quite a kink in our evolutionary journey. Science and technology are the mommy and daddy of most of our severe problems. No other species has developed a fascination with endless growth. The other critters have remained in balance for millions of years, limited by predators and food supply, nature's brilliant time-proven design.

The Huesemanns note that we took a different path. "Humans have used powerful technologies to escape these natural constraints, first by using weapons to eliminate large predators, then by inventing agriculture to increase food supplies, and finally by employing sanitation and medical technologies to increase their chances for survival."

Our devious experiments at controlling and exploiting nature have created a thousand nightmares. We've zoomed right past seven billion, giving the planet quite a fever. Still, the mainstream mindset is convinced that life is always getting better and better, and that technology will overcome any challenges on our joyride to utopia. We have no doubt economic growth can continue until the sun burns out, and nothing will ever slow us down. According to Huesemann's Law of Techno-Optimism, "Optimism is inversely proportional to knowledge."

The mainstream mindset is so weird — it celebrates the benefits of technology, and steps around the stinky messes, pretending not to see them. Innovation is never a free lunch. Every benefit has costs, and it's impossible to predict every unintended consequence. When serious problems are discovered, we tend to resolve them with additional innovation, which generates additional unintended consequences. We can delay paying the bills for our mistakes, but every debt must and will be paid. It's something like quicksand.

A century ago, the benefits of the automobile were immediately apparent, and the staggering unintended consequences were not. This technology has caused huge damage to our health, our families and communities, the ecosystem, and the unborn. Car problems are still growing, as billions of people in the developing world are eager to live as foolishly as Americans. The car and the television are our two biggest techno-bloopers, according to the Huesemanns.

Foolish fantasies are the deliberate consequence of the mass media and advertising, which are tremendously successful at persuading folks that the purpose of life is to transfer as much stuff as possible from nature to landfills. "Needs" are what is necessary for survival and health, like food, shelter, and community. "Wants" are things we have no need for, stuff we have sudden impulses to acquire. They are infinite in number, constantly changing, generally frivolous, and often useless.

The path to consumer nirvana and high status involves devoting a substantial portion of our lives to doing various sorts of work. For many, the work is less than meaningful or satisfying. The reward is trade tokens, which are used to acquire wants, and each purchase provides a brief consumer orgasm. The thrill is soon gone, the gnawing returns, and we are compelled to go back to the mall and get another fix.

No matter how hard we thrash our credit cards, we never arrive at our destination — wholeness and contentment. "We are chasing a mirage, thereby remaining forever dissatisfied and unhappy." In the last 50 years, rates of depression in the U.S. have increased ten-fold, and continue to rise (rates among the Amish are far lower).

Depression is also a result of our mobility and isolation. Until the industrial era, most people spent their entire lives in stable communities, and formed long-term social bonds with the people around them. Before the hell of automobiles, daily life included pleasant face-to-face encounters with others. Before the hell of glowing screens, people spent little time sitting alone.

Technology has a daffy response for any problem. It's far easier to develop techno solutions than social solutions. Rather than attempting the social challenge of creating a way of life that isn't so lonely and dreary, technology can simply chase away depression and anxiety with happy pills. It's easier to build new road systems than it is to convince people to give up their cars. It's easier to provide life-saving surgeries than it is to encourage people to vacate their couches and eat a healthy diet.

The Huesemanns harbor special loathing for the medical industry. It's extremely expensive, and remarkably ineffective. Intelligent, low cost preventative care is not the focus. New treatments are constantly being developed. The dead generate no profits, so we keep very sick people alive on machines; we transplant organs. Death must be delayed by any means necessary, regardless of cost. "If it can be done, it should be done." We need to remember that old age and death are normal and natural.

The last section of the book provides the theoretical solutions to our predicaments. This plan requires world leaders that will eagerly cooperate in rapidly and radically reconfiguring the way we live and think. It requires a human society that is spiritually connected to nature, people who abhor pollution and mindless consumption, folks willing to make enormous sacrifices in order to ensure the wellbeing of future generations of all species. Energy will be renewable, nonrenewable resources will be shunned, and all wastes will be safely biodegradable. The Huesemanns warn us that the transition might not be easy.

The Evolution of Technology

Humans are the most sophisticated toolmakers in the family of life. We've gone from stone hammers to hydrogen bombs. We've become so addicted to our technology that we can no longer survive without it. If we eliminated electricity, the modern way of life would disintegrate before our eyes.

Humans no longer sit in the pilot seat of our global civilization. The autopilot runs the show. Our complex labyrinth of technology herds us through a chute. It's no longer possible to make sharp (intelligent) turns, because the system has immense momentum and no brakes. We can't banish cars, plows, or electricity today. We're trapped on a runaway train.

How and why did we get into this mess? That's the subject of George Basalla's book, *The Evolution of Technology*. Scholars were debating this issue, and Basalla had an urge to jump into the ring, molest the illusions of his inferiors, and set the record straight.

His first task was to demonstrate that innovation evolved by synthesizing or altering existing innovations. Famous inventions were never original, unique, unprecedented acts of pure magic that fell out of the sky, like acts of God. The myth of the heroic inventor is just 300 years old. Henry Ford referred to his monster child as a quadracycle. It was not much more than a four-wheeled bicycle. The mother of invention was evolution, not revolution.

His second task was to explain the various ways in which our dance with artifacts has evolved, and this consumed most of the book. Readers are taken on an illuminating journey to realms that our industrial society has erased from the maps and forgotten.

We've all seen the graph of population growth over the last 10,000 years. Technological evolution follows a similar curve. For most of the hominid journey, our artifacts were little more than sticks and stones, and their evolution happened very slowly. A state of the art stone hammer might be no different from a hammer used 500,000 years earlier.

It is important to understand that for almost the entire hominid journey, our ancestors enjoyed a relatively sustainable way of life, and that this era corresponds exactly with the long, long era when technological evolution was essentially in a coma. This is not a coincidence.

Unfortunately, our system of education is writhing in a bad trip after inhaling the loony fumes of the myth of progress. This intoxicant was conjured by buffoons 200 years ago, and its side effects include disorientation, anxiety, and uncontrollable self-destructive impulses. We continue to hallucinate that the zenith of the human journey is today, and that the Golden Age is yet to come. We have a remarkable ability to completely tune out what is perfectly obvious, and vitally important.

The Tikopians and Sentineli are island societies that keep their numbers in check, and live very lightly, using simple artifacts. These communities stay in balance with their land, and are content. They do not suffer from a persistent itch for more and more. Technological innovation is entirely off their radar. They have no need for it, and experimenting with it could permanently destroy them.

Native American potters and basket weavers created artifacts that were careful, error-free reproductions of traditional designs. Apprentices worked hard to imitate the work of their elders, and their success earned respect. Their culture had a healthy resistance to change, because their time-proven traditions kept them on a good path.

The Muslim world is extremely wary of new inventions, which are considered evil until they demonstrate actual benefits. The Arabic word for *novelty* also means *heresy*. The Prophet warned that those who imitate infidels turn into infidels — stay on the true path.

China invented the compass, gunpowder, and printing, and put them to practical use. When Europeans brought this knowledge home, it sparked immense innovation that led to major changes in their way of life. The vast Chinese civilization was stable and conservative. It was not nimble, fast-paced, and highly competitive like Europe. Europe was a chaotic and unstable collection of competing nations. Society had far less resistance to new artifacts.

The wheel was first used in Mesopotamia, about 5,000 years ago. In many societies, it became a popular artifact, used for commerce and warfare. "A wise king scattereth the wicked, and bringeth the wheel over them." (Proverbs 20:26)

The native civilizations of North and South America were able to grow and die without using wheeled transport. Many groups in the Near East eventually abandoned the use of wagons, because camels were a faster and easier way of moving stuff. Wild tribes often just carried stuff home on their backs via footpaths, or paddled canoes — wheels required far more effort: cleared roads, bridges, and wagons.

The industrial civilizations of Europe and America have extensively used wheels in their artifacts. Our cultural myths celebrate the wheel as a super-sacred icon. Basalla concluded, "the wheel is not a unique mechanical contrivance necessary, or useful, to all people at all times." The ability to whoosh across the landscape on a bicycle is not required to meet our biological needs. No sustainable society used wheels, because hunters and gatherers had no need for them.

Basalla's book contained zero evidence that he was an eco-terrorist determined to smash civilization, or even a mild-mannered tree-hugger. The book just seemed to be unusually objective, as if it had a good cleansing soak in a potent myth-o-cide. It felt like he was a shaman conveying vital messages from the realm of the ancestors, whilst being cleverly disguised as a history professor. To the mainstream mind, these messages constitute heresies. But the messages contain the medicine we need to blow the locks off our minds, so we can escape, go home, and heal.

Agriculture and architecture are new novelties, not necessities. Technology is not necessary for any animal to meet its needs. Yes, other animals use tools, but none of them use fire, or use tools to make tools, or refine the designs of existing tools.

Obviously, we could not live like hurricanes without artifacts, and we could not survive in many regions where humans are an invasive exotic species, but we could enjoy a tool-free future in tropical regions, like our ancient African motherland (or a future Siberian jungle?).

We praise technological progress, but it's an illusion. There is no evidence that humankind is genuinely bettered by techno innovation. Often, it batters us, instead. We are tropical primates, and we can survive without manmade artifacts in tropical ecosystems.

Plants have a long history of thriving for millions and millions of years without any assistance from humans. Agriculture is unnecessary. All other animals survive without cooking, which is also unnecessary.

"Fire, the stone axe, or the wheel are no more items of absolute necessity than are the trivial gadgets that gain popularity for a season and quickly disappear."

Basalla's insights bounce off the minds of the mainstream world, automatically rejected by bulletproof denial. But these fresh notions are a sure sign that clear thinking is beginning to seep into the stagnant halls of history departments, those dusty museums where the dying Cult of Progress will make its last stand.

The path to sustainability is blocked by ideas — toxic illusions, metabolized into highly contagious beliefs, resulting in mass insanity. At the gate of the path to healing, foolish ideas must be left in the recycle bin. There is no shortage of better ideas.

Original Wisdom

Original Wisdom is an unforgettable book. Like all humans, author Robert Wolff was born a wild animal, ready to enjoy a pleasant life, romping around in a tropical wilderness. He grew up in Sumatra, the son of Dutch parents. His father was a doctor. The young lad suffered the misfortune of being educated by the dominant culture. It trained him for an unnatural life of schedules, destinations, and anxiety. His wildness was paved over, and his consciousness became disconnected from All-That-Is.

Wolff was interested in healing, and hoped to become a doctor, but World War II interrupted his plans. After the war, he became a social psychologist, and worked on a number of government projects. Work included numerous visits to rural villages in Malaysia, where life was very laid back. The people were "soft, gentle, polite." Villagers were the opposite of city people, who tended to be "crude, loud, insensitive."

Oddly, the patients in Malaysian mental hospitals included whites, Indians, and many Chinese — but no Malays, who were half of the population. Malay villages had a healthy sense of community. They accepted the presence of people who were odd; there was never a thought of sending them away. Everyone knew the village thief, and no one reported him to the police, because he belonged where he was. Malays respected one another.

Wolff was grateful that he had learned to speak several languages, because this ability expanded his awareness. Languages are unique products of the cultures in which they evolve. Different cultures perceive reality in different ways, and many ideas cannot be accurately translated from one language to another. Consequently, it was clear to him that the Western worldview was not the one and only way of interpreting reality. Most Western people never learn this. Insanity seems perfectly normal to the inmates of the loony bin.

His career began in the 1950s, the dawn of the most horrific era in human history. Population grew explosively, as did the ecological blitzkrieg. Traditional cultures were being exterminated by a plague of bulldozers. Wolff worked hard to learn and record the knowledge of traditional healers. He believed that their skills were the time-proven results of thousands of years of trial and error. A tremendous treasure was on the verge of being lost forever.

He remembered the days before antibiotics, when Western doctors were little better than witch doctors. He detested modern healthcare, where doctors practiced medicine, not healing. They were highly skilled at temporarily postponing death via extremely expensive treatments — even if the additional weeks or months of existence were meaningless. Not long ago, most of those with fading spirits would simply have been allowed to pass to the other side in peace.

In his crusade to preserve ancient knowledge, he met a number of healers who had not been the apprentices of venerable elders. They acquired their skills via inner knowing. Intuition told them what herbs to use, and how to prepare them. These healers told Wolff to relax; a treasure was not being lost. The wisdom was always accessible. When it was needed, someone would find it. This notion gives Western folks cramps, because they process reality via thinking.

One day, Wolff learned about a tribe of hunter-gatherers who lived in a remote mountain forest, the Sng'oi (or Senoi or Sakai). Meeting them opened the door to a series of life-changing experiences, a great healing. They were masters of intuition and inner knowing. They lived in a spiritual reality, "where things were *known* outside of thinking."

Their camps were not close to the road. Whenever Wolff arrived unannounced for a visit, one of the Sng'oi would be waiting for him in the forest. The guide would stand up and, without a word, lead him to the village. This baffled Wolff. How did they know he was coming? When asked, they told him that they had no premonition of his arrival. They had experienced a feeling to go to a place and be there. When Wolff appeared, they understood why they were there.

They knew each other's unspoken thoughts, communicating telepathically. Their shaman could sometimes foresee future events. In the mornings, the Sng'oi discussed their dreams. Once, Wolff described a dream. Its message, they told him, was that he was needed at home. He returned to his family, and learned that a child had had a medical emergency.

"They had an immense inner dignity, were happy, and content, and did not want anything." They loved to laugh and joke. They were often singing and smiling. Angry voices were never heard. Each new day was a blank slate — no plans, no jobs, nothing that had to be done. They floated, inspired by feelings. Life in a tropical rainforest was not a tough job.

One evening, while sitting in a group, Wolff went into a trance, and spoke to the others, an experience he did not remember. A Sng'oi shaman recognized that Wolff had shamanic powers, and offered to open spiritual doors for him. His name was Ahmeed, and his job description was "to bring new knowledge to the People." Wolff accepted his offer.

The learning process involved long, silent walks in the forest, with no food or water. Wolff was frustrated, because he was thinking like crazy. It was impossible to still his frantically racing mind. He could not hear his inner voice. At the end of the walks, he was exhausted; his mind fried.

Eventually, his thinker got more and more flaccid, and he learned to pay attention. Some days, he could float away from his mind, and vividly experience the sounds and smells of the forest. Everything changed. The world became intensely alive. He ceased being an observer, and became a living part of All-That-Is.

After months of practice, he gradually remembered how to be a human being. "The all-ness was everywhere, and I was part of it. I cannot explain what went on inside me, but I knew that I had learned something unbelievably wonderful. I felt more alive than I had ever felt before. All of me was filled with being." He felt great love for the people. The trees and mosquitoes were his family.

Back in the civilized world, Wolff was no longer the same person. Inner knowing could be painful, and sometimes had to be turned off. He could sense the feelings of the people around him, and this could be overwhelming. "It was frightening to discover how many people think nothing at all, but feel waves of anger, resentment, and bitterness — although they act as if they are deaf and blind to their own feelings."

As the years passed, Wolff became whole and confident, as his humanness recovered. Being human was so much healthier than being civilized. That's his message. Even adults can heal. It's never too late to try. "*Knowing* inside is not something unusual; it is how we are. All humans can have that connection with All-That-Is. The connection is within us." Cultures without the connection are on a bleak path.

Much of the book is available online, in a document titled *What It Is To Be Human* (wildwolff.com).

Cadillac Desert

Marc Reisner's classic, *Cadillac Desert*, takes us for a walk on the wet side, revealing far more than you ever wanted to know about dams, flood control, irrigation, and municipal water systems — and the serious long-term drawbacks that came along with building thousands of water projects in the frenzied pursuit of short-term wealth and power. It's a brilliant, funny, and annoying exposé of government corruption. It's an ecological horror story. It's a collection of powerful lessons for our society, lessons on how not to live, warning signs.

The western regions of the U.S. tend to be dry. Agriculture is risky where annual rainfall is less than 20 inches (50 cm). Locations like Phoenix, Reno, or El Paso, which get less than seven inches (18 cm), are especially poor places to settle, let alone build cities.

Native Americans in the west were blessed with excellent educations, and they wisely lived, for thousands of years, in a manner that was well adapted to the ecosystem, without trashing it. Europeans suffered from dodgy educations that celebrated the magnificent civilizations of the Fertile Crescent, which successfully transformed lush oases into moonscapes and went extinct. Almost all of these dead cities were hard-core irrigation addicts.

Around the world, many civilizations arose in arid regions. Desert soils were often highly fertile, because the nutrients were not leached out by centuries of significant rainfall. Desert farmers did not need to clear forests before planting. All they needed to do was add water. Irrigation turned their deserts green, but it also accelerated the growth and demise of their societies.

By the late nineteenth century, Los Angeles was growing rapidly, but it was doing this by mining the groundwater, a practice that had no long-term future. The city finished the Owens Valley project in 1913, which brought in water from 223 miles away (359 km), and included 53 miles (85 km) of tunnels. Drought hit in 1923, and the head of the water department frantically urged the city to stop the growth immediately, even if this required killing everyone in the Chamber of Commerce. They ignored him, so he began pressing for an aqueduct from the Colorado River.

To make a long story short, America built a couple thousand major dams between 1915 and 1975. Many were built during the Depression, to put the unemployed to work. In congress, water projects became an extremely popular form of "pork." A great way for me to get your support for my bill would be to amend the bill to include a water project in your district. This got out of control, to ridiculous proportions.

Many worthless projects were built at great expense to taxpayers and ecosystems. Corporate America refused to invest in dams, because they were unlikely to pay for themselves, let alone generate reliable profits. So, the west became a socialist utopia, dominated by militant free market conservatives who adored massive government spending in their region, and fiercely opposed it everywhere else.

By the time Jimmy Carter became president in 1976, the national debt was close to a trillion dollars, and inflation was in double digits. It was time to seriously cut spending, and Carter hated water projects, because they were so wasteful. He attempted to terminate 19 water projects, and promptly became the most hated man on Earth. He was a president with above average principles, a serious handicap.

Ronald Reagan took a different principled approach — no more free lunches. He thought that those who benefitted from the welfare should fully repay the government for the generous help they received, both capital costs and operating expenses. States should pay a third of the costs of reclamation projects, up front. Pay? Countless fat cats burst into tears. The keg was empty, and the party ended.

I was amazed to learn that Carter was special because of his sense of history. "He began to wonder what future generations would think of all the dams we had built. What right did we have, in the span of his lifetime, to dam nearly all of the world's rivers? What would happen when the dams silted up? What if the climate changed?"

Well, of course, great questions! As victims of narrow educations, our graduates lack a clear understanding of environmental history, a defect for which we pay dearly. What right did we have to build 440 nuclear power plants before building waste storage facilities? What right did we have to destroy the climate? What right did we have to leave a trashed ecosystem for those coming after us? A sense of history is powerful medicine, an essential component for an extended stay on this planet.

We know that any dam that doesn't collapse will eventually fill with silt and turn into an extremely expensive waterfall — no more power generation, no more flood control, no more irrigation. Every year millions of cubic yards of mud are accumulating in Lake Mead, the reservoir at Hoover Dam. Many reservoirs will be filled in less than a century. In China, the reservoir for the Sanmexia Dam was filled to the brim with silt in 1964, just four years after it was built.

We know that irrigation commonly leads to salinization. Salts build up in the soil, and eventually render it infertile, incapable of growing even weeds. This often happens after a century of irrigation. Salinization played a primary role in the demise of the ancient Fertile Crescent civilizations. China's Yellow River Basin is an exception, because of its low-salt soil. It's a serious problem in the Colorado River Basin, the San Joaquin Valley, and many other places. It's sure to increase in the coming decades, following a century-long explosion of irrigation around the world.

We know that mining the water in the Ogallala aquifer will eventually become impossible. This ocean of Ice Age water lies primarily beneath Texas, Kansas, Colorado, and Nebraska. Following World War II, diesel-powered centrifugal pumps enabled farmers to pump like there's no tomorrow. A 1982 study predicted problems after 2020. When the irrigation ends, many will go bankrupt, many will depart, and some will return to less productive dryland farming, which could trigger another dust bowl. Water mining has become a popular trend around the world, a short-term cash cow.

Stonehenge was built between 4,000 and 5,000 years ago, and it was a durable design. It had no moving parts, no electric-powered controls, and it was not required to prevent billions of gallons of water from normally flowing downstream to the sea. How long will our dams last? The Teton Dam did a spectacular blowout two days after it was filled.

Typhoon Nina blasted Asia in the summer of 1975. Near China's Banqiao Dam, a massive flood resulted from 64 inches (163 cm) of rain, half of which fell in just six hours. The dam collapsed, and the outflow erased a number of smaller dams downstream. Floods killed 171,000 people, and 11 million lost their homes.

In 1983, a sudden rush of melt water blasted into Glen Canyon Dam, damaging one of its spillways. The dam did not fail that day. It did not take out the Hoover Dam downstream with a huge wall of water. It did not pull the plug on agriculture and civilization in southern California.

As we move beyond the cheap energy bubble, and the extraction of sequestered carbon fuels goes downhill, industrial civilization will wither. It won't be able to make replacement parts for dams, turbines, the power grid, and so on. Will the nation of the United States go extinct some day? The status quo in California is dependent on the operation of many pumping stations, which depend on the operation of hydropower dams. The Edmonston station pushes water uphill 1,926 feet (587 m), over the Tehachapi Mountains, using fourteen 80,000 horsepower pumps.

As I write, the west coast is experiencing a serious drought. Reservoirs in California are dangerously low. Droughts can last for decades, or longer. There is a good chance that climate change will increase the risks of living in extremely overpopulated western states. So might earthquakes.

A wise man once gave this advice to California governor Edmund Brown: "Don't bring the water to the people, let the people go to the water."

Deep Water

The completion of the Hoover Dam in 1935 was a head-snapping experience — something like the moon landing, or the atomic bomb — history-making techno-craziness. It was the greatest construction project in human history, and the world's biggest power plant. It was a giant leap forward in humankind's crusade to enslave and abuse Big Mama Nature, and leave behind enormous messes for the kids.

Legions of hustlers were thrilled to exploit fabulous new opportunities for becoming rich whilst not getting their hands dirty. From 1935 to 2000, about 45,000 large dams were constructed in 140 nations. In his book, *Deep Water*, Jacques Leslie takes readers to India, Africa, and Australia to explore the dark world of the dammed.

In India, we meet Medha Patkar, a charismatic full-throttle activist determined to stop the Sardar Sarovar Dam on the Narmada River. It would flood the homes of 200,000 to 300,000, many of whom were indigenous tribal people. Tribal folks were happy to live in the roadless forest, where the Hindus didn't molest them. In the Hindu world, tribal people were assigned a status even lower than the untouchables. Tribes had zero political power.

The primary villain in this book was the World Bank, which poured billions of dollars into dam projects, to spur what is comically referred to as sustainable development. Crooked bureaucrats in India were highly skilled at diverting a good portion of this flood of money into their own pockets. The politicians of India were so corrupt that they made American officials almost look virtuous. Social and environmental concerns went out the window.

In India alone, dams have displaced somewhere between 21 and 55 million people (40 to 80 million worldwide). In the relocation game, officials promised the sun and moon to the families to be displaced, like five acres (2 ha) of good land and a government job. What they actually ended up getting was screwed. Their fields were under water, and they were prohibited from fishing in the reservoir. Often the tribes scattered to the winds, and ended up in urban nightmares.

India's population is projected to be larger than China's by 2050. The privileged folks are eager to enjoy a planet-trashing consumer lifestyle; they have little concern for what happens to the politically invisible. The nation has already built 4,300 large dams, and has plans for 700 to 1,000 more. Dam building is easier and more profitable than population management.

The next section of the book takes us to Southern Africa, where we meet anthropologist Thayer Scudder, who spent decades as a consultant specializing in the resettlement of unlucky people who resided in future reservoirs. He was skilled at creating high quality resettlement plans, and disappointed to see them all mostly ignored. Once again, the natives were screwed, the officials pocketed a lot of money, and the ecosystem was damned.

Scudder had no doubt that dams were cool, in theory. In theory, it was not impossible to create water projects that were fair, equitable, beneficial, and environmentally sensitive. On the other hand, he believed that 70 percent of the world's 45,000 large dams should have never been built. Decade after decade, he nurtured a fantasy that some day he would be involved in creating just "one good dam." Instead, the great triumphs of his long career were his successes in killing a few stupid projects.

The last stop is Australia, where we meet water commissioner Don Blackmore, and get a thorough analysis of his frustrating struggle to keep the dying ecosystem of the Murray-Darling Basin on life support. It's the continent's only major river system, but its annual flow is a wee trickle compared to the Amazon. Australia was an especially unsuitable place to transplant the British way of life, and many experiments have fallen far short of their lofty goals, agriculture for example. Much of the continent is arid, droughts are common, the ancient soils are low in nutrients, and the supply of fresh water is far from dependable.

Before the colonial invasion, thirsty Australian forests prevented most precipitation from reaching the water table in the Murray Basin. When the white lads chopped down 15 billion trees to create cropland, the water table surged upward, as much as 75 feet (23 m), mobilizing the salts stored in the soil, and poisoning large areas of land. The soils in the basin contain 100 billion tons of salt. It would be a terrible place to attempt large-scale irrigation, but they did.

Radical reductions of water diversions would slow the growing damage, but without water, farming is impossible. Climate change presents a new wild card. It could add major strains to a system that's already staggering.

Leslie spent a day with an Aborigine man, Tom Trevorrow. He lives in the Coorong, a 90-mile (145 km) lagoon near the mouth of the Murray. When he was young, the land was thriving with abundant wildlife. Today, with 75 percent of the water diverted upstream, the Coorong is very salty, and the habitat for birds, fish, and trees is devastated. He wants the dams removed. "The River is a living thing. When you start interfering with it, everything dies."

Aborigines managed to survive with an unrestricted free-flowing river for 50,000 years. They survived because they learned how to live with the land, an extremely intelligent strategy. They were not obsessed with unhealthy impulses to temporarily control and exploit nature. Our civilized ancestors forgot this wisdom.

This book is a powerful parable. Readers are given a backstage tour of the hideous world behind the dazzling magic show of endless growth and sustainable development. The heroes of our culture, the wealthy pioneers of progress, without their makeup and glittering costumes, are sad creatures.

Every one of the world's 45,000 large dams will die, sooner or later. About 5,000 large dams are more than 50 years old. As they age, the costs of maintenance rise, eventually eliminating profits. Investors must make an important decision — should they abandon the dam, or come up with billions of dollars to safely decommission it? It often costs more to decommission a major hydropower dam than it did to build it.

Many dams are nearly impossible to safely decommission. Exactly where do you dispose of billions of tons of accumulated sediment, mud often loaded with pollutants? Abandoned dams become the responsibility of taxpayers, who may not have the expertise, funds, or desire to safely decommission them. Earthquakes may decommission some dams. So might terrorists or wars. Old age and normal decay will certainly remove many.

The good news here is that we enjoy a surplus of super-important lessons to learn. We currently have access to outstanding tools for learning and teaching. We have a ridiculously out-of-balance culture to practice on, and little to lose. We have been presented with a fabulous opportunity to become the most beloved generation of ancestors ever.

Savage Grace

Jay Griffiths' book, *Savage Grace* is a powerful celebration of wildness and freedom. It celebrates societies that work, societies that have complete respect for their ecosystems, societies that have survived for thousands of years without suffering destructive whirlwinds of mass hysteria.

Griffiths is a brilliant heretic and a proud one. Her book shows us what happens when madness collides with wildness. It helps us understand the dark injuries that destroyed our own freedom, and put us on the path to what we have become. It is 350 pages of full-throttle outside the box thinking, written with passion and eloquence.

Griffiths was born in deepest, darkest England, a devastated island that was once a magnificent rainforest. She was blessed with the precious gift and curse of having an active mind. She excelled at asking penetrating questions that were not proper for young ladies (or lads) to ask. The wardens were not amused.

During her teen years, she hung out with fundamentalist Christians, but what they were teaching could not survive rational scrutiny, and her mind was highly allergic to blind faith. Painful clashes inspired her to run away. She abandoned the normal life for which she had been trained. "I lost a walled city but found a wildness and freedom. I never regretted it."

She wandered around the world, but life was not always easy. "Following a passionate freedom can mean loneliness, penury, humiliation, for we live in a world where the caged hate the free." By and by, she floated away into a healthy dance with depression. Depression is one of life's valuable idiot lights, warning us that it's time to pay attention and alter our course.

One day, the phone rang, and a friend invited her to Peru, where she could hang out with shamans, use powerful medicine, and recover her lost soul. So she did, and it worked. The heavy black clouds soon dispersed. She spent the next seven years working on her book, travelling from the Amazon to New Guinea, Australia, and Arctic Canada.

We routinely teach our children that wild people are primitive, and that their way of life is inferior and undesirable. In so doing, we erect a brick wall that prohibits fresh wild notions from flushing the crud out of our constipated imaginations. We teach our children to live like there's no tomorrow, to shop till you drop, to leave nothing behind for future generations.

Griffiths understands that the brick wall must be smashed, for the sake of all life. Her mind is a sledgehammer. She takes us on visits to wild ecosystems that stood in the path of the all-devouring global economy. She listened to the wild people, in a caring and respectful manner, hearing their pain, rage, and despair. They had a healthy way of life before the invasion. They needed nothing from us. They simply wanted to be left alone.

She took long treks through the jungle with wild people who possessed immense knowledge of the plants and animals. They perceived that all flora and fauna have spirits (except for domesticated plants). They saw that all wild beings were animated by the same life force, but different species appeared in different forms. We were all equal. When humans lived like equals, rather than masters, they didn't gang rape their ecosystem, because that would have been inconceivable.

After days of hiking through a perfectly healthy land, a treasure of abundant life, they stumbled upon the town of Maldonado, the cash economy, the modern world — electric lights, pop music, abundant booze and drugs, discarded syringes, splatters of puke, and overflowing outhouses. Everyone seemed to be mad. "To me, the forest had been wildly beautiful and the town was a hideous wasteland."

One chapter was devoted to the vast wildness of the sea, the place where all life began. The surface of Mars is better known to us than the floor of our oceans. The underwater world is a realm of magnificent diversity. Cetaceans, like whales and dolphins live in an incredibly intelligent manner, exactly as evolution prepared them to live, wild and free, without technology.

The ocean is a place where primates have little business, beyond the shoreline. Civilized primates have become abusive, ravaging the sea life, and filling the waters with toxins, sewage, garbage, and noise. Climate change is making the oceans so acidic that catastrophic harm now seems very likely. Wild people didn't do this — even when they lived too hard, the harm they caused was far, far less than the harm caused by our way of life.

Missionaries were high on the list of people that Griffiths most resented, because their mission was to destroy wild cultures, and convert wild people into literate, employed, Christian consumers. In Peru, four different missionary groups, using helicopters and speed boats, competed to find uncontacted tribes. They knew that they would import deadly diseases, but they didn't care. In some places, half of the people died within two years of their arrival. The priests blamed female shamans for the illness, and the angry people killed the shamans.

Common gifts for the converts included axes, tobacco, clothing, and mirrors. Mirrors enabled people to see their own faces, and become more aware of their individuality. Jesus saved individuals, not communities. God lived in heaven, and the Earth was a realm of wickedness, so it didn't matter, it was worthless. Missionaries built roads into the jungle, which were soon used by miners, loggers, and other destroyers. Separated from the family of life, the modern heart gets hard.

Missionaries forced the natives to surrender their sacred objects, which they burned. Within two generations, traditional knowledge became extinct, because it was no longer being passed down to the young, who spent their days in classrooms. Cultural genocide was emotionally shattering. In one Brazilian tribe, over 300 natives committed suicide.

In Australia, the invasion of civilization has been devastating for the Aborigines and their home, but the elders maintain a sense of patience, for the noxious cities are nothing more than ugly scabs. Whites have never possessed the spirit of the land, which remains alive beneath the parking lots and shopping centers. With time, the disease will pass; the land will heal and thrive once again, to the best of its ability.

Humans are not domesticated, we are genetically wild animals, but so many have been tamed. "Tamed creatures are dolt-minded and dumb, insipid and bland," Griffiths tells us. "The tame are trained only to hear the voice of their tamer, having ears only for command." Our wild genes scream in despair, as we go berserk with cage rage. "Sensible habits and good road safety skills will keep you alive till eighty. So what? If you didn't know freedom, you never lived."

The myth of human superiority has given birth to an enormous ecocidal monstrosity, and its ongoing self-destruction will result in unimaginable harm. If we cannot find a way to return to our humble place in the family of life, we will have no future. That's the message here.

The Population Bomb

In 1968, biologist Paul Ehrlich achieved infamy by publishing *The Population Bomb*, one of the most controversial eco-books ever printed. Ehrlich has been condemned to spend eternity with Thomas Malthus, in a dungeon reserved for doom perverts. To this day, professors still use the two lads as great reasons to never take seriously anyone who asserts that there are limits to growth. We all know, of course, that humankind has no limits. We have technology!

Actually, Malthus never predicted catastrophic famine. He simply stated the obvious — when population reaches overshoot, the death rate will automatically rise to restore balance, one way or another (starvation, disease, conflict). A thousand people cannot prosper if forced to share ten cheeseburgers a day. The overshoot ceiling rises when food is abundant, and falls when food is scarce. Malthus was not a doomer. His cardinal sin was declaring the obvious — that there are limits to growth.

Ehrlich, on the other hand, actually did predict catastrophic famine, and soon. The first lines in his book are, "The battle to feed all of humanity is over. In the 1970s and 1980s hundreds of millions of people will starve to death in spite of any crash programs embarked upon now." Millions indeed starved, but not hundreds of millions. Everyone agrees that this prediction was inaccurate or premature.

When Ehrlich was writing, India was sliding toward catastrophic famine. Only ten nations produced more food than they consumed in 1966. In America, the postwar baby boom led to a freakish population spike of 55 million in 20 years. The streets of 1968 were jammed with scruffy rebels protesting the Vietnam War, and our materialist way of life. It was hip to be loud, brash, and vigorously opposed to the status quo.

At the same time, the Green Revolution was just getting rolling, and no one could foresee how well it would succeed at temporarily boosting grain production. Norman Borlaug was the wizard of the Green Revolution, and his holy mission was to reduce world hunger. He hoped that his new magic seeds would provide us with 10 or 20 more years to resolve our population issues. We didn't even try. Those who recommend strict population control measures are called callous. But the leaders who take no action on population are also callous.

Naturally, much more food led to many more people. In 1968, there were 3.5 billion people, by late this morning there were 7.3 billion. World hunger sharply increased, and many other problems worsened. The Green Revolution had wonderful intentions, but its unintended consequences far exceeded its benefits, because we refused to seize the opportunity to confront and subdue the 800-pound gorilla.

The bottom line here is that Ehrlich's predictions of catastrophe within a specific timeframe were wrong, but he succeeded in bringing a lot of attention to real and growing problems — population, pollution, and environmental destruction. At the same time, he succeeded at pissing off almost everyone.

Liberals hated him because he wanted to set population goals for poor nations, and withhold food aid from those who did not meet their goals. He contemplated the notion of withholding food aid to nations that had zero chance of becoming self-sufficient. He did not endorse the "right" of families to breed as they pleased — a right that was not handcuffed to responsibilities.

Religious people hated him because he believed that contraception and abortion should be legal everywhere, and that all children should receive rigorous training in sex education and family planning. They hated him because he believed that fetuses were nothing more than potential humans.

Environmentalists hated him, because he was a lightning rod for criticism. They believed that his fondness for bold statements made it hard for folks to trust anything greens said. He was a popular scapegoat to blame their failures on. If Ehrlich had never been born, would we be living in a sustainable utopia today?

Conservatives hated him because he wanted to regulate pollution and pesticide use. He advocated compulsory population control, because voluntary family planning has never been successful at stabilizing or reducing population. Ehrlich detested their insane obsession with perpetual economic growth, which thrived on population growth, and disregarded ecocide. But they loved him for being so loud and so bizarre. He made it easy for them to label all greens as hysterical nutjobs.

Modern society is suffocating in information. Everyone in a hunter-gatherer clan knew the entire collection of their cultural information. Today, we don't know a millionth of our cultural information, because knowing it all is impossible. So, climatologists are freaked out about rising temperatures, while the masses are blissfully ignorant. Petroleum geologists are freaked out about the approaching end of the cheap energy bubble, while the masses are not.

Within the realm of his specialty, Ehrlich could perceive enormous threats that society was unaware of, and this freaked him out. He was compelled to rattle cages. If he had written a dry, mature, scholarly discourse on population, with 300 footnotes, it would not have reached a general audience and provoked lively and widespread discussion. In modern society, suffocating in information overload, you get attention by flaming and shouting, like the election ads for candidates. Whether or not it is honorable, it works. In my opinion, Ehrlich's ideas were sincere, and a bit inflamed, but not devious fabrications.

Ehrlich's book was read by many, and it drew needed attention to a crucial issue. A taboo subject was let out of the closet, for a while. Others were inspired to write books. Green organizations boldly called for serious action. Sadly, this inspired many checkbook activists to put away their checkbooks, and population quickly became a non-issue. So, the issue of overpopulation was handed over to Big Mama Nature to resolve, and she will.

While his ideas continue to outrage many, they do have a basis in cold, hard reason. We could reward couples who don't marry until 25, and those who space their children at least five years apart. Childfree people could be eligible to win lottery prizes. "There has been little effective criticism of the medical profession or the government for their preoccupation with death control… death control in the absence of birth control is self-defeating."

It would have been cool if humans were purely rational, realized their mistake, and took bold action to avert disaster. Ehrlich sighed. "By now you are probably fed up with this discussion. Americans will do none of these things, you say. Well, I'm inclined to agree." He wrote because there was a wee chance for success.

Don't read this book to learn about overpopulation and its side effects. Hundreds of newer books are more up to date. Read this book to contemplate morals, ethics, taboos, ideologies, and communication. Contemplate his critics, and why they are so determined to banish discussion on an issue that is a major threat to humankind and the planet (see the reader comments on Amazon.com). The anger and pain that continues to swirl around this book provides a fascinating study in human nature — long-term survival vs. a mentally unstable anthropocentric culture.

Ehrlich is an intelligent and charismatic fellow. In 2008, on the fortieth anniversary of *The Population Bomb*, he reread his book and blushed a bit. He had learned a few new things in the preceding forty years, but his overall impression was that in 1968 he had been far too optimistic. He presented his current perspective in a lecture at Stanford, *From the Population Bomb to the Dominant Animal* (54 min. online).

The Population Explosion

Following the publication of *The Population Bomb* in 1968, the new predicament of overpopulation was inducted into our gruesome mob of predicaments. World leaders snapped to attention, contemplated their options, realized that promoting population control was political suicide, and chose to step around the hopeless issue. The house was not on fire today, just some smoke.

The big exception was the Chinese, whose one-child program successfully prevented 350 million births. It was sometimes heavy-handed, but ignoring runaway growth would have guaranteed a super-heavy disaster. China had the same amount of cropland as the U.S., but four times the population, and the cropland was wearing out after many centuries of farming. The last thing they needed was more mouths to feed.

In 1968, there were 3.5 billion people, twenty years later 5.3 billion. Paul and Anne Ehrlich realized that *The Population Bomb* had failed to inspire miraculous change, so they wrote *The Population Explosion* (1990). The problems they had predicted earlier were now appearing in many places, and a new generation needed an excellent primer on overpopulation and its side effects. This second book did not repeat the 1968 error of predicting timeframes. It was much more substantial than the first, and is still illuminating to read today. Readers will recognize that the raging bloody chaos of the twenty-first century is an obvious consequence of soaring overshoot.

In this second act, the Ehrlichs took readers into the ecological equivalent of an amusement park funhouse, where loud and scary ghouls and goblins frighten us at every turn — except that their eco-spooks were genuinely dangerous. The trends in food production and population were not in any way encouraging. In 1970, population was growing by 75 million per year. By 1990, it was 95 million.

At the same time, staggering amounts of irreplaceable topsoil were being lost, aquifers were being depleted, and fields were being taken out of production because of erosion, desertification, salinization, waterlogging, and urban sprawl. The Green Revolution surge in food production was peaking, whilst population continued to soar, setting the stage for crisis. "We shouldn't delude ourselves: the population explosion will come to an end before very long."

North America produced 75 percent of the world's grain exports, and the U.S. was the world's number one exporter. In 1988, a severe drought reduced U.S. grain production from 300 to 200 million tons. That year, Americans consumed more than they produced. A stable climate was essential for crop production. So was healthy topsoil, which was being lost at an estimated 24 to 26 billion tons per year. So was the cheap energy bubble, which powered the food system.

In 1990, the Ehrlichs were aware that global warming might become a serious problem some day, one that might disrupt agriculture, and spark major famines. They knew that fossil energy was finite, and that we would be insane to burn it all. But Peak Oil and climate change were not presented as current threats in this book. The inevitable return to muscle-powered agriculture is certain to take a huge bite out of food production, and an unstable climate will ensure unstable harvests.

Most of humankind lives in the northern hemisphere, in regions having a temperate climate. These regions are where most of the world's grain is produced. Tropical regions are far more troublesome to farm, and they are home to most of the world's hungry folks. There is no frigid winter to reduce the number of crop pests. Soils in tropical forests are typically thin. Rains are often heavy, sweeping away soil, fertilizer, and pesticides. The magic seeds of the Green Revolution do not thrive in the humid tropics.

A fascinating chapter reveals why it is so hard for us to take action on long-term issues. It's almost impossible to see, hear, touch, or smell greenhouse gasses, overpopulation, acid rain, aquifer depletion, soil destruction, or mass extinction. These are not sudden, attention-grabbing events, like a charging rhino. They are slow motion processes that are mostly perceptible via charts, graphs, and books. We are tropical primates, and we evolved to pay close attention to the here and now, in the immediate vicinity.

Slow motion threats cannot be chased away with angry complaints or magical thinking. We can't seem to get interested in making enormous sacrifices today in the hope of theoretical benefits somewhere down the road, maybe. Exponential growth can blindside us, because it's slow at first, and gradually spins into a devastating whirlwind. Evolution did not prepare our legendary big brains for highly unstable civilized living.

The Ehrlichs are more homocentric than ecocentric. Here's a real boner: "The population problem is rooted in one of humanity's greatest triumphs — overcoming natural controls on population size: predators, starvation, and disease." Triumphs? Overcoming natural controls was the blunder that hurled us onto the path of doom! Replace "triumphs" with "mistakes" and the line makes sense. Natural controls work beautifully. There are not 7.3 billion chimps staring at cell phones.

From 1968 to today, the main goal of the Ehrlichs has been to prevent the collapse of our global civilization. In *The Population Explosion*, they fire hose readers with torrents of grim information. Readers are likely to conclude that today's global civilization is already far beyond the point of no return. The solutions recommended require countless miracles, by next year, if possible — world leaders fully cooperating to rapidly reverse the course of humankind.

In a 2014 essay, they concluded that the odds of preventing collapse are now less than one percent. Every civilization collapses, and not one has ever been anything close to sustainable. Instead of rescuing civilization, wouldn't a wiser goal be to quit destroying the ecosystem? The early civilizations destroyed themselves by overexploiting renewable resources, like water, forests, and topsoil. The newer ones are repeating the traditional mistakes, and extracting nonrenewable resources at an exponential rate.

Sadly, the super-loony consumer lifestyle has been successfully marketed as being extremely cool. Everyone in China, India, Africa, and everywhere else is eager to live as wastefully as possible, like Americans, but finite resources make this impossible. Instead, Americans need to learn how to live like the people who pick their coffee beans, and we will, sooner or later.

Here's an essential sentence: "The complacency with which our education system at all levels accepts the production of citizens hopelessly unequipped to understand the population explosion and many other aspects of the modern world is a national disgrace."

The Wayfinders

Long, long ago, Teutonic storytellers told tales by the fire. Many of them mention Odin, a deity who was a wisdom seeker, singer, poet, and warrior. Odin had two ravens, Huginn and Muninn, who daily flew out over the world, observed the events, and returned to report the news. The names of his birds meant "thought" and "memory." Odin cherished these ravens. He knew that the loss of thought would be terrible, but that the loss of memory would be far worse. Thought is clever and useful, but memory is essential and indispensable. When thought is disconnected from memory, the result is the world outside your window.

Wade Davis is very tuned into the high cost of forgetfulness. Modern folks have not only forgotten who we are, and where we are from, but we are busy erasing the surviving remnants of much ancient knowledge. There are about 7,000 languages in the world today, and half are approaching extinction.

When we wander amidst an endless herd of consumers, it's easy to forget that our worldview is just one of many. Our culture is a freak in human history, because of its blitzkrieg on future generations of all species. Most perceive this to be perfectly normal; it's all they know. In his book, *The Wayfinders*, Davis takes us on a fascinating tour, visiting lucky people who have not been cut loose from their past.

We have been trained to perceive other cultures as inferior and primitive. When the British washed up on the shore of Australia, they failed to recognize and respect the incredible genius of the Aborigines. Through tens of thousands of years of trial and error, the natives learned how to live in balance with a damaged ecosystem that was hot, dry, and lean. The white colonists have attempted to transplant a European way of life, which is starkly inappropriate, and can only exist temporarily.

The Aborigines have a network of travel routes that were sung into existence by the ancestors. The songs describe the landmarks that travelers will find along the route. If you know the song, you know the route. Songs are maps. The routes are called songlines. The entire continent is spiritually alive, and the people have a remarkable awareness of place, and a profound reverence for it.

The Polynesian culture is found on thousands of islands scattered across a vast region of the Pacific. The Spanish first encountered them in 1595, when they arrived in the Marquesas, a society of 300,000 people. Within a month, 85 percent of the people died from European diseases. For some reason, the islanders thought that the visitors were demons.

Polynesians were highly skilled at sea travel. They built excellent catamarans, using Stone Age technology, that were 50 percent faster than the floating monstrosities from Spain. Even with their state of the art sextants and charts, Europeans remained primitive navigators who got nervous when they drifted beyond sight of land.

Davis went on a voyage with Polynesians who remembered the ancient knowledge, and had no techno-gadgets. The navigators always knew exactly where they were, and could travel hundreds of kilometers, across open ocean, directly to their destination, a tiny island. They paid careful attention to the wind, clouds, stars, wave patterns, sky colors. They noted the water's salinity, phosphorescence, plant debris, and temperature. Sharks, dolphins, porpoises, and birds provided information. For example, white terns indicated land within 200 kilometers (124 mi.), and boobies stayed within 40 kilometers (25 mi.) of land.

On the Sahara, the people who understand the desert do not get lost. They can read the winds, the texture of the sand, and the forms of the dunes. They can smell water. In Canada, the vast province of Nunavut is home to the Inuit people. They were geniuses for surviving in a harsh climate with Stone Age technology. Travelling by dogsled in the long months of darkness, they never got lost, because they were experts at reading the snow.

These older cultures learned how to adapt to their ecosystems, because this encouraged survival. They were blessed to inhabit ecosystems that did not provide ideal conditions for the birth of industrial nightmares. Unfortunately, they have been "discovered." They now live in the shadow of spooky people from industrial nightmares. Many natives have been absorbed into the consumer monoculture, and have lost their identity.

All species routinely produce mutations. The mutants that can smoothly blend into the ecosystem, and live in balance with it, have a decent chance at continuing in the dance of evolution. Disruptive and dysfunctional mutants eventually end up on the bus to Extinctionville.

Experts now believe that the San people of the Kalahari may be the oldest culture on Earth. As humankind migrated out of Mother Africa, folks found themselves in ecosystems quite different from their tropical place of origin. Different regions inspired different cultural mutations.

Social Darwinists typically imagine a hierarchy of cultures in which industrial civilization is placed at the gleaming pinnacle. Every student in our culture has this dodgy notion repeatedly pounded into his or her brain. It is a sacred myth that is commonly mistaken for truth. Colonists from the gleaming pinnacle felt obligated to illuminate primitive people, pull them into the wondrous world of wage slavery, and provide them with brassieres and Bibles.

Well, Big Mama Nature is in a rather furious mood these days, and she's in the process of pounding an unforgettable lesson into our cheesy civilized brains. It's called reality — reaping what you sow. Our culture is a mutant, an immaculate failure. We could not be farther from the pinnacle of successful adaptation, or closer to the tar pits of Extinctionville.

Davis takes us on many intriguing side trips. In remote regions of the Sierra Nevada de Santa Marta we find cultures that escaped from the colonial invaders, and have not been severed from their roots. They call themselves the Older Brothers, the guardians of the world. We are the immature Younger Brothers, the zombie-like demolition crew. They are sure that the Younger Brothers will eventually wake up — when Big Mama Nature pulls the rug out from under us. They invite us to join them, and live with respect for life.

Our culture is a menace to all life on Earth. A culture of perpetual growth is both insane and suicidal. We need to stop destroying ancient cultures. Every culture that goes extinct removes important knowledge for living on Earth. Older cultures provide living proof that there are other ways of thinking and living, and they can inspire us to search for the long-forgotten wisdom that lies outside the walls. Stable long-lasting cultures are far more interesting than flash-in-the-pan burnouts. Imagination gets better mileage than despair or denial.

Overshoot

William Catton's book, *Overshoot*, describes the process by which most modern societies have achieved *overshoot* — a population in excess of the carrying capacity of the habitat. It examines the long human saga, and reveals embarrassing failures of foresight that make our big brains wince and blush. Catton drives an iron stake through the heart of our culture's goofy illusions of progress. Readers are served a generous full strength dose of ecological reality with no sugar coating.

Humans evolved to thrive in a tropical wilderness. In the early days, we lived lightly, like bonobos, in a simple manner that supported a modest population density. As the millennia passed, we learned how to increase carrying capacity by adopting ever-more-clever technology, like spears, bows and arrows, and atlatls. Better tools enabled us to acquire more food from a wider variety of sources. Conservative bonobos remained on the time-proven path designed by evolution. But technological innovation tossed our ancestors out of evolution's safety net, requiring us to create cultural safety nets, based on mindful foresight and enlightened self-restraint. Our path became slippery.

Much later, we slipped into soil mining — agriculture — which sent our carrying capacity into the stratosphere, temporarily. When topsoil is not molested by digging sticks, plows, overgrazing, or defor-estation, it does a fantastic job of maintaining itself. But molested soils erode and deteriorate. New topsoil is created over geological time. So, from a human timeframe, disturbed soil is a nonrenewable resource.

Soil mining often leads to water mining and forest mining. It has a long history of spurring population growth, bloody conflict, and per-manent damage to ecosystems. This was a big fork in the path. Up to this point, we increased carrying capacity by *takeover*, expanding into new habitat and pushing out other species. Now, we have added *draw-down* to the game, by depleting resources, both renewable and nonre-newable, a dead end approach.

When communities lived with enlightened self-restraint, salmon and bison could be renewable sources of food for tens of thousands of years, or more. Using dead branches for firewood did not degrade for-est vitality. On the other hand, iron, oil, and topsoil are not renewable. Their extraction does not contribute to the long-term carrying capacity of the habitat. What they provide is *phantom carrying capacity*, a boost that can only be temporary.

A habitat's carrying capacity is limited by the least abundant neces-sity. The limiting factor is usually food, but it can also be water, fire-wood, oil, and so on. Writing in the late 1970s, Catton perceived that 90 percent of humankind was dependent for survival on phantom car-rying capacity. Today, that figure is certainly higher, with billions of people dependent on oil-powered agriculture and market systems. As the rate of oil extraction declines in the coming decades, there will be many growling tummies.

Columbus alerted Europeans to the existence of an unknown hemisphere, the Americas. This New World was fully occupied by Stone Age nations that survived by low-tech hunting, fishing, foraging, and organic soil mining. They had no wheels, metal tools, or domesticated livestock. European colonists, with their state of the art technology, vigorously converted wilderness into private property devoted to the production of food and commodities. This greatly expanded the carrying capacity of the Americas for humans. Colonists exported lots of food to Europe, boosting carrying capacity there. Population exploded on both sides of the Atlantic.

A bit later, we developed a tragic addiction to sequestered carbon (fossil fuels) — solar energy that had been safely stored underground for millions of years. This accelerated the Industrial Revolution. Cool new machines allowed us to expand cropland, increase farm productivity, and keep growing numbers of people well fed. The population of hunter-gatherers grew 0.09% per generation. With the shift to agriculture, population grew 0.78% per generation. Since 1865, it's growing 27.5% per generation.

For four centuries, much of the world experienced a ridiculously abnormal era of innovation, growth, and excess — the Age of Exuberance. This created a state of mind that perceived high waste living as normal, and expected it to continue forever. We were proud that our children would be able to live even more destructively than we could. Our glorious leaders worked tirelessly to increase drawdown and worsen overshoot.

We have no limits. We'll grow like crazy until the sun burns out. This is known as the cornucopian paradigm. Cornucopians hallucinate that withdrawals from finite nonrenewable savings are *income*, and that wealth can be increased by withdrawing even more nonrenewable *savings*. Cornucopians proudly refer to growing overshoot as *progress*. Ecology, on the other hand, insists that our ability to survive above carrying capacity, in overshoot, can only be temporary. We can refuse to believe in limits, but limits don't care if we believe in them.

Catton was writing soon after the oil shocks of the 1970s and, at that moment, he thought that the Age of Exuberance was over. Our poor children would have a bleak future, a sickening descent into primitive barbarism — no SUVs, ATVs, RVs, PWCs, or McMansions. It was fun having the wonders of industrial society, like bicycles, metal pots, books, and running water. But these luxuries were provided by a system that has been surviving for 200 years on an exponential drawdown of nonrenewable resources. It's a way of life that survives by burning up posterity's savings. Catton warned us, "It was thus becoming apparent that nature must, in the not far distant future, institute bankruptcy proceedings against industrial civilization, and perhaps against the standing crop of human flesh."

Sadly, the consumer hordes can't wrap their heads around the notion that the Age of Exuberance is wheezing. Yes, things are a bit rough now, but recovery is just around the corner, probably tomorrow. The crazy cornucopian pipedream has become the primary worldview in most societies. It is still injected into the brains of every student, numbing the lobes related to enlightened self-restraint, often permanently.

We become anxious and angry as we slip and slide into more and more limits. Catton noted that a worrisome reaction to this is to blame someone, to identify scapegoats, hate them, and kill them — but this is pointless. "The end of exuberance was the summary result of all our separate and innocent decisions to have a baby, to trade a horse for a tractor, to avoid illness by getting vaccinated, to move from a farm to a city, to live in a heated home, to buy a family automobile and not depend on public transit, to specialize, exchange, and thereby prosper."

While Catton was writing, 40 years ago, a new paradigm was beginning to appear on the radar — the ecological paradigm. This reality-based mindset made it much easier to understand our predicament, and to envision intelligent responses, but probably not brilliant solutions. Society is not rushing to embrace the ecological paradigm, because any mention of limits is still pure heresy to the dominant paradigm.

Ecology is not frivolous theoretical nonsense. It's as real as life and death. In the game of ecology, there is no "get out of overshoot free" card. There is no undo command. Ignoring overshoot leads to die-off, an unpleasant return to carrying capacity. After the fever comes the healing. This is an essential book for literate animals younger than 100 years old. It is one of the most important books I have ever read, and I highly recommend it.

Limits to Growth

The Club of Rome was formed in 1968. It included big shots and experts from 25 nations. Social and environmental challenges had grown beyond the ability of individual countries to manage. It was time to study the big issues, and develop strategies for dealing with them. Their research began with the Project on the Predicament of Mankind.

In 1972, *Limits to Growth* was published, authored by Donella Meadows, Jorgen Randers, and Dennis Meadows. They developed a computer model that allowed them to tinker with variables like population, food, pollution, and resources, and then create possible scenarios for the coming decades. This allowed them to understand which variables were best for leveraging desired improvements.

The book concluded that we were on a path to big trouble, but it was not too late to avert disaster. World leaders did not leap to action, so 20 years later the second edition was published, *Beyond the Limits*. It announced that humankind was beyond overshoot, and it was time to slow down. Despite millions of copies sold, consumers kept consuming, and leaders kept snoozing. In 2004, the third edition was published, *Limits to Growth — The 30-Year Update*, the subject of this review. All three books present two very important ideas.

(1) Our planet is finite, so economic and population growth cannot continue forever. There are limits to growth. Nothing could be more obvious to anyone who has more than two brain cells, but our culture stubbornly refuses to admit this. It is impossible to ever have enough. We are hell-bent on perpetual growth, by any means necessary, at any cost. Sorry, kids! Even the most prestigious universities remain hotbeds of the perpetual growth cult.

(2) Humans have moved beyond the limits. We are currently on a path that cannot continue for more than a generation or two. Sorry, kids! Exponential population growth continues, and exponential growth in resource consumption is growing even faster. Climate is becoming unstable. Cropland is being destroyed. Rivers and aquifers are

being drained. Forests are vanishing. Fossil energy is finite. And so on. There are no silver bullet solutions, but there are countless ways to challenge and weaken the doom monster.

Naturally, the perpetual growth cult is yowling and screeching. They denounce the *Limits to Growth* research, asserting that the "predictions of the future" were wildly inaccurate, and therefore all of their ideas are pure balderdash. Of course, those who have actually read the book(s) know that the authors were careful to repeatedly remind readers that the various *possible scenarios* of the future were not *predictions*.

For example, on the issue of trends in population growth, the range of possible scenarios runs from worst case (huge growth) and best case (minimal growth), with the most likely scenario somewhere between the extremes. Reality in 2015 largely validates the quality of the scenarios presented in the book.

So, there are limits to growth, and we are beyond the limits. This begs the question: what next? The hurricane of predicaments that comprise humankind's war on the planet is enormously complex. We have countless options, and the better ones include acknowledging reality, learning, clear thinking, mindful discussion, slowing down, consuming much less, fewer kids.

With regard to what next, the book gets fuzzier. The intended audience is not the billion hungry souls living on less than two dollars a day. The authors are writing to the educated, wealthy elite — folks who will yowl and screech if anyone makes a move toward their air conditioner, refrigerator, or vehicle collection.

For them, sustainability implies *terrible sacrifice*, an unbearable reduction of their planet-killing standard of living. It is impossible for them to imagine a way of life that is simple, sane, relaxed, healthy, and enjoyable. Our culture tirelessly promotes maximum waste status seeking. We are taught to imagine unforgettable shopping safaris, bringing home important trophies, glowing with pride.

Because this elite audience is jittery and spooked, the discussion becomes more acrobatic and dubious. For example, "A global transition to a sustainable society is probably possible without reductions in either population or industrial output." Not all growth is bad. Poor folks need some growth so they can escape from poverty, and discover the magic of family planning. The authors were not of one mind, Jorgen saw dark storms ahead, and Donella believed in love and hope.

Of the ten scenarios presented in the book, only one results in a sustainable future, which is inhabited by eight billion happy humans. This scenario includes the highest number of major changes. In it, "the system brings itself down below its limits, avoids an uncontrolled collapse, maintains its standard of living, and holds itself very close to equilibrium."

Our predicaments have been accumulating for centuries. The Agricultural Revolution sharply disturbed our relationship with the family of life, and the Industrial Revolution greatly magnified these imbalances. Consequently, it's time for the Sustainability Revolution. The book mentions three ways of contemplating sustainability.

Most well-known is the Brundtland Report, which defines sustainable development as "...development that meets the needs of the present without compromising the ability of future generations to meet their own needs." It fails to point out the huge difference between wants and needs. Needs are about the necessities for survival: food, clothing, and shelter. Consumers often perceive needs as everything money can buy.

Another approach is the Herman Daly Rules. (1) Renewable resources such as fish, soil, and groundwater must be used no faster than the rate at which they regenerate. (2) Nonrenewable resources such as minerals and fossil fuels must be used no faster than renewable substitutes for them can be put into place. (3) Pollution and wastes must be emitted no faster than natural systems can absorb them, recycle them, or render them harmless.

The Daly Rules are clearer, and they imply backing away from industrial society and traditional agriculture. His second rule is perplexing. It's OK to use energy and minerals to make solar panels, but what would we need electricity for? Rule two would seem to prohibit using energy and minerals to make computers or refrigerators, because they are not renewable, and they require the existence of a vast and unsustainable industrial society. Readers are warned that a sustainable society "would be almost unimaginably different from the one in which most people now live."

The authors favor a third approach to sustainability, the Ecological Footprint model, which compares the impact of human activities to the planet's carrying capacity. They calculated that humankind's current footprint requires an area 1.2 times the Earth — we have exceeded the planet's carrying capacity by 20 percent, and this is unsustainable. The footprint is defined as "the total area of productive land and water ecosystems required to produce the resources that the population consumes and assimilate the wastes that the population produces, wherever on Earth that land and water may be located." The footprint model is vague and imprecise.

The scenarios in the book are based on measurable variables, like cropland area, industrial output, energy reserves, population, and so on. They do not include unknowns like war, floods, earthquakes, epidemics, and climate instability.

A serious weakness in their computer model is the assumptions used to project crop yields. Nine billion could be fed in 2100 if cropland area was not diminished, if food production doubled worldwide, if degraded land was restored, if erosion did not continue, if irrigation capacity did not diminish, and if there was adequate energy and fertilizer. These assumptions are impossible to take seriously. Agriculture is highly unsustainable already.

No book provides the solutions we wish for — a healthy future, with a high standard of living, quickly achieved via easy, painless changes. *Limits to Growth* is a classic, and it takes a unique approach to describing our predicaments, and evaluating responses to them. It's stimulating brain food, easy to read, with annoying splotches of magical thinking. It assumes that the harmful aspects of modern civilization can be voluntarily eliminated via intelligent reforms enacted by international cooperation, and that billions of us can live happily ever after.

Thinking Animals

Paul Shepard grew up in rural Missouri, during an era that lacked television, internet, and cell phones. He was lucky to live in a community where progress had not yet erased the wildlife. Young Paul was fascinated by wild animals. He collected butterflies and bird eggs. He hunted and fished. He adored the great outdoors. It was a happy time.

World War II hurled him into the mass hysteria of modernity. He survived D-Day and the Battle of the Bulge. Later, he spent 20 years at Pitzer College, close to the monstrous megalopolis of Los Angeles. During his lifetime, population tripled, and nuclear bombs fried cities. It was easy to see that old-fashioned rural society was starkly different from the industrial nightmare. Modern society was insane. Why? Shepard explored this question in *Thinking Animals*, and in his other groundbreaking books.

Over the passage of millions of years, evolution gradually increased the intelligence of many species. As predators got better at tracking, stalking, and killing, the herbivores got better at being menacing defenders and escape artists. For this balancing act to work, predators had to be slightly more clever than prey. If predators got too good at hunting, or prey got too good at escaping, the ecosystem would plunge into chaos. For both teams, intelligence and awareness were essential.

Our two-legged ancestors were not natural born carnivorous predators like lions, tigers, and wolves. The two-legs had to play two roles: hunter and prey. This required them to have the aggressive mindset of stalkers and killers, as well as the hyper-awareness of delicious walking meatballs.

Living in a healthy ecosystem was vastly more stimulating and meaningful than sitting in climate-controlled enclosures, staring at glowing screens. Everything was alive, intelligent, alert. The sky, land, and water were filled with living things. The air was rich with music and fragrances. Paying complete attention was a full time job. A jaguar might be hiding behind any rock. Just over the hill, a group of deer might be taking a nap.

The core of Shepard's message was that we evolved in a world where we were surrounded by a variety of wild animals, and this played a central role in the development of big brains and human intelligence. A healthy wild ecosystem was a fantastic place to live, and the greatest teacher of all, because it taught us how to be authentic human beings.

Complex language played a major role in activating our developmental turbo-thrusters. We named everything, and complex language made it easy to transfer large amounts of vital information from one generation to the next. We kept getting smarter and smarter. Wow! It was amazing… for a while.

By and by, too smart two-legs began fooling around with a fateful experiment in plant and animal domestication. For Shepard, everything was cool until the dawn of domestication, the rebellion against evolution. The wild ecosystem was replaced by a manmade landscape inhabited by herds of enslaved castrated animals and freaky colonies of mutant plants.

It has become common to believe that humans are the masters of the world. Of course, the discovery of evolution, made famous by Darwin, blew this homocentric nonsense completely out of the water. Two-legs, indeed, are animals, but most continue to deny this embarrassing fact.

Wild animals are fascinating to observe, and they taught our wild ancestors many skills for living on the land — concealment, stealth, stalking, tracking, ambush, and so on. Wild critters lived perfectly well by their wits and abilities. They had no desire to be our friends, nor any need for humans whatsoever (beyond our tasty flesh). They were wild, free, intelligent, and alert.

Domesticated animals were the opposite. Wild traits were undesirable, so they were erased via selective breeding. This resulted in pathetic, pudgy, dim-witted, docile mutants (Shepard called them "goofies"). Wild animals, on the other hand, are only submissive during their immature phase.

Modern humans, like barnyard animals, are deprived of growing up wild and free in a healthy ecosystem. Humans are jammed into complex societies where submission to authorities is required to maintain order in the crowd. Complex society is as unnatural as living on Uranus. We have a strong tendency to retain infantile or adolescent aspects long past childhood. Many spend their entire lives in an immature state.

Despite this misfortune, our bodies and minds are the product of millions of years of hunting, foraging, and studying nature. Our genes are at home in the wild, and every newborn is a wild animal, eager to enjoy a life of freedom. For millions of years, wild animals were a primary focus of our ancestor's attention. We need to live among them in order to develop as normal, healthy animals. Spending our lives in abnormal circumstances damages us. We become frustrated, alienated adults, lacking a confident sense of self. Many become hardened and rigid.

Living in a vast mob of strangers, we lack a strong sense of belonging, and this hampers our ability to form social bonds with others. In an effort to compensate, we buy millions of pets. Pet keeping was extremely rare until recent times. "Only in this perspective of the rarity of the pet does the pet explosion in modern cities take on its full strangeness." Pets may dull the pain of modern life, but "keeping pets is a hopeless attempt to resurrect crucial episodes of early growth that are lost forever."

Healthy childhood development requires successfully accumulating a sequence of time-critical experiences. Adults who attempt to reconnect with their missing childhood wildness might be partially successful, at best. "The mind, like the body, is an organ with multiple ripenings, and going back is a pathetic, exceedingly difficult undertaking." To bypass this mess, kids should be raised very close to nature. "The point of this book is to assert that animals have a very large claim on the maturing of the individual and his capacity to think and feel."

Thinking Animals was published in 1978, and it is an important book. Eighteen years later, Shepard published *The Others*, which took a fresh look at the subject. It takes the discussion to a deeper level, and it's easier to understand. I reviewed it in *Sustainable or Bust*.

Silent Spring

Silent Spring is a classic, a powerful broadside against synthetic pesticides. Now, more than fifty years old, the book still packs a solid roundhouse punch. With one book, one woman enlightened millions and spurred a loud outcry. One woman inspired big changes. Many of the pesticides she slammed have been banned or highly restricted.

Following World War II, Americans had big heads. We had won the war, invented a terrible new weapon, our economy was booming, and life was great! We succeeded at whatever we tried. We were giddy with euphoria. Then, Rachel Carson rolled a hand grenade into our dining rooms. Suddenly, Sunday dinners at grandma's looked far less delicious. What were we eating? Would it kill us?

During the war, researchers working on chemical warfare agents discovered substances that were highly toxic to insects. After the war, greedy minds became fascinated by these super-poisons, and visions of profits danced in their heads. A new industry was born, and we were blissfully ignorant of the unintended consequences to come. The production of synthetic pesticides increased five-fold between 1947 and 1960.

To control the elm bark beetles that caused Dutch elm disease, two to five pounds of DDT were sprayed on elm trees. This killed the natural predators of the beetles, as well as 90 species of birds, and assorted mammals. Worms ate the poison leaves, and the robins that ate the poison worms quit reproducing. Elms kept dying. More elms survived in places not sprayed.

To control gypsy moths, a million acres a year were sprayed with DDT. Sprayers were paid by the gallon, not the acre, so some places were sprayed multiple times. Bees died. Cows ate DDT grass and produced DDT milk that was consumed by DDT humans. Regulators did not block the sale of poison milk. At the end of the expensive project, the gypsy moths returned.

To control fire ants, millions of acres were sprayed with two new poisons: dieldrin and heptachlor, which were far more toxic than DDT. Newborn calves died after their first drink of milk. Piglets were born dead. Opossums, armadillos, raccoons, quail, songbirds, turkeys, livestock, poultry, and pets died. In the end, there were more ants in Florida than before.

We know little about what these toxins do to the complex microorganisms in healthy topsoil. Many of them interfere with nitrogen-fixing bacteria, which provide an essential nutrient for all living things. Some organisms are wiped out, leading to explosions of other organisms. The chemicals persist in the soil for years, and build up with each new application. Soil beneath an apple tree can contain 113 pounds (51 kg) of DDT. Old-fashioned arsenic pesticides keep the soil toxic forever.

Yes, it's a bummer that all spawning salmon died when New Brunswick's Miramichi River was sprayed with DDT, while the terrible spruce budworms laughed at the embarrassed entomologists. When Ontario sprayed to kill blackflies, they wiped out blackfly predators, enabling the fly population to explode seventeen-fold. The same thing happened in Florida, where large areas in coastal regions are now uninhabitable because of hordes of pesticide-resistant mosquitoes.

"Resistant" is a keyword in this comedy of errors. Big Mama Nature routinely produces organisms that are resistant to insecticides, herbicides, fungicides, antibiotics, and antivirals. We can throw one poison after another at life, and life will become resistant to it. Winning the war on life is impossible. Resistance can develop in as little as two months. The average time is three years. Insects are reproductive champions, and can promptly refill the land with resistant offspring. The breeding process in humans is much slower, so it may take us thousands of years to become resistant to pesticides.

Silent Spring delivered two powerful messages. It alerted us to the nightmare world of pesticides. It also turned big floodlights on the incredible incompetence of our experts and regulators. In 1960, almost everyone was blissfully ignorant about the toxic chemicals in their lives. In those days, most folks still trusted their elected officials. They trusted the experts who told them that DDT was harmless, and chlordane was a miracle of scientific genius. Today, for good reason, we automatically doubt any statements made by leaders or experts, because what they tell us frequently has little or no relationship to the full truth.

Carson did not believe that the use of pesticides should be banned entirely, but she did recommend that we shift toward less toxic alternatives, like pyrethins and *Bacillus thuringiensis* (Bt). Not surprisingly, malarial mosquitos are becoming resistant to bed nets treated with pyrethin-based insecticides, and many crop pests are now resistant to Bt.

She was fascinated by research in sterilizing male bugs, so that female bugs would not be able to tell the studs from the duds. Chemosterilants were used to render millions of houseflies impotent. Male gypsy moths found their lovers via sexy scents. So, researchers sprayed this scent all over the place, and were delighted to observe the fluttering lads falling deeply in love with wood chips that smelled like hot babes. Ultrasonic sounds could be used to kill blowflies, mealworms, and yellow fever mosquitoes.

About half of the insects called pests are immigrants from foreign lands. Here, they were not controlled by their natural predators from the old country. Carson recommended importing the predators and parasites of notorious immigrant pests. Moving organisms from one region to another is a mistake that has often led to unintended disasters, like the rabbits of Australia, the potatoes of Ireland, smallpox, and so on. She thought that it was OK for humans to try to sit in the ecosystem's driver's seat.

Carson was fighting breast cancer as she finished her book, and she died in 1964, two years after it was published. If she had lived longer, I think she would have recognized the serious shortcomings of the anthropocentric worldview of her era. Living like the masters of the planet has been a reliable recipe for countless catastrophes, and it's the core reason why seven-point-something billion people are standing on very thin ice today.

Ecological thinking is the antidote. Forget control — adapt! Carson was intrigued by the brilliant rascal Paul Shepard, who could have exorcised her anthropocentric demons, had she lived longer. She quoted Shepard, who summed it up nicely: "Why should we tolerate a diet of weak poisons, a home in insipid surroundings, a circle of acquaintances who are not quite our enemies, the noise of motors with just enough relief to prevent insanity? Why would want to live in a world which is just not quite fatal?"

Living Within Limits

Garrett Hardin was famous for his 1968 essay, *The Tragedy of the Commons*. He thought that folks who kept their cattle on common lands had little concern for the condition of the pasture, while privately owned pastures benefitted from the careful stewardship of wise ranchers.

I was perplexed by his notion that property owners love and protect their land. Everyone understands that privately owned cropland is degraded with every pass of the plow, year after year, despite being managed by government rules and regulations. Private land is often permanently ruined by mining, logging, and manufacturing enterprises. In 1998, in response to critics, Hardin published *Extension of the Tragedy of the Commons*, in which he admitted that a better title for his essay would have been *The Tragedy of the Unmanaged Commons*.

For years, I dismissed Hardin as a free enterprise gadfly. I realized I was wrong when I read *Living Within Limits*. He was an enthusiastic critic of economic growth and population growth. In this book, Hardin had a heroic goal — radically reforming industrial civilization before it disintegrated. He read mountains of books, and generated an enormous stream of rational ideas and recommendations.

He plowed through multiple editions of Malthus, and concluded that the good Reverend was 95 percent right, which delighted me. Hardin summarized the message of Malthus as, "Disaster is a natural outcome of perpetual population growth, but disaster can be forestalled if society can find the will to put an end to population growth." Poor Malthus has been widely hated for 200 years, most commonly by those who have never read him. His great sin was in questioning the trendy belief that civilization was in the fast lane to utopia.

Hardin learned that enlightening the befuddled world was a frustrating endeavor. Questioning sacred norms instantly turned you into a dangerous nutjob. Alas, the modern world was as rational as a loony bin — despite the fact that we were the most highly educated generation that ever walked the Earth. The notion that there were limits was impossible to accept. He believed that the only thing that's truly limitless is debt (and maybe foolishness).

Here we are, well into the twenty-first century, still pissing away billions of dollars in the ridiculous pursuit of colonizing other planets. We need more space to grow, more resources to mine, fresh ecosystems to destroy. Would you volunteer for a 400-year voyage in a small metal capsule?

Here we are, still feverishly determined to pursue economic growth by any means necessary. Almost all economists suffer from the hallucination that endless economic growth is possible and desirable; resources are unlimited. But the sun is setting on the cheap energy bubble, which will eventually bring growth to a halt, and shift it into reverse. Well, let's not think about that.

Here we are, several years beyond the peak of the global production of conventional oil, paying little attention to the foreseeable challenges ahead — at some point, production will continuously decline, whilst prices will continuously rise. M. King Hubbert, a Shell Oil geologist, predicted this in 1948, and the crowd chuckled. Of all the oil we will ever consume, 80 percent of it will have been extracted during a 56-year binge, roughly from 1969 to 2025. Let's not think about that.

Here we are, still refusing to seriously consider the huge problem of overpopulation. Our boundless optimism has no doubt that miraculous technology will solve any problem. For almost the entire hominid journey, the rate of population growth has been close to zero. The rate rose a bit when ancestors got interested in tools, it rose more with the advent of agriculture, and it skyrocketed during the cheap energy bubble — the temporary situation that we live in today, and consider to be normal. Hardin imagined that we will be happier when the herd shrinks to a half billion or so, as it was in 1492. But even then, many depended on unsustainable soil mining for survival.

The problem is that, one by one, we've eliminated many of the controls that used to keep our population in balance. We killed off most man-eating predators. We developed a food production system that reduces the risk of famine. We built sanitation systems to prevent pandemics of fecal-oral diseases. We invented vaccinations and antibiotics to cure or prevent contagious diseases. We made great advances in death control, but failed to balance them with advances in birth control.

Today, birth control is essentially voluntary. Hardin insisted that voluntary efforts have always failed in the long run. An effective solution can only be based on some form of coercion. Talking about reproductive rights without equal regard for reproductive responsibilities is foolish.

Hardin also detested immigration. America is a high waste society, and it's highly overpopulated. Is it truly our obligation to care for everyone? There are two billion poor folks in the world. Shall we invite them all to join us? Or, should we send them lots of food?

Overpopulated poor countries are living beyond their carrying capacity, and this cannot not fixed by sending them food. More food reliably results in even more hungry people. Hardin thought this was dumb — we should simply mind our own business, let nature take its course, and allow balance to be restored. He thought that the leaders of poor countries had an obligation to take responsibility for their overpopulation, and develop appropriate solutions. It's their job.

It's been over 20 years since Hardin's book was published, and everything has rapidly gotten worse. There is clearly a sense of frustration and despair in his words. We're heading for a bloody disaster, and nobody cares! The problems are obvious, as are intelligent responses. (Scream!)

I used to feel that pain. The pain was rooted in the expectation that modern society should behave in a rational manner, as we were taught in school. I've since realized that this expectation was absurd. We are who we are, and we'll change when we run out of options. In theory, humankind is not fatally flawed. Almost all of our ancestors lived in a relatively sustainable manner. Most developed voluntary methods of birth control that worked quite well. In theory, we can learn from our mistakes, and return to living in balance. In the end, it's either balance or bye-bye, pick one.

By definition, an unsustainable population can only be temporary. The same is true for continuous economic growth. Time will fix these mistakes, with or without our assistance. We should have listened to Hardin, but we didn't, so we'll leave more scars on the planet. The scar of an unbalanced climate may not heal for a long, long time. It's quite possible that warming will force the human journey into a new and very different direction.

A Sand County Almanac

Aldo Leopold's book, *A Sand County Almanac*, is near the top of many lists of environmental classics. It was published in 1949, and it has sold more than two million copies. He was born in Iowa in 1887, when Earth was inhabited by just 1.4 billion humans. It was an era before radio, television, automobiles, airplanes, computers, DDT, nuclear fission, and antibiotics. Most roads were dirt. Vast ancient forests still thrived. On the first page, Leopold informs us that this is a book for people who cannot live without wild things.

Part one is a series of twelve sketches, one for each month. They describe how the land changes during the circle of the seasons — the return of the geese, the mating ritual of the woodcocks, the rutting of the deer, the bloody snow where predators snatched prey. They describe what life was like in simpler times, before the sprawl, the malls, the highways, the tsunami of idiotic consumer crap. People were more in touch with the life of the land, because it had not yet been deleted.

In 1935, Leopold bought a farm in Wisconsin. The previous owner had tried and failed to make a living tilling the lean sandy soil. The place was cheap, far from the highway, worthless to civilization, but a precious sanctuary for a nature-loving professor. Luckily, the soil mining enterprise perished quickly, before it had time to exterminate the wildness.

Leopold loved the great outdoors. He loved hiking and hunting. Birds fascinated him. He spent many years working for the U.S. Forest Service, and later became a professor of game management at the University of Wisconsin. Sadly, he lived in a culture that was waging full-scale war on nature, and this drove him mad. It was so senseless. During his life, the population had grown from 1.5 to 2.4 billion, an era of staggering out of control disruption.

Part two presents observations, made in assorted times and places, about the damaged relationship between Americans and nature. This relationship was often abusive, because it lacked love. There often was no relationship at all. Many folks had no sense of connection to the rest of the family of life. For them, nature was nothing more than a treasure chest of resources that God created for the amusement of ambitious nutjobs.

Leopold was saddened by the trends. He learned to never revisit places that had amazed him in his youth. It was too painful to see the damage that commerce and tourism were tirelessly inflicting. It was best not to turn sweet memories into heartbreaking nightmares.

He was raised in an era when it was perfectly normal to kill wolves, coyotes, and other predators at every opportunity. These "vermin" killed too many game animals, depriving hunters of their rightful harvest. The most famous essay in this book is *Thinking Like a Mountain*. Having just shot a wolf, the gunman noticed a fierce green glow in its eyes. With the wolves eliminated, the deer multiplied in numbers, stripping the vegetation off the mountain, and wrecking the ecosystem. Deer lived in fear of wolves, and the mountain lived in fear of deer.

Part three is essays describing the need for a land ethic. Cultures have ethics to define right and wrong. Traditionally, these defined person-to-person interactions, or the interactions between individuals and society. Leopold lamented that American culture lacked a land ethic, rules for living with the natural world, the family of life. In our culture, as long as the land was not claimed and defended by someone else, you were free to do whatever you pleased.

Mainstream education was close to useless, because it was incapable of recognizing the glaring defects in the mainstream worldview. It loaded young minds with the crash-prone software of infantile self-interest. Generation after generation was being programmed to spend their lives as robotic servants to our economic system. The education system and the economic system were the two primary threats to the health of the land. Today, 65 years later, the lunacy has become a roaring hurricane. Leopold would be horrified and furious.

Leopold was a pleasant lad, glowing with love for the natural world, and a gifted storyteller. But this should not be the only ecology book you ever read. Since 1949, there has been an explosion of research in anthropology, archaeology, ecology, and environmental history. Many important discoveries have been made about hunter-gatherers, agriculture, deforestation, civilization, finite resources, climate change, and ecological sustainability. Today's deep ecologists will sneer at a few statements in the book, but in 1949, no one was more radical than Leopold.

At the time, he knew we were on a bad path, and we needed to pay serious attention to where it was taking us. He clearly understood the goal. He wrote, "Conservation is a state of harmony between men and land." He was sketching out a concept now known as ecological sustainability. Here's his land ethic in a nutshell: "A thing is right when it tends to preserve the integrity, stability, and beauty of the biotic community. It is wrong when it tends otherwise." Great!

Since the book was published, population has skyrocketed from 2.4 to 7.3 billion. Our leaders, educators, and the vast human herd remain lost in a dream world where perpetual growth is the only channel on the glowing screens. This madness has paralyzed our culture, and condemned our descendants, but it's running out of time. Hopefully, in its aftermath, important lessons will be learned and never forgotten.

Leopold's book was written "for people who cannot live without wild things." As the swelling mobs surge into vast cities, our disconnection from wild nature is almost complete. We have forgotten who we are, and where we came from. Well, we're wild animals, and we came from wild nature, like every other critter. Darwin revealed this embarrassing secret, but it still makes us uncomfortable, since it clashes with our deepest, darkest myths, our grandiose illusions of superiority.

Anthropocentric myths have ancient roots in every civilized culture, and they are like venomous brain worms that turn us into planet thrashing monsters. In 1949, few expressed doubts about these myths, but Leopold did. He often dreamed that the progressive movement would eventually grow, flourish, and address the primary challenges of our time, but reality hasn't cooperated.

His vision of a land ethic would have been a first step, but not a miraculous cure. No other animal needs a formal system of rules and regulations to discourage self-destructive behavior. Like our chimp and bonobo cousins, the others have never forgotten who they are, or how to live. Thinking like an animal has worked perfectly for millions of years. Thinking like a conqueror has been a disastrous failure.

Thoreau

Henry David Thoreau had a mind that was intelligent, complex, and rigidly righteous. He was born in Concord, Massachusetts in 1817, into a family of uppity Unitarian abolitionists. After attending Harvard, he worked as a schoolteacher for a few years. Later, he lived with Ralph Waldo Emerson, serving as a tutor, handyman, and editorial assistant. Emerson took him under his wing, and encouraged his literary efforts. Emerson owned land on Walden Pond, and he allowed the young man to build a cabin there. Living by the pond led to experiences that inspired Thoreau's classic, *Walden*.

Thoreau built the cabin at age 27, and moved out at 30. His thinking was not yet set in concrete, and it wandered to many regions in the world of ideas, tirelessly searching for eternal truth. He read the ancient classics in Greek and Latin, and discovered that enlightened philosophers preferred paths of voluntary simplicity. He adored Native Americans, because they thrived in wildness and enjoyed a simple life. He worshipped nature, and loved spending time outdoors.

Unfortunately, he was born during a diabolical hurricane of what is now called Sustainable Growth™. Concord was becoming discord, as the ancient forest was replaced with gristmills, sawmills, cotton mills, a lead pipe factory, and a steam powered metalworking shop. It was rare to stroll by Walden Pond in daytime and not hear whacking axes. Railroads were the latest fad for rich folks. Countless trees were hacked to death to provide millions of railroad ties. By 1850, just ten percent of the land around Concord was forest, and wild game was getting scarce.

Obviously, the residents of Concord were not philosophers aglow with timeless wisdom. They were also not wild folks who had lived in the same place for thousands of years without destroying it. These new people acted crazy! They were possessed, out of their minds, infected with the highly contagious status fever. They burned up their precious time on Earth in a furious struggle to appear as prosperous as possible — fancy houses, cool furniture, trendy clothes. If a monkey in Paris put on a traveler's cap, then every monkey in America must do likewise.

Thoreau was not impressed. "A man is rich in proportion to the number of things which he can afford to let alone." In 1845, he moved into his tiny new cabin. He hired a farmer to plow two and a half acres (1 ha), and then planted a bean field. Using a hoe to control the weeds proved to be far more challenging than his fantasy of humble simplicity. The net income for a summer of sweat and blisters was $8.12, far less than envisioned. He learned an important lesson, and this experiment was not repeated.

A low-budget life of simplicity required a low-budget diet. Thoreau's meals majored in water and unleavened bread made from rye and corn meal. Over time, he lost interest in hunting and fishing. "I had rarely for many years used animal food, or tea, or coffee, etc.; not so much because of any ill effects which I had traced to them, as because they were not agreeable to my imagination."

The second summer included a pilgrimage to Maine. He had a gnawing hunger for genuine wilderness that Concord could not satisfy. He also wanted to meet real live Indians, and be invigorated by their purity. Alas, Mount Katahdin was a rugged wilderness without trails, and the philosopher from Harvard was shocked by how difficult it was.

Big Mama Nature gave him a swift dope slap. In *The Maine Woods*, he recorded her harsh words. "I have never made this soil for thy feet, this air for thy breathing, these rocks for thy neighbors. Why seek me where I have not called thee, and then complain because you find me but a stepmother?" This nasty wilderness "was a place for heathenism and superstitious rites — to be inhabited by men nearer of kin to the rocks and to wild animals than we."

His experience with the Indians also disappointed him. After 200 years of colonization, their traditional culture had long been bludgeoned by smallpox, whiskey, missionaries, and civilization. "Met face to face, these Indians in their native woods looked like the sinister and slouching fellows whom you meet picking up strings and paper in the streets of a city. There is, in fact, a remarkable and unexpected resemblance between the degraded savage and the lowest classes of the great city. The one is no more a child of nature than the other."

Sadly, Thoreau never experienced a community that was fully wild, free, and at one with the land. He returned to Walden, a tame and comfortable place, and buried some fantasies. He wasn't at home in wilderness, and he wasn't at home in civilization. Could he find peace somewhere in between? He soon packed up his stuff, left the cabin, and returned to the Emerson home. He had learned a lot from 26 months of solitude, but he was wary of getting stuck in a rut.

After eight years of work, and seven drafts, *Walden* was published in 1854. It caught the world's attention, and he finally had a steady stream of income. Thoreau's sister died of tuberculosis in 1849. His father died of tuberculosis in 1859. In 1862 it killed Henry, at the ripe old age of 44.

He had spent his life trying to find a beautiful, healthy, and ethical way of living. His education prepared him for a life in civilization instead, loading his mind with myths, hobbles, and blinders. Thoreau was well aware that his society was on a dead end path. Its citizens robotically submitted to the peer pressure of their culture. They could imagine no other way to live. The only thing they could change was their clothes. Consequently and tragically, "The mass of men lead lives of quiet desperation."

His core message was "explore thyself" — question authority, question everything, every day. Never assume that you are crazy, and never assume that your society is normal and sane — it is not! Stay away from status fever, and the living dead that suffer from it. Go outdoors! Live simply! Live! Live! Live!

Thoreau's world was deranged. But viewed from the twenty-first century, it looks far less crazy than our nightmare. He gathered chestnuts by the pond, a species that would later be wiped out by blight. The skies were often filled with passenger pigeons, now extinct. Millions of buffalo still thundered across the plains. He drank water directly from the pond. There were no cars or aircraft. Most folks moved by foot or horse. They did not live amidst hordes of strangers; they knew each other. None spent their lives inside climate-controlled compartments, staring at glowing screens.

Henry would have hated our world. His mission was to live as mindfully as possible. "I went to the woods because I wished to live deliberately, to front only the essential facts of life, and see if I could not learn what it had to teach, and not, when I came to die, discover that I had not lived."

Desert Solitaire

Edward Abbey was an eco-wordsmith whose work is often compared to the classics of Aldo Leopold and Henry Thoreau. His book *Desert Solitaire* has been called "the *Walden* of the southwest." Abbey was born in Pennsylvania, and went to school in New Mexico. In 1956 and 1957 he spent the summers as a ranger at the Arches National Park, near Moab, Utah. It was a mind-altering experience. The young ranger fell in love with the desert, and kept extensive diaries.

Like Leopold and Thoreau, he had profound reverence and respect for the natural world. All three watched in agony as industrial civilization worked so hard to mindlessly destroy it. While the other two were respectable gentlemen, Abbey was a funny, rude, rowdy, loose cannon.

In 1845, Thoreau diagnosed the problem as a deficiency of timeless wisdom and intellectual refinement. In 1949, Leopold recommended establishing a set of common sense rules to discourage gung-ho American halfwits from obliterating the future. By 1968, Abbey was furious about the absurdity of it all. Our culture was insane. It was time to mercilessly beat the monster to a bloody pulp, but the monster was winning, and it was shape shifting into an invincible mass extinction steamroller.

At the Arches, Abbey's ranger station consisted of a picnic table, house trailer, generator, and pickup truck. It was far from the main entrance, and the dirt road was dusty, primitive, and pocked with potholes. He spent the six-month tourist seasons in a place of immense beauty, constantly in awe of the magnificence of this gorgeous desert paradise. The multi-colored sandstone had been sculpted into astonishing forms by a million years of snow and rain. "I am twenty miles from the nearest fellow human, but instead of loneliness I feel loveliness. Loveliness and a quiet exultation."

The only turd in the tranquility was the daffy tourists, determined to see every national park in two weeks. They yowled and whined about the terrible road. They were Americans, by God, and paved roads and vast parking lots were guaranteed in the Constitution. Many of these "wheelchair explorers" never stepped out of their cars, except to take a few snapshots and contribute to the litter. Where's the Coke machine?

They were unable to comprehend the treasure that surrounded them. Their spirits did not soar, overwhelmed with amazement at the power of this sacred land. It was as if their souls had been anesthetized by living in an industrial nightmare. They were like fish that no longer felt at home in the water, preferring to reside on dry land and devote their lives to flopping and shopping.

Worse, the vision of the Park Service was to update its scruffy old parks into gleaming Disneyland National Parks — modern, clean, and convenient. In 1956, President Eisenhower signed a bill to create the interstate highway system. America sold its soul, and its future, to the automobile. Abbey was bummed. He knew that the Arches were doomed. After two summers, he quit, not wishing to stick around and watch the inevitable wreckage of progress.

He was right. Several years later, planners designed a new and improved infrastructure that would allow the Arches park to accommodate 75,000 visitors per year — a vast increase from Abbey's frontier days. In 2012, the park had over a million visitors. Traffic jams, noise, and air pollution have become serious problems.

Anyway, the book contains a collection of stories and rants. The most important story was *Down the River*, which described floating down the Colorado River as the Glen Canyon Dam was being built. Abbey and his buddy Ralph were among the last humans to observe the incredible canyons before they were submerged beneath the new Lake Powell reservoir. It reminded me of our generation, taking a final cruise through what remains of the natural world, before it is composted by the unintended consequences of our brilliant techno-miracles.

Oddly, the reservoir was named after John Wesley Powell, an early explorer who actually loved the beautiful river. "Where he and his brave men once lined the rapids and glided through silent canyons two thousand feet deep the motorboats now smoke and whine, scumming the water with cigarette butts, beer cans and oil, dragging the water skiers on their endless rounds, clockwise."

Abbey and Ralph were delighted to leave modernity behind, "...the stupid and useless and degrading jobs, the *insufferable* arrogance of elected officials, the crafty *cheating* and the slimy advertising of the businessmen, the tedious wars... the foul, diseased, and *hideous* cities and towns we live in..." and on and on. They had sweet fantasies of spending the rest of their days floating downstream in canyon country. They also had sweet fantasies of blowing up the dam — fantasies that Abbey later expanded in his smash hit, *The Monkey Wrench Gang*.

The U.S. built several thousand major dams in the twentieth century. These projects created many jobs during the Depression, unleashed flash floods of political sleaze, and made mobs of fat cats richer. Glen Canyon Dam was intended to be a "cash register dam," generating big revenues from hydropower sales, which could then be used to pay for vast irrigation projects. The dreams were far brighter than the subsequent realities.

Hoover Dam was finished in 1936, creating the Lake Mead reservoir. Today, this reservoir is at 37 percent of capacity, its lowest level since the 1930s, when it was being filled. Farther upstream, the Glen Canyon Dam was finished in 1963, creating the Lake Powell reservoir. Today, this reservoir is at 54 percent of capacity. The flow of the Colorado River has been below average since 1999. In 2002, the flow plunged to 25 percent of normal and 2003 was a bit higher.

There is growing concern that falling water levels will eliminate the thrust necessary to spin the power turbines at Glen Canyon. While water levels fall, sediment levels are rapidly rising, as the river delivers 30,000 dump truck loads per day. Eventually, sediment will permanently choke the power turbines. While many wring their hands about the toll of ongoing drought, lots of water is also being lost due to evaporation and bank seepage (water soaking into porous sandstone). Droughts can come and go, but rising temperatures seem to be here to stay for a long, long time — and some believe that this is the primary cause of falling water levels.

Up to 34 million people depend on water from the Colorado River basin. The rapid development of Cheyenne, Albuquerque, Salt Lake City, Phoenix, Tucson, Los Angeles, and San Diego was inspired by a cyclone of magical thinking. Our well-educated nation suffers from a pandemic of ecological ignorance, and critical shortages of foresight.

Abbey had the ability to stand firm against the whirlwinds of magical thinking that constantly roar through our communities, making everyone sleepy and dreamy. He understood that humans were not above and apart from the rest of nature, that anthropocentricism was a glaring symptom of lunacy. It was obvious to him that new technology was best left in the box and promptly buried. The culture that poisons our worldview is completely out of its mind. Where's the Coke machine?

Wisdom Sits in Places

Wal-Mart, McDonalds, Shell, Safeway, the highway matrix — everyone knows these culturally significant features of our landscape. Less well known are the natural features of the land: the hills, prairies, ponds, and streams. Our landscape watched the mammoths roam, it watched the furious madness of civilization, and it will watch the manmade eyesores dissolve into ancient ruins.

Waking up in the civilized world each morning is a jolt — jets, sirens, the endless rumble of machines. Most of us live amidst hordes of two-legged tumbleweeds, nameless strangers. We are the people from nowhere, blown out of our ancestral homelands by the howling winds of ambition and misfortune. Our wild ancestors never lived here. Carson McCullers wrote, "To know who you are, you have to have a place to come from."

I've found the entrance to a different version of reality, a temporary place of refuge, an escape from the madness. It's called *Wisdom Sits in Places*, and it was written by Keith Basso, an ethnographer-linguist. In 1959, he began spending time in the Apache village of Cibecue, in Arizona. He discovered a culture that had deep roots in the land, and a way of living that was far from insane.

The Apache culture also had entrances to other realms. Many places on their land had names, many of these named places were associated with stories, and many of these stories had ancient roots. Everyone in Cibecue knew the named places, and their stories. The voices of the wild ancestors could be heard whenever the stories were told, and their words were always conveyed in the present tense. "Now we are in for trouble!" Past and present swirled together.

The stories were a treasure of time-proven wisdom. They often provided moral messages that taught the virtues of honorable living, and the unpleasant rewards of poor choices. When people wandered off the good path, stories reminded them of where this would lead. They helped people to live well. Because of the power in the stories, the natives said, "The land looks after the people."

Most scholars who spend time learning about other cultures were raised in the modern world of nowhere. These experts would study languages, ceremonies, food production, clothing, spirituality, and so on — but they paid too little attention to the relationship between culture and place, because this notion was absent in their way of knowing. Often, the reports they published were missing essential components.

From 1979 to 1984, Basso worked on a project that blew his mind. The Anglo world had zero respect for sacred places when there was big money to be made. But natives didn't want their sacred places destroyed, so they hired experts to document their culturally significant sites. Elders took Basso to see these places, and record their stories. He created a map that covered 45 square miles (116 sq. km), and had 296 locations with Apache place names.

Ruth Patterson told Basso about her childhood in the 1920s and 1930s. In those days, families spent much time on the land, away from the village. They herded cattle, tended crops, roasted agave, and hunted. As they moved about, parents taught their children about the land. They pointed out places, spoke their names, and told the stories of those places. They wanted their children to be properly educated.

Apaches used traditional stories for healing purposes. Nothing was more impolite than directly criticizing another person, expressing anger, or providing unrequested advice. Instead, the elders used stories to "shoot" healing notions. During a conversation, they would mention the names of places having stories that would be good for the wayward person to remember. Then, hopefully, he or she would reflect on the stories, understand their relevance, and make the changes needed to return to balance.

One time, three wise women sat with a woman who was too sad. The first wise woman spoke a sentence that mentioned a place name. Then the second mentioned another place. So did the third. The sad woman recalled mental pictures of those places, and heard the ancestors' voices speak the stories of those places. She reflected on their meanings, and the clouds lifted. She laughed. This was a gentle, effective, and brilliant act of healing. They called it "speaking with names."

One day, Dudley Patterson was talking about stories and wisdom. Basso asked him, "What is wisdom?" Patterson replied, "It's in these places. Wisdom sits in places." In a long and beautiful passage, he told Basso how his grandmother explained the pursuit of wisdom. Everyone is different. Some are smart, some are half-smart, but only a few achieve wisdom. Wisdom is acquired via a long dedicated quest; no one is born with it.

When elders become wise, people can see them change. They become calm and confident. They are not fearful, selfish, or angry. They keep promises. They pay careful attention, always listening for the voices of the ancestors. Patterson's grandmother summed it up something like this:

"Wisdom sits in places. It's like water that never dries up. You need to drink water to stay alive, don't you? Well, you also need to drink from places. You must remember everything about them. You must learn their names. You must remember what happened at them long ago. You must think about it and keep on thinking about it. Then your mind will become smoother and smoother. Then you will see danger before it happens. You will walk a long way and live a long time. You will be wise. People will respect you."

Years later, when Basso sat down to write his book, Cibecue had changed. The road to the village had been paved, and there was a school, supermarket, medical clinic, and many new houses. Big screen televisions were a new source of stories, sent from the spirit world of corporations, not ancestors. People were spending far less time wandering about, old trails had grown over, and the younger generations were losing their connection to the land and its old-fashioned stories. They preferred the new information provided at school, which was useful for survival in civilization.

So, the book invites us to contemplate a society far different from our own. It calls up ancient memories. Everyone's wild ancestors once lived in a way something like the Apaches. It's inspiring to remember this. Observing the world from a tribal perspective allows us to realize how far we've strayed. The people from nowhere are paying a terrible price for the frivolous wonders of modernity, and the wreckage it leaves behind. I am reminded of a line from Chief Seattle, "You wander far from the graves of your ancestors and seemingly without regret."

Basso wrote, "We *are*, in a sense, the place-worlds we imagine." Prince Charles said it a bit differently: "In so many ways we are what we are surrounded by, in the same way as we are what we eat." In the traditional Apache world, the people were surrounded by a beautiful culture that encouraged respect, caring, and wisdom. In the modern consumer world, we're surrounded by a wisdom-free nightmare of hurricane-force infantile energy reminiscent of a Godzilla movie. But all hurricanes die. Our Dark Age will pass. Think positive!

Mao's War Against Nature

When I was young, I discovered pictures from China, where the streets were filled with people riding bicycles. I was overwhelmed by this display of human intelligence. Had they learned from our mistakes and taken a higher path, or had their culture taught them to respect life? I was living in Kalamazoo, where the streets were a nightmare, jammed with impatient nutjobs in speeding wheelchairs. The air was thick with methylene chloride, and the river was a PCB cesspool. If only our leaders were Chinese… sigh! Like I said, I was young.

In 1949, Mao Zedong led a revolution that overthrew the Chinese government. The victors created the People's Republic of China, a communist state. China had suffered from a long era of exploitation by foreign powers. Mao was eager to create a prosperous industrial utopia as rapidly as possible, by any means necessary.

In 1972, Richard Nixon visited Mao and reestablished relations between the U.S. and China. Judith Shapiro was among the first Americans allowed to work there. She taught English. The outside world knew little about Red China, but Shapiro soon learned that the Maoist era had been a turbulent freak show. She described this period in her book, *Mao's War Against Nature*.

Every environmental history book is a horror story, describing how clever humans survived by using technology and aggression to devour nonrenewable resources, deplete renewable resources, ravage ecosystems, and leave the bills for their children. Shapiro's book stands out, because it examines an era of unbelievable ecocide. Maoist China repeated the classic mistakes of other civilizations, but in fast forward mode.

Mao's high-speed modernization project was called the Great Leap Forward (1958-60). He wanted to produce more steel than Great Britain within 15 years. Peasants rapidly constructed several million primitive backyard furnaces. A hundred million people worked day and night melting tools, pots, and scrap into blobs of useless metal. Most of the furnaces were wood-fired, and deforestation was widespread. In those days, the peasants still believed the dream — that their heroic efforts would bring a new era with powerful tractors and railroads. They worked enthusiastically.

At the same time, there was a huge drive to increase grain production via bone-headed strategies. They were told that if they planted ten times as many seeds in a field, the yield would be ten times higher. Sadly, the densely grown plants rotted. But local leaders were deeply engaged in a competition to report astonishing gains in grain production, and their claims were far in excess of reality.

Because it would have been impossible to store all the grain reported, folks were ordered to make steel. The 1958 crop largely rotted in the fields, while the steel-making peasants consumed their grain reserves. In 1959, drought arrived, and the Great Famine began. Between 35 and 50 million died by 1961 — the biggest manmade famine in history.

The war on nature had another front, the Four Pests — rats, sparrows, flies, and mosquitoes. Sparrows were an enemy of the people because they ate too much grain. Schoolchildren ran around the countryside, destroying their nests and smashing their eggs. They banged pots whenever a sparrow landed. Before long, there were far fewer sparrows, and far more of the insects they used to eat. Farmers soon realized that sparrows were great allies. The birds were removed from the pest list, and replaced by bedbugs.

A core component of the Mao era was disregard for expertise. Mao hated intellectuals, scientists, and anyone else who questioned his fantasies. "Mao and his followers all too often fell into the trap of believing that because they declared something possible or true, it would be so." Time-proven ideas were annoying superstitions that obstructed the fast lane to utopia. Knowledgeable people who voiced doubts about stupid ideas were promoted to exciting new careers in breaking rocks, exterminating forests, or worse.

When the president of Beijing University warned about the danger of rapid population growth, he was denounced and relieved of his responsibilities. Overpopulation could only be a problem in evil capitalist societies — never in a socialist paradise. China was already overpopulated in 1949, and it grew with spooky speed. Mao refused to believe the census numbers. In 1958, family planning programs were ended, and not resumed until 1971. Mao died in 1976, and in 1979, the one-child policy was implemented.

When a respected engineering professor at Qinghua University warned that the planned Sanmenxia Dam on the Yellow River was stupid, and would promptly fill with silt, he was denounced and relieved of his responsibilities. The dam was built, and the reservoir filled with silt two years later, flooding a nearby town. Mao rushed to build thousands of dams, of which 2,976 had collapsed by 1980. Many were built with soil alone, by untrained peasants. Floods caused by two dam failures in 1975 killed an estimated 230,000 people.

Rubber was a strategic resource, and Mao did not want to rely on imports from capitalists. During the Cultural Revolution, hundreds of thousands of educated urban youths from bad families (i.e., intellectuals, rightists, capitalists) were shipped to the virgin rainforests north of Laos. This region was too far north for rubber, but the experts understood it was dangerous to protest. So, ancient forest was cleared, and planted with rubber. Much of it died during the winter of 1974-75. They replanted, and the trees died again. They replanted a third time, with the same result.

Looking at this era from the outside, it's easy to see the foolishness. The only news the peasants got came from government sources — propaganda. The culture had a long tradition of obedience to superiors. Free speech and dissent were not cool. "Political campaigns so distorted human relationships that family members were driven to denounce and beat each other, neighbors spied on neighbors, schoolchildren drove teachers to suicide, and the world was turned upside down for countless millions."

As I read, I couldn't help but contemplate how foolish our own culture would appear to intelligent outsiders. How much of our news stream is truthful? What stories are missing? Why do we disregard the warnings of climate scientists? How can a "well-educated" population remain so ecologically illiterate? It's 2015, the polar bears are dying, and the streets of Kalamazoo are still jammed with speeding wheelchairs. Why?

The Chinese were manipulated to pursue an ideology, and the program resulted in enormous environmental harm. It seems like consumer societies are manipulated via advertising and peer pressure to cause enormous harm via lifelong competition for status. We must continually acquire more impressive homes, cars, televisions, and on and on. A couple years ago, it was awesomely trendy to wear clothing printed with skull motifs. The following year, the skulls vanished, and the trend robots rushed to fill their wardrobes with the latest new fashions.

Anyway, Shapiro's book is stunning. Mao is dead, and so is his ideology. The new game is the high speed pursuit of personal wealth. She mentions a few signs of hope, but it seems clear that the post-Mao era is causing far more environmental harm. The population is still growing. The pollution is horrendous. In every nation, the war on nature is winning. What would intelligent people do?

The End of Nature

Long, long ago, in scorching-hot 1988, Bill McKibben was busy writing *The End of Nature*, a book that cranked up the global warming warning sirens. It was the first climate change book written for non-scientists, and it was a smash hit. It makes an eloquent effort to convince those entranced by the dominant culture to radically change their thinking and lifestyles, this week if possible, because the biosphere is more damaged than we think.

It's about living with great care, fully present in reality, and pursuing the healing sanity of voluntary self-restraint. The root issue is that we're blindsiding nature. This doesn't mean we're eliminating all life on Earth. It means that humankind has spawned powerful cultures that no longer blend in smoothly with the rest of the family of life.

If we look at the world of 500 years ago, we can observe a number of blotches resulting from human activities, but the atmosphere remained fairly close to its original condition, as did the oceans, and much of the planet's land surface. The seas were loaded with fish, and millions of bison thundered across North America. Overall, the world largely remained the domain of Big Mama Nature. It was able to shake off the punches from human activities.

In the last 200 years or so, this has changed. Human cleverness is now capable of causing disturbances that are global in scale. These include DDT, ozone holes, radiation, acid rain, and an unstable climate. The dominant culture is discharging pollutants that affect the biosphere everywhere. Humankind has (temporarily) forced nature out of the pilot's seat. This is what is meant by "the end of nature."

In recent decades, our techno-juggernaut has invented a new and dangerous way of interfering with nature, genetic engineering. It provides us with countless opportunities for making disastrous, permanent, irreversible mistakes. Since the beginning of life on Earth, evolution has done an amazing job of preserving the family of life as it moves through an obstacle course of perpetual change. Now, bioengineers have broken into the control room, intent on making permanent changes to the future of life, with the objective of boosting corporate profits.

Genetic engineering gave McKibben intense nightmares. Some manmade organisms might survive for millions of years, affecting the biosphere longer than nuclear waste. Certainly, GMOs are unnecessary for our long and challenging return to balance with nature. It's a technology with fabulous potential for creating multitudes of unintended consequences; bizarre surprises that the mad scientists could have never imagined. What could possibly go wrong?

McKibben is a good thinker, a good writer, and a good-hearted human being. He's an environmental wordsmith who is also a Christian, providing a perspective that is not common in green literature. The end of nature deeply offended his beliefs. Many Christians don't get much farther than the instructions to "multiply and subdue," which imply that God made the world for us to dominate and exploit. McKibben knew that the scriptures could be annoyingly inconsistent. He was fond of the largely ignored Book of Job, which teaches that humans are not the center of the universe, and wilderness is not ours to trash.

As the dominant culture furiously pounds the planet, glaring questions arise — why doesn't God stop us? Did he die, or move away? McKibben sidesteps the sixth chapter of Genesis, where God realized that creating humans was a huge mistake, because they turned out to be remarkably wicked. God corrected his blooper by bringing "a flood of waters upon the earth, to destroy all flesh, wherein is the breath of life, from under heaven; and every thing that is in the earth shall die." Today, humans are the ones executing the end of nature, not the Creator. No other species is so clever — or so willing to mindlessly imitate a pissed-off sky god.

The End of Nature is also notable because it does not reek with a pungent anthropocentric stink. The path to healing requires the abandonment of human superiority, a deadly brain fever. McKibben concurs with Dave Foreman, who said, "Each of you is an animal, and you should be proud of it." It's nearly impossible for us to accept that we are delicious two-legged meatballs wandering around in the food chain, and that the rest of creation is at least as important as we are.

Green wordsmiths rarely reveal a profound love for the natural world, maybe because it's unprofessional, or because they have no spiritual connection to life, the norm in this society. The focus for many green thinkers is finding a way to maintain our "high standard of living" while leaving no scars on the ecosystem, an absurd and impossible quest. Usually, their primary objective is generating enough electricity to keep their gizmos glowing and humming. Food is lower on the list, and population reduction is nowhere to be seen.

Lately, hysterical electricity addicts have been hallucinating that nuclear energy is the silver bullet solution. McKibben noted that if we quit burning fossil fuels to generate electricity, and switched to nuclear, our carbon dioxide emissions would only drop 30 percent, because much of our economy cannot run on electricity (ships, planes, trucks, trains, etc.). Furthermore, carbon dioxide is only half of the greenhouse gases we are releasing. Alas, there is no free nuclear lunch.

McKibben loved nature. While writing, he lived in the Adirondacks, and he gushed with adoration for the surrounding forest and mountains. Outdoors, he felt the presence of God far more than when he sat indoors among a congregation of holy rollers. God created nature, not cities. The scriptures repeatedly remind us that one of God's great delights was annihilating cities.

McKibben confessed that he's also an American who enjoys the cool things that modern living provides, and he has no desire to live in an unheated cabin. Modern living is so comfortable. Unfortunately, it's pounding nature to bits. There is a vast chasm between the way of life we are addicted to, and a sustainable life. If we were rational, we would leap into "an all-out race to do with less." Instead, we desperately cling to a blind faith in technological miracles that will magically eliminate all need for living intelligently.

A memorable portion of the book describes the author's sincere struggle to find answers, tirelessly wrestling with hordes of demons and inconvenient truths. He tries so hard to find workable approaches, but there are no quick and easy solutions. Centuries will pass before balance returns. But our biggest obstacles are psychological, and radical change is not impossible, in theory.

The nations of the world actually cooperated in sharply reducing the use of DDT, and ozone-eating CFCs, because the risks clearly exceeded the costs. Fossil energy is different. Billions of people literally cannot survive without oil. Therefore, the radical changes we need will not happen anytime soon, if ever. We can continue living like there's no tomorrow, or we can make a heroic effort to encourage a gentler collapse — McKibben's preference.

To recharge his sanity, he enjoys stepping outdoors at night, and gazing at the stars. The rest of the universe is still as wild and free as it ever was. What could be more inspiring?

The Tender Carnivore

Paul Shepard was an animal with a PhD who made the astonishing discovery that he really was an animal, and so was everyone else. This sort of thinking makes us sweaty and nervous, because we prefer to believe that we are the creator's masterpiece — not the cousins of disgusting baboons and orangutans. It's insulting to call someone's kid a cute animal.

Two-legged primates evolved as hunters and gatherers in healthy wild habitats, living in small groups. These intelligent animals were perfectly at home in natural surroundings, but today's two-legs are overwhelmed by the intensity and complexity of modern life. Industrial civilization does not feel like home. Could this be why we are frantically shopping the planet to smithereens? Shepard spent his life trying to solve this riddle.

Historians have produced glorious stories of the incredible ascent of humankind, from hungry dirty peasants to futuristic cell phone zombies. In the process, they whited out 99 percent of the human journey, the era before we went sideways. Restricted to this heavily edited history, our culture has "unwittingly embraced a diseased era as the model of human life." This has nurtured "a malignant self-identity."

We can't know who we are if our past has been whited out. In his book, *The Tender Carnivore*, Shepard pulls back the curtains and presents readers with the 14 million year version of our story. Notably, the book leaps outside the wall of flatulent myths, and speaks from a viewpoint where wild people are normal healthy animals, and planet thrashers are not. His ideas provide an effective antidote to the trance, a charm to break the curse.

The book includes a timeline of the human saga. By 40,000 years ago, we had 240 tools, and numbered 3.3 million. By 10,000 years ago, we had domesticated sheep, goats, and cereals, and there were 5.3 million. By 6,000 years ago, we had irrigation, pottery, metal, war, states, wheels, trade, ideology, and writing — and there were 86 million. The human enterprise was getting dangerously out-of-balance.

Tree monkeys are relatively safe from predators, so males and females are about the same size, and the troop is sexually promiscuous. Ground monkeys, like baboons, are far more vulnerable to predators, so they are larger, and live in tight groups. They kill and eat other animals. The males are much bigger and stronger than the females, and they are hot-tempered.

Ground monkeys are "the most aggressively status-conscious creatures on Earth." High-ranking males have primary access to females and food. They are constantly watched by low-ranking males, who wait for signs of aging and weakness, and opportunities to drive the big boy out of the harem. They are high-strung animals who constantly adapt to a hierarchy that is always changing.

Civilized humans are also high-strung animals that live in status-conscious troops where some folks are cooler than others. In sedentary societies, where personal wealth varies, the status game is amplified by hoarding status trinkets — cars, televisions, and other valuables. Unfortunately, high social status is defined by super-trendy trinkets that have high environmental costs. Status trumps the health of the planet. Shepard says that we are obsessed with immature goals and follow trends like a dumb herd.

The ape family includes chimps and gorillas. They inhabit forests, and spend the daylight hours on the ground. Chimps live in groups of about 40, and use a few very simple tools. They are nice, mild mannered animals, Shepard says. But when Shepard was writing, Jane Goodall's chimp research was just beginning.

It turns out that chimp groups are ruled by an alpha male, who aggressively dominates the females. They are also violent killers. Goodall saw one chimp group completely exterminate another group. Bonobos are their closest relatives, and they are strikingly different.

Bonobo groups are matriarchal, extremely promiscuous, and far less violent.

A number of anthropologists have reported that, among recent hunter-gathers, males are not dominators, with some exceptions. But many would agree that, during the civilized era, the status of women often got the shaft. Shepard's overview of primate history suggests that male domination and abuse was not invented by Middle Eastern deities. Evolution can get rough.

When scientists raised chimps in their homes, along with their own children, the chimps were at least as intelligent as children, until the children were three or four, learned language, and left the chimps in the dust. Language promotes mental development, spurring reasoning and knowing. Yet, without language, lions and wolves are superior hunters. Intelligence is an evolutionary experiment. It allows us to better comprehend the complexity of the world, but it also enables us to better destroy it.

Ideally, when adolescence concludes with a successful initiation into adulthood, the youth becomes a confident fully human animal that is well integrated with the non-human environment. He clarifies his self-identity, moves closer to his peer group, and away from his parents. When initiation is botched or omitted, the youth remains trapped in adolescence, chronically narcissistic, enraged at humankind and nature for failing to help him become a complete human. "Everyone who fails will be intellectually, emotionally, and socially retarded for the rest of his life."

Because humans evolved to be ground-dwelling wild omnivores, the hunter-gatherer way of life "is the normal expression of his psychology and physiology. His humanity is therefore more fully achieved, and his community is more durable and beautiful." When removed from a healthy wild environment, folks "live in constant crisis, stress, and poor mental health."

Throughout the book, Shepard directs a fire hose of ideas at readers, and some are stronger than others. This one is false: "Hunters and gatherers, by contrast, do not make war." When Knud Rasmussen trekked from Greenland to Siberia in the 1920s, he reported several regions where warfare was common, in his book *Across Arctic America*.

It is also false that all humans are inherently violent. Elizabeth Marshall Thomas, Richard Lee, and Colin Turnbull all reported that Pygmy and Bushman hunter-gatherers were not warlike. People with adequate space and resources like to sing and dance. The Inuit described by Rasmussen lived in extremely low population density, but the lands they inhabited had an extremely low carrying capacity. Crowding is a reliable cause of stress and frantic agitation.

In the last chapter, Shepard looks toward the future. He presents us with imaginative, impractical, and sometimes daffy solutions (he later confessed that he was not entirely serious here). Rather than burning oil, we could use yeast to convert it into high-protein food. Agriculture and domesticated animals must go. Human settlements should be limited to a five-mile strip along the coasts, returning the interiors of continents to nature. In the wild lands, only foot travel would be allowed. Only hand weapons could be used for hunting, no guns or dogs. And so on.

The book was written in the good old days of the early 1970s, when there were fewer than four billion, and the future seemed somewhat stable. Peak Oil and climate change had yet to walk onto the stage. We seemed to have time to repair things. This is a 40-year old book, with a few rough edges, but well worth the time.

The Big Flatline

Jeff Rubin is the former chief economist at a major Canadian investment bank. His book, *The Big Flatline*, gives readers an opportunity to see the cheap energy bubble through the eyes of someone from the executive suites. He spent 20 years flying around the world, hanging out with the rich and powerful, and this was a mind-altering experience. In the process, he lost the rose-colored glasses that are mandatory in his field, and this cost him his job.

Rubin's overview of the current geopolitical state of affairs is fascinating. Energy costs far more than it did a decade ago. Oil was $30 a barrel in 2004, and $147 in 2008 (crash!). Since energy is the driving force behind the global economy, this sharp increase is a game changer. When energy is cheap, we can grow like crazy, but triple-digit oil prices slam down on the brake pedal.

High energy prices are not a passing storm, over the long run they're here to stay. Perpetual growth is never a free lunch. The inevitable approach of genuine scarcity guarantees rising prices. In the world of geology, *resources* are the amount of oil in the ground, and *reserves* are the amount of oil that can economically be extracted. For example, the Canadian tar sands contain 1.6 trillion barrels of oil resources, but only 170 billion barrels of reserves (eleven percent of total).

As an economist, Rubin focuses on the price trends in energy, but the energy industry is paying close attention to EROEI (energy returned on energy invested). In the good old days of high-profit gushers, it was common to invest one calorie of energy to extract 100 calories of oil (100:1). By 2010, typical EROEI was about 17:1, and some are predicting 5:1 by 2020. Most fossil energy will stay in the ground forever, because of low or negative EROEI. Imagine having a job that paid $100 a day, but the bridge toll for getting there was $105.

Rising prices enable the extraction of difficult and expensive nonconventional energy (tar sands, shale oil, deep sea). At some point, declining EROEI makes extraction pointless, regardless of market prices. Consequently, most of the oil in Canadian tar sands will be left where it is. (The EROEI of tar sands now in production is about 3:1, and 5:1 for shale deposits.)

The world of coal is a similar story. Coal resources are enormous, but coal reserves are far less than proclaimed by industry cheerleaders. Anthracite is premium coal, and its production peaked in 1950. Grade B bituminous coal peaked in 1990. There is abundant grade C coal, lignite, which contains only a fifth of the energy in anthracite, and is especially filthy to burn. Since grade C coal is so low in energy, it cannot be shipped long distances profitably. The coal industry is also constrained by EROEI, and much of this resource will be left in the ground forever.

As we zoom toward a no-growth or negative growth economy, it would be intelligent to prepare for it, to make the transition less turbulent. We aren't. The end of growth is intolerable, inconceivable, and unacceptable. There is only one path forward, by any means necessary — a beautiful recovery followed by an eternity of perpetual growth and heavenly prosperity. Rubin gives us a dope slap. Recovery is impossible. The era of wasteful excess is behind us. Turn your brain to the ON position, pay attention, and prepare for a new reality.

Following the 2008 crash, governments borrowed vast sums of money bailing out pathologically reckless banks. The trendy deregulation movement of the '80s and '90s dismantled prudent time-proven rules that prohibited bankers from behaving like spoiled two-year olds with other people's money. Bailouts created enormous strains for many nations. As a consequence, "central banks are running printing presses almost nonstop to kickstart economic growth." As the value of the dollar declines, we'll pay even more for energy, and dig a grave for growth.

Flooding the economy with new money will do nothing to encourage recovery, because it does not address the core problem, energy limits. But it is creating catastrophic levels of debt that are guaranteed to inflate the misery down the road (beyond the next election cycle, hopefully). Greece has a dim future, and Ireland, Portugal, Spain, and Italy are not far behind. Debt-crippled economies will be helpless sitting ducks when the next recession strikes.

In the first half of the book, Rubin describes the global mess, as he understands it, and he does a great job. It's important information, and it's coming from a lad close to the inner circle of the banking industry, not wild-eyed radical extremists from the Sierra Club. It's a triple-shot of full-strength reality, and it brings many issues into sharp focus.

In the second half, he makes a heroic effort to recommend strategies for responding to the mess. His goal is a fairly smooth transition to a static economy, which he presents as a realistic possibility. For readers who have not been making a serious effort to understand the complex challenges of the Earth Crisis, Rubin's analysis will be soothing. The future isn't roaring with danger. Everything will be mostly OK, sort of.

The magic of the marketplace will rescue us by continually raising the prices on our bad habits, forcing us to live slower and lighter. If governments raise taxes on energy, we'll use less. We don't need more regulations on corporations. If governments do nothing, we'll still use less, because of ever-growing energy costs.

Mature people should be mindful of climate change, because it is not a trivial problem, but our fear of climate disaster exceeds the actual threat, according to Rubin. The gloomy IPCC warnings are based on silly energy resource projections — in a hundred years, we will *not* be consuming more energy than today. We'll be forced to quit our addiction to hydrocarbon fuels before emissions have time to cause catastrophic problems.

Manufacturing jobs will come back home, as rising energy prices drive up the cost of moving products across long distances. The benefits of cheap Asian labor will be lost to rising shipping costs. Transportation costs will also encourage the recovery of localized economies. The food we eat will travel far fewer miles. Local farm labor needs will provide exciting new careers for folks discarded by obsolete industries.

Trained as an economist, Rubin has an outlook focused on cost trends in the here and now. He doesn't slam nuclear energy, because it produces respectable output numbers every day. It doesn't matter that we have yet to figure out a safe and permanent way of disposing the waste, which can remain extremely toxic for millions of years. It doesn't matter that deactivating reactors can cost as much as building them, because the bill is sent to taxpayers and unborn generations, not today's stockholders.

Critical thinkers who are well informed about the complex challenges of the Earth Crisis are not likely to be persuaded by Rubin's vision of the future, but his discussion of the present is excellent. This should not be the only book you ever read.

Rubin concludes with wise advice: "As the boundaries of a finite world continue to close in on us, our challenge is to learn that making do with less is better than always wanting more."

Plagues and Peoples

Nobody comprehends the universe, because it is almost entirely out of sight. We also can't see the universe of microorganisms here on Earth, or fully comprehend their powerful influence. Historian William McNeill learned that disease has played a major role in the human journey, and he wrote a fascinating introduction to our intimate companions, the parasites, in *Plagues and Peoples*.

All critters eat. Hosts provide food, and parasites consume it. Large-bodied parasites, like wolves, are *macro-parasites*. Wolves kill their hosts. *Micro-parasites* include bacteria and small multi-celled organisms. If they quickly kill their host, the banquet is short. A more stable strategy is to simply take a free ride on a living host, like the billions of bacteria that inhabit our guts, share our meals, and don't make us sick.

In healthy ecosystems, stability is the norm. Species coevolve, which encourages balance, like the dance of oak trees and squirrels, or the foxes and rabbits. Balance is disturbed by natural disasters, like when an invasion of organic farmers overwhelms an ecosystem with their plows, axes, and enslaved animals. A farming community is a mob of macro-parasites that weakens or destroys its ecosystem host over time. When parasites disturb balance, McNeill calls this *disease*. "It is not absurd to class the ecological role of humankind in its relationship to other life forms as a disease."

The ruling classes in civilizations behave like macro-parasites when they siphon nutrients away from the working class hosts that they exploit. To survive, the elites must keep enough farmers alive to maintain an adequate supply of nutrients. Elites rely on violence specialists to protect their host collection from other two-legged macro-parasites, like the bloodthirsty civilization across the river. In this scenario, the worker hosts are suffering from a type of disease (the elites) that is called *endemic*, because it allows them to survive.

Disease that kills the host is *epidemic*. "Looked at from the point of view of other organisms, humankind therefore resembles an acute epidemic disease, whose occasional lapses into less virulent forms of behavior have never yet sufficed to permit any really stable, chronic relationship to establish itself."

Our chimp and bonobo cousins continue to have a stable relationship with their ecosystem. Consequently, there are not seven billion of them. Like them, our pre-human ancestors evolved in a tropical rainforest, a warm and wet ecosystem with immense biodiversity. This diversity included many, many types of parasites, and they lovingly helped to keep our ancestors in balance. Life was good. "The balance between eater and eaten was stable, or nearly so, for long periods of time."

Then, some too-clever ancestors began fooling around with technology. With spears, we were able to kill more prey, and foolishly eliminate many of the rival predators that helped keep our numbers in check. By and by, our ancestors began leaving Africa, moving into cooler and drier climates. We left behind many tropical parasites, and explored new lands that had far fewer parasites. We suffered less disease. We moved into new regions as skilled hunters, and encountered game animals that had no fear of us. With clever new technology, like clothing and huts, our ancestors could sidestep their biological limitations and survive in non-tropical habitats.

Antelope and tsetse flies are unaffected by the sleeping sickness parasites they carry. These relationships are old and stable, but a blind date with a new parasite can be fatal. With the advent of animal domestication, there were many blind dates. We began living in close proximity to other species, and their parasites, to which we had no immunity. This gave birth to the deadly new diseases of civilization, and led to a long era of epidemics.

"Most and probably all of the distinctive infectious diseases of civilization transferred to human populations from animal herds." Aborigines, who did not enslave herd animals, did not suffer from infectious disease. The same was true for Native Americans, even those who lived in the densely populated regions of Mexico, Central America, and the Andes.

Humans share many diseases with domesticated animals: poultry (26), rats and mice (32), horses (35), pigs (42), sheep and goats (46), cattle (50), and dogs (65). In addition to the diseases of civilization are ancient rainforest diseases like malaria and yellow fever, which were introduced to the Americas by the slave trade.

From 500 B.C. to A.D. 1200, as civilizations developed in different regions of Eurasia, each area developed pools of civilized diseases, some of which became quite popular. India has a wonderful climate for parasites, and it may be where smallpox, cholera, and plague parasites first entered human hosts. Bubonic plague slammed into a virgin population in the Mediterranean basin. The plague of Justinian (A.D. 542-543) hit hard, maybe killing 100 million, about half of Europe.

From 1200 to 1500, the isolated disease pools of Eurasia eventually connected with the others, creating one large pool of civilized diseases. Nomads, like the Mongols, transported parasites back and forth between China and Europe. Parasites also travelled by ship. Black Death began in China around 1331. Between 1200 and 1393, China's population dropped by half. The disease arrived in Crimea in 1346, spread across Europe, and killed about a third of the people. Muslims believed that those killed by the plague were martyrs, chosen by the will of Allah. They mocked the Christian infidels who successfully limited the spread via quarantines.

Between 1300 and 1700, a number of epidemic diseases became domesticated. To survive, parasites required a steady supply of new hosts without immunity — these were mostly children. A population of 500,000 or more was needed to produce enough new hosts to support an ongoing infestation of measles. If a disease was too virulent, it would eliminate its hosts and die off. Over time, a number of serial killers softened into childhood diseases, like mumps, smallpox, and measles.

From 1500 to 1700, Old World diseases discovered the New World. Europeans and their African slaves were walking disease bombs, but they were mostly immune to the parasites they carried. Native Americans were a virgin population, having no immunity whatsoever to the new parasites, they were blindsided by catastrophic epidemics. The population of Mexico and Peru dropped 90 percent in 120 years.

Since 1700, science has made great advances in death control (not balanced by equal achievements in birth control). Vaccinations have been effective in controlling smallpox and polio. Antibiotics have temporarily provided several decades of relief from a number of infectious parasites. Sewage treatment and water purification systems have also provided temporary relief, during the cheap energy bubble.

Industrial society, with its radically unhealthy way of life, has nurtured new diseases of civilization, like cancer and heart disease. Influenza is a powerful wild card, because it rapidly mutates, sometimes into highly virulent forms. By the time effective vaccines are massproduced, the pandemic may already be over. Many new viral diseases, like Ebola and AIDS, are appearing, as the human swarm meets new and exciting rainforest parasites.

The plague bacterium still lives harmlessly in burrowing rodents and their fleas. Over the years, it has spread around the world. By 1940, it was carried by 34 species of burrowing rodents in America, and 35 species of fleas. By 1975, it was found across the western U.S., and portions of Canada and Mexico. Black rats are the vector that moves the parasites into humans. As long as the gas-guzzling garbage trucks keep running regularly, we'll be safe, maybe.

Modern consumers have had little exposure to epidemic disease, but our elaborate, energy-guzzling systems of death control only provide temporary protection. Sewage treatment, water purification, effective antibiotics, and industrial agriculture have a limited future as we move beyond the cheap energy bubble.

The Eye of the Crocodile

In February 1985, Val Plumwood was having a lovely time canoeing by herself in Australia's Kakadu National Park. The ranger had assured her that the saltwater crocodiles, notorious man-eaters, never attacked canoes. It was a perfect day, gliding across the water in a beautiful land, no worries.

She was a scholar and writer who focused on feminism and environmental philosophy. The Earth Crisis was pounding the planet, and it was obvious to eco-thinkers that this was caused by a severely dysfunctional philosophy. Her book, *The Eye of the Crocodile*, is a fascinating voyage into the realm of ethics, values, and beliefs.

Plumwood understood that the ancient culture of the Aborigines was the opposite of insane, and she had tremendous respect for it. It presented a time-proven example of an ethic that had enabled a healthy and stable way of life for thousands of years. Australia was blessed with a bipolar climate that often swung between drought and deluge, making low-tech agriculture impractical. The land escaped the curse of cities until you-know-who washed up on shore. (As her canoe gently drifted, a floating stick slowly moved closer.)

Plumwood grew up in a rural area. She was home schooled, and enjoyed a fairy tale childhood outdoors, delighted by the "sensuous richness" of the forest. She was unlike most of her generation, because she "acquired an unquenchable thirst for life, for the wisdom of the land." Thus, her appreciation of the Aboriginal culture was not merely intellectual — it was real and deep. Unlike most of her generation, she enjoyed a spiritual connection to the land. (The floating stick had two beautiful eyes.)

The stick with two eyes was a crocodile, nearly as big as the canoe, and it was five minutes to lunchtime. Suddenly, the reptile began ramming her canoe. She rushed toward shore, but the crocodile leaped and grabbed her between the legs. Three times, it pulled her underwater, trying to drown her. Miraculously, she managed to escape, severely injured, and survived.

It was a mind-blowing life changing experience. Intellectually, she had understood food chains, predators, and prey. But this was the first time in her life that she was nothing more than a big juicy meatball — impossible! She was far more than food! The crocodile strongly disagreed. Its sharp teeth drove home the message that she was not outside of nature. She was a part of the ecosystem, an animal, and nourishing meat — no more significant than a moth or mouse.

She wrote, "In the vivid intensity of those last moments, when great, toothed jaws descend upon you, it can *hit you like a thunderclap* that you were completely wrong about it all — not only about what your own personal life meant, but about what life and death themselves actually mean."

She was blindsided by the realization that an entire highly educated civilization could be wrong about subjects so basic — animality, food, and the dance of life and death. The crocodile painfully drove home the point that the modern culture was living in a fantasy. Our highly contagious culture was ravaging the planet, and we didn't understand why. Each new generation was trained to live and think like imperial space aliens.

Plumwood was educated by the space alien culture, but the crocodile was a powerful teacher from the real world, the ecosystem. Darwin revealed that humans were animals, but this essential truth harmlessly bounced off a long tradition of human supremacist illusions. It was easy to see that those who were demolishing the planet were radicalized space aliens who believed that human society was completely outside of nature, and far above it.

The Aboriginal people inhabited the real world. They were wild two-legged animals who had learned the wisdom of voluntary self-restraint. For them, the entire land was alive, intelligent, and sacred; even the plants, streams, and rocks — everything. Nobody owned it.

Mindfully inhabiting a sacred place required a profound sense of respect.

Space aliens drove them crazy. Colonists in spandex jogged mindlessly across sacred land, listening to electronic pop music. Reverence was absent. They did not belong to the land, and were unaware of its incredible power. Some of the traditional folks wanted to ban these disrespectful intrusions. The colonial era had been a disaster.

The space alien worldview had many layers of hierarchy. At the summit were the elites. Below them were women, peasants, slaves, and the colonized. Beneath the humans were animals. Some critters, like dogs, cats, and horses, had special status. If they obediently submitted to human domination, they were not meat. Below them were meat class animals that had no consciousness. Especially despised were man-eating animals, and critters that molested human property. They were mercilessly exterminated. Beneath animals was the plant world, a far older realm.

The foundation of the dominant worldview was human supremacy, and this mode of thinking had been the driving force behind a growing tsunami of ecological devastation. Plumwood saw two alternatives to supremacist thinking.

(1) *Ecological animalism* was the realm of crocodiles, Aborigines, our wild ancestors, and the rest of the natural world. All life was food, including humans. In an ecosystem, "we live the other's death, die the other's life." Our bodies belonged to the ecosystem, not to ourselves. The spirits of animate and inanimate beings had equal significance.

(2) *Ontological veganism* did not believe in using animals or eating animal foods. This ethic was an offshoot of human supremacy. It did not condemn the dogma of human/nature dualism. It denied that humans were meat, despite the fact that a number of large predators have been dining on us for countless centuries. It believed that animals were worthy of moral consideration, but the plant people were not.

Ontological veganism was queasy about predation; it would prefer a predator-free world. It believed that human hunting was cultural (animal abuse), while animal predation was natural (instinctive). But every newborn human has a body carefully designed by evolution for a life of hunting. We are capable of smoothly running for hours on two legs, and we have hands, arms, and shoulders that are fine-tuned for accurately throwing projectiles in a forceful manner. What you see in the mirror is a hunter.

Plumwood was a vegetarian because she believed that the production of meat on factory farms was ethically wrong. She had no problems with Aborigines hunting for dinner. All of the world's sustainable wild cultures consumed animal foods. She was well aware that her plant food diet was not ecologically harmless.

Cultures rooted in human supremacy have achieved remarkable success at rubbishing entire ecosystems. This is not about flawed genes. It's about a bunch of screwy ideas that we've been taught. Sustainable cultures perceive reality in a radically different way. Luckily, software is editable. Plumwood recommended that creative communicators bring new ideas to our dying culture; stories that help us find our way home to the family of life. This is an enormous challenge.

Plumwood also wrote an essay, *Prey to a Crocodile*, which is not in the book. It provides a detailed discussion of the attack. The rangers wanted to go back the next day, and kill the crocodile. She strongly objected. The crocodile had done nothing wrong. Predation is normal and healthy. She had been an intruder.

The Great Warming

Recent decades have been a golden age for archaeologists. New technology has provided tools for better understanding the past. Researchers can now identify the climate trends of past centuries by analyzing the layers in tropical coral, tree rings, glacial ice packs, and lakeshore and seabed sediments.

Climate has played a primary role in influencing the course of human history. It could enable the rise of mighty empires, and later reduce them to dusty ruins. Big changes can happen suddenly, without warning, and have devastating effects. Mighty scientists may huff and puff and stamp their feet, but climate will do whatever it wishes.

In 2000, archaeologist Brian Fagan published *The Little Ice Age*. This book examined an era of cooler weather spanning from 1300 to 1850, and its effects on northern Europe. In those days, most folks lived from harvest to harvest, with few safety nets. In 1315, it barely stopped raining, and the heavy rains continued through 1316 and 1317, followed by horrendous weather in 1318. At least 1.5 million folks checked out. The famine of 1344 to 1345 was so extreme that even the super-rich starved.

Preceding the Little Ice Age was the Medieval Warm Period, which spanned from 800 to 1300. Fagan described this era in *The Great Warming*, published in 2008. Far less was known about this time, because fewer written records have survived. But new climate data has been filling in a number of missing pieces, revealing many forgotten events, important stuff.

When it was in the mood for mischief, the Little Ice Age was a harsh bully. Fagan had expected the warm period to be the opposite, and in some regions, it was, sort of. In Europe, there were fewer late frosts, and the growing season was three weeks longer. There were vineyards in England and southern Norway. Surplus wealth enabled the construction of grand cathedrals.

Whilst the weather was rather pleasant, the era suffered from a devastating spasm of innovation. The diabolically powerful moldboard plow, which was able to turn heavy soils, replaced the primitive scratch plow. A new harness allowed horses to replace pokey oxen as beasts of burden. The new three-field fallowing system enabled two-thirds of the fields to be growing crops every year, instead of just half of them, with the old two-field system.

By using these new technologies, vast regions of highly fertile heavy soils could now be converted into highly productive cropland. The only obstacle was the vast ancient forests, and their untamed wildlife. Loggers grabbed their axes and exterminated more than half of Europe's forests between 1100 and 1350.

Expanded cropland area, combined with a balmy climate, produced much more food, and this always resulted in a mushrooming mob. Between 1000 and 1347, the population of Europe grew from 35 to 80 million, despite short life expectancies. It got so crowded that folks in 1300 were worse off than their grandparents in 1200.

In other regions, the warm period brought unpleasant weather. The Mayans of the Yucatan lowlands experienced extended droughts and abundant misery. "Hot, humid, and generally poorly drained, the Maya lowlands were a fragile, water-stressed environment even in the best of times," Fagan observed. "It's hard to imagine a less likely place for a great civilization."

The Mayan city of Tikal may have had 300,000 residents. It was entirely dependent on rainfall for water. Their ecosystem did not have dependable sources of water, like rivers or underground aquifers. They developed amazing systems for storing rainwater, and these worked really well, usually, but not during multi-year droughts. The drought of 910 lasted six years, and generated social unrest, which led to the collapse of many Mayan cities.

At the same time, severe droughts in western North America followed similar patterns. Irrigation systems at Chaco Canyon enabled more than 2,000 folks to survive in an arid region for several centuries. This worked well in wetter years. After 1100, droughts intensified, and within 50 years, the city was abandoned.

California was home to hunters and foragers. Acorns were half of the diet for many tribes. Oaks could produce as much food per acre as medieval European farms, and foragers could acquire a year's supply in several weeks. Fewer acorns fell in drought years, and extended droughts killed the oak trees.

Stumps at Mono Lake indicate that a severe drought began in 1250 and lasted for over a hundred years. Fagan noted "None of today's droughts, which last as long as four years, approach the intensity and duration of the Medieval Warm Period droughts." He called them *megadroughts*. They baked away the surface waters and soil moisture.

The Yellow River (Huang He) has an appropriate nickname, *China's Sorrow*, because it is one of the world's most trouble-prone rivers. Fagan said "the Huang He basin (has) been a crucible for human misery for more than seven thousand years." About 45 percent of the Chinese population lives in the basin. From year to year, precipitation can vary by 30 percent. A dry June is a bad omen.

To reduce the risk of famines, the Chinese built complex irrigation systems, which the Yellow River enjoyed burying with silt. The yellow loess soil of the region was highly fertile, easy to till, and 200 feet deep (61 m) on average. It was also light and easily erodible. Once upon a time, forests held the soil in place, but deforestation had catastrophic consequences. The river carried an enormous load of yellow silt downstream, and this created perfect conditions for disastrous floods, which have killed many millions over the centuries.

This region has long been a spooky place to live, but the warm period was worse, "a time of violent climatic swings nurtured thousands of miles away that brought either lengthy dry cycles or torrential rainfall that inundated thousands of acres of the Huang He basin."

Today, the global climate is hotter than the Medieval Warm Period. The warming trend has been steadily building since 1860. Glaciers are melting and folks are getting increasingly nervous about rising sea levels. While this is indeed a bummer, Fagan warns that extended drought is a far greater threat. Extended drought withers agriculture, toasts pastures, and dries up lakes and rivers. Seven-point-something billion people will be extremely vulnerable when we move beyond Peak Food, and into the climate surprises of the coming decades.

The Future

Al Gore's book, *The Future*, is fascinating and perplexing. The world is being pummeled by enormous waves of change, and most are destructive and unsustainable. What should we do? To envision wise plans, it's important to know the past, and understand how the present mess evolved. The book presents a substantial discussion of six mega-trends that are influencing the future:

EARTH INC is the global economy, dominated by a mob of ruthless multinational corporations. It's pushing radical changes in the way we live, work, and think. Many leaders in the world have become its hand puppets, shamelessly selling influence in exchange for treasure and power. Earth Inc. is the monster that's killing the ecosystem.

GLOBAL MIND is the worldwide web that enables communication between people everywhere. Two billion now have access to it. It provides access to a cornucopia of fresh information — knowledge from sources outside the walls of culture and propaganda. The Global Mind is our single hope for inspiring rapid, intelligent, revolutionary change.

BALANCE OF POWER is changing. Following World War II, the world was happy, as America provided virtuous leadership that helped maintain stability in the world. Today, the U.S. is no longer respected. Power is shifting away from Western nations to new power-houses, and from national governments to corporate interests.

OUTGROWTH is the explosion of unsustainable growth in almost everything — population, pollution, consumption, soil mining, water mining, extinctions, and on and on. Earth Inc. is fanatically obsessed with perpetual growth, and aggressively flattens anything that stands in its path. Bummer growth must be replaced with the magically harmless growth of Sustainable Capitalism.

LIFE SCIENCE is providing us with technology to manipulate biological processes in new ways. We'll cure more diseases and live much longer. Our ability to deliberately alter the genes of any living organism allows us to play a significant role in controlling the planet's evolutionary journey. Of course, evolution must be manipulated cautiously, to hopefully avoid embarrassing calamities that were impossible to foresee.

THE EDGE is the catastrophically dysfunctional relationship between humankind and the ecosystem. On the down side, trashing the atmosphere and climate has created a monster we cannot control. On the plus side, it's inspiring many enlightened efforts to guide civilization back into balance with the ecosystem.

Al Gore is a charming lad with a good sense of humor. The son of a senator, Gore has spent much of his life amidst the barbarian tribes of Washington. He eventually became the vice president and a wealthy tycoon. While at Harvard, one of his professors was a pioneer in climate change research, a big juju subject, and a primary influence on Gore's career path. Gore is a senior advisor to Google, and a board member at Apple. He is exceptionally well informed about the digital world, climate change, ecological challenges, global politics, and the shenanigans of the rich and powerful.

In the book, Gore sometimes jabbers like a politician giddy with optimism. Yes, things are a big mess, and the status quo is in need of speedy, intelligent, radical reform. We can fix it! Politicians rarely win elections when their objective is damage control (Jimmy Carter's mistake). The way to win is to wear a big smile and promise hope, solutions, and better days ahead.

Much of the book is impressive, but its optimism for the future is not well supported by compelling arguments and evidence. Readers

117

learn that it's not too late to nip climate change in the bud. We simply need to reduce greenhouse emissions by 80 to 90 percent. But how could we do this without blindsiding the system that enables the existence of seven-point-something billion people? Easy! Create a carbon tax. Shift subsidies from fossil energy to renewables. Require utilities to use more alternative energy. Create a cap and trade system. If every nation eagerly did this next week, our worries would be over.

Population continues to grow exponentially. Gore recommends that we "stabilize" population. It would be risky to actually reduce population, because this might trigger a "fertility trap," a terrible downward spiral of population free-fall. When there are too many seniors, and not enough taxpayers, pension systems collapse.

But stabilizing an enormous population raises serious questions about how much longer we can continue to feed so many people. Agriculture is currently engaged in "strip-mining topsoil" on a staggering scale. Each kilogram of Iowa corn costs 1.5 kilograms of topsoil, a precious nonrenewable resource.

Gore asserts that this can be corrected by a transition to crop rotation, and to organic low-till technology. But low-till cropping is designed for conventional agriculture, and works well with heavy applications of herbicide. Organic low-till is still in the experimental phase, and is extremely difficult to do successfully, because weeds are not wimps.

While water usage is increasing, water resources are declining, because underground aquifers are being depleted in many highly productive farming regions. Gore recommends drip irrigation, wastewater recycling, and cisterns for rainwater storage. Considering the current scale of water mining, and the cost of high tech irrigation, it's hard to see these options as effective solutions. When the water is used up, farm productivity drops sharply, or completely.

Meanwhile, another monster is rising on the horizon — global phosphorus reserves are moving toward a crisis. Because phosphorus is an essential plant nutrient, this will have huge effects on conventional agriculture. Oh, and we also need to get the world's nations united behind reversing deforestation, fish mining, and mass extinction.

Gore says that it would be insane to burn the fossil energy we've already discovered, because this would worsen the effects of climate change. But we're unlikely to stop. Experts argue about when Peak Oil will arrive, but it will, and it will be followed by an era of increasing turbulence, as industrial civilization is painfully weaned. Most of the easy oil has already gone up in smoke, and what remains is far more difficult to extract. Expensive oil means expensive food, and many poor people can barely afford food today. Spikes in food prices led to food riots in 2008 and 2011.

Gore adores civilization's two magnificent achievements, democracy and capitalism, but he laments that both have been "hacked" by the evil slime balls of Earth Inc. If we don't fix this, we're doomed. It's time to fetch our pitchforks and chase the slime balls away. The solution to our problems is to restore dynamic democracy, and then create a magical utopia of Sustainable Capitalism, which will allow Sustainable Growth to continue forever! The best is yet to come!

The book provides an impressive discussion how we got into this mess. It's unique in that it comes from a card-carrying member of the global elite, not a hungry dirty radical. Readers are given a rare opportunity to enjoy the view from the top of the pyramid. I hope that the second edition clarifies some questionable assumptions in this otherwise fascinating book.

The Human Web

Cultural cheerleaders constantly shout about how lucky we are to live in an age of miracles, a utopia of technology and progress. Everything is just great (if you cram most of reality under the bed).

But the folks who rip off their blinders know better. They can perceive huge and growing crises that cannot be well addressed via the pursuit of shopping and entertainment. They can see that it's time to learn, to think, and to change. Understanding how we got into this bog of predicaments requires learning, lots of learning. For this, we need our superheroes, the historians.

William McNeill, and his son John, heard the cries for help and came to the rescue. William once tried to boil the human journey down to one book, but it was 829 pages, too big for general readers. John's vision was human history in 200 pages, and he teamed up with his father to write it. The finished product was 350 pages, and titled *The Human Web*.

The book slices human history into time blocks, and provides snapshots of the world during each period. It's not a sleep-inducing recital of kings, empires, wars, and dates. It's about trends — in technology, weaponry, religion, worldviews, and environmental impacts. The McNeills framed their discussion based on a model of *webs*, which are networks of communication and trade. Throughout the book, they take readers on an interesting promenade through the ages. Let's take a peek at a few of their topics.

For most of the human journey, our hunter-gatherer phase, webs were small nomadic clans. They weren't completely isolated. For example, the freakishly powerful new technology of bows and arrows made it much easier to deplete game and enemies. It managed to gradually spread from web to web until it was used everywhere except Australia. This was version 1.0 of the worldwide web. Technology that expands food production or kill-power has always been popular and highly contagious. Webs that don't adopt the latest technology are likely to be more vulnerable to webs that do.

As humans migrated out of Mother Africa, into non-tropical ecosystems, new challenges and opportunities forced many changes. Survival depended on flexibility and innovation, and we got quite slick at this. By 40,000 years ago, we had become a potent "weed species" of invasive exotics, like dandelions, rats, and houseflies. Nothing could stop our spread.

With the emergence of agriculture 12,000 years ago, webs got bigger, and interacted more with neighboring webs. Around 6,000 years ago, the emergence of cities led to metropolitan webs. Things and ideas spread faster and farther. Strong webs frequently expanded by absorbing weaker webs. By 2,000 years ago, the highly successful Old World web included most of Eurasia and North Africa. Finally, by 500 years ago, most of the world's webs merged into the cosmopolitan web, which spanned the entire globe.

We began domesticating animals about 6,000 years ago. Along the way, we learned a new trick, milking them. "Herdsmen, in effect, substituted themselves for kids and lambs as consumers of milk — an extraordinary perversion of natural biological relationships." By going into the dairy business, a herder could extract four times more calories from their enslaved animals, compared to simply eating them.

Salvation religions grew in popularity because they made life more tolerable for the oppressed majority. Everyone, including women and slaves, had souls, so nobody was completely worthless. Those who obeyed the divine rules while alive were promised eternal life in paradise.

Trading by barter was often clumsy. I might not want to trade my wheat for your rutabagas. The invention of money made trading much easier. This greatly increased the exchange of goods, and the injuries caused to ecosystems. Emperors also loved money, because taxes paid in rutabagas were a hassle. When peasants were required to pay taxes with money, they had to acquire money by selling stuff, forcing them to produce commodities.

In A.D. 1000, most of Western Europe was largely forest, and lightly populated. Then the moldboard plow came into use. It enabled farmers to till heavy soils. Cropland rapidly expanded as forests shrank. A similar explosion occurred in India and China, as rice farming spread between A.D. 200 and 1000, spurred by irrigation, iron tools, and the use of oxen. Population growth accelerated.

In the good old days, communities were not diverse. Members of small webs shared the same worldview, so there was far less friction. With the invention of the printing press, cities were flooded with information from many cultures, and many of the new ideas conflicted with traditional beliefs. Both the Pope and Luther howled, and tried to block the rising tide of science and other heresies. Today, science is attempting to standardize the global mind, at the expense of multinational religions and other myth systems.

Civilization is addicted to agriculture. Soil mining, forest mining, and water mining are unsustainable. We know this, but it's impossible for us to go cold turkey and quit the habit. Similarly, we have become extremely addicted to the unsustainable use of fossil fuels, and our modern way of life would be impossible without them. Nonrenewable resources do not last forever. Our super-sized global society is lurching toward its expiration date.

The most disturbing trend in this book is a non-stop, ever-growing arms race, driven by an obsession with perpetual growth. It seems to be impossible for unsustainable societies to stop pursuing more and better ways of smashing each other. During the industrial era, there has been explosive growth in death technology. In the twenty-first century, we are now capable of wiping out most of humankind in a single day, with the push of a button.

The last chapter provides two summaries. John, the son, writes first. He sees history as an ongoing race for complexity, requiring ever-increasing flows of energy and information. In remote areas, simple cultures still work, but when complex cultures thrust into their sacred home, the days of wildness and freedom are soon over. Complexity provides immense competitive advantages, as long as the inflow of extracted resources continues. But the inflow is now beginning to sputter. Consequently, "the chances of cataclysmic violence seem depressingly good."

Then William, the father, writes. The path that led us to having one worldwide web was driven by a collective pursuit of wealth and power. He wondered how long this web could survive on our current energy flows. William thought that for long-term survival, we needed to return to small face-to-face communities, "within which shared meanings, shared values, and shared goals *made life worth living for everyone*, even the humblest and least fortunate." He concluded, "My personal hunch is that catastrophes — great and small — are sure to come and human resilience will prove more than we can imagine."

This book is part of a significant shift in the modern perception of reality. It is pushing aside the magical thinking that assured us that technology and wise leaders could be trusted to smooth the path before us. Very late in the game, it's finally acceptable for respected scholars like the McNeills to state the obvious. They point to big storms ahead, ready or not.

Constantly wishing away the swarms of contradictions makes us crazy. When we stop wishing, and open our eyes, the world suddenly snaps into sharp focus, and makes perfect sense — we are not in utopia; we are lost. Finally, we have a call to action. How can we get home? It's time to pursue understanding, and stir in generous amounts of imagination. Our experiment in controlling and exploiting ecosystems has been a disaster. On the path forward, adapting to ecosystems is likely to work far better. It's worth a try.

Something New Under the Sun

A verse in the Bible proclaims, "There is no new thing under the sun" (Ecclesiastes 1:9). These words come from a low-tech era when nomadic herders diminished their ecosystem so slowly that little change was noticeable to the passing generations. *Something New Under the Sun* is the title of John McNeill's environmental history of the twentieth century. It describes a high-tech era when industrial society got thoroughly sloshed on cheap energy, and went on a berserk rampage, smashing everything.

With the emergence of agriculture, the relationship between humankind and the ecosystem took a sharp turn onto a bumpy bloody unsustainable road. There are a few places where agriculture wrecks the land at a slower pace. A region spanning from Poland to Ireland typically receives adequate rain in gentle showers, the lay of the land is not steep, and the heavy soils are not easily eroded. When the farming methods from this region were exported to North America, where heavy rains are common, it resulted in severe erosion.

Many agricultural systems flamed out and vanished long ago. China has beat the odds, and remained in the farm business for over 3,000 years. This is often cited as proof that sustainable agriculture is possible. But McNeill points out that their longevity is the result of sequentially replacing one unsustainable mode with a different unsustainable mode. They will eventually run out of tricks and flame out. A process that regularly pulverizes soils and depletes nutrients cannot have a long-term future, and irrigated systems usually flame out faster.

Food is one thing that humans actually need. McNeill describes how agriculture has become far more destructive in the last hundred years. It produces more food, degrades more land, and spurs population growth, which seriously worsens many other problems. Readers learn about erosion, heavy machinery, synthetic fertilizers, salinization, pesticides, herbicides, water mining, and so on. Our ability to continue feeding a massive herd will face huge challenges in the coming years.

In addition to troublesome agriculture, we stirred fossil energy and industrialization into the pot, and it exploded. The twentieth century was like an asteroid strike — a tumultuous pandemonium never seen before, that can never be repeated. Tragically, this era of roaring helter-skelter is what most people today perceive to be "normal." Life has always been like this, we think, because this is how it's been since grandma was born. *History Deficiency Syndrome* leads to a life of vivid hallucinations, but there is a highly effective antidote: learning.

The "normal" mindset is trained to focus on the benefits of modernity, and to be indifferent to the costs. With a bright torch, McNeill leads his readers down into deep catacombs where industrial civilization stores the skeletons of the twentieth century's blunders. He takes us on an extended tour of the embarrassing side effects of progress — deforestation, bio invasions, eutrophication, mass extinctions, nuclear accidents, acid rain, smog, ozone depletion, toxic pollution, greenhouse gases, and on and on.

It's a great introduction to reality; vital knowledge that most students never receive. Society has rendered these blunders largely invisible in our schools, workplaces, newsrooms, churches, and homes. They stay in the catacombs. In the normal daylight world, we are constantly distracted by a fire hose of frivolous information, ridiculous balderdash, and titillating hogwash. The myths thrive. The world was made for humans. We are the greatest.

McNeill points out that a major cause of twentieth century mass hysteria was that millions of people were enslaved by "big ideas." Some ideas are absorbed by cultures and never excreted, even stupid ideas, like the obsession with perpetual economic growth, our insatiable hunger for stuff and status, our stunning disregard for the generations yet-to-be-born.

"The overarching priority of economic growth was easily the most important idea of the twentieth century." We created a monster that we could not control — it controlled us. Economists became the nutjob gurus of the wacky cult of growth, and society guzzled their hallucinogenic Kool-Aid. Crazy economists, who preached that society could get along without natural resources, won Nobel Prizes. They became respected advisors to world leaders. In every newscast, you repeatedly hear the words "growth" and "recovery."

Environmentalists often sneer at the multitudes who fail to be enraged by the catastrophe of the week. They assume that the herd understands the issues. But the daily info-streams that flood into the mainstream world have almost nothing in common with McNeill's model of reality. Few people in our society have a well-rounded understanding of our eco-predicaments, including most environmentalists. This world would be a much different place if McNeill's perception of history became the mainstream, and folks could readily comprehend the harms caused by our lifestyles. Ignorance is enormously costly.

One wee bright spot in the twentieth century was the emergence of Deep Ecology, a small group of renegade thinkers that enthusiastically denounced the dead end path of anthropocentricism. For the first time in 300 years, Western people were spray-painting rude insults on the cathedrals of Cartesian thinking — "We do not live in a machine world of soulless dead matter!" Deep Ecology succeeded in channeling bits of wisdom from the spirits of our wild ancestors.

The book is thoroughly researched, well written, and hard to put down. It's fascinating to observe the spectacular ways that brilliant innovations backfire. Human cleverness is amazing, but it is dwarfed by our amazing un-cleverness. We weren't made to live like this. On the final pages, McNeill does not offer an intoxicating punch bowl of magical thinking. Our future is highly volatile, even the near future is uncertain. History has little to say about sudden mass enlightenment and miraculous intelligent change. "The reason I expect formidable ecological and societal problems in the future is because of what I see in the past." We live in an interesting culture.

Snake Oil: Fracking's False Promise

When a dark and furious storm is racing in, and the tornado sirens are howling, smart folks stop staring at their cell phones, and head for shelter. But what if the cell phones were streaming messages that the storm warnings were a hoax, and there was nothing to fear? Twenty years ago, Peak Oil was a ridiculous absurdity conjured up by notorious idiots on the lunatic fringe. Ten years ago, it had become an acceptable topic for polite conversation. Today, an extremely effective disinformation campaign has inspired many to toss their energy concerns out the window.

This made Richard Heinberg hopping mad, so he wrote *Snake Oil* to set the record straight. He's been blasting the warning sirens for more than ten years, via a series of books. Nobody sane disputes that fossil energy is finite and nonrenewable. Nobody sane disputes that our current path has an expiration date. The argument is over when that date arrives. For most folks, something that may become a problem 50 to 100 years from now is simply not worth thinking about. Heinberg is getting strong whiffs of trouble right now.

The production of conventional oil and gas is close to peak, but new technology has enabled production of unconventional oil and gas. We are now extracting oil and gas from shale. We're cooking oil out of tar sands bitumen. We are drilling in deep waters offshore. This energy is far more expensive to produce.

Today, for each barrel of new oil we discover, we consume four or five barrels pumped from elderly fields. In 1930, oil was as cheap as four cents per barrel. In 2002, a barrel of oil cost $25, and in 2012, it was $110 (with a $150 spike in 2008). Deep water drilling is economically possible when the price is $90 or more. Existing tar sands projects can continue production at $60, but new tar sands projects need at least $80. Almost all drilling requires $70. The era of cheap energy is over.

Every gold rush produces a few winners and legions of losers. In order to drum up the necessary investment funding, it is customary to make highly exaggerated estimates of the immense wealth just waiting to be reeled in by wise guys (like you). I recall hucksters once proclaimed that the Caspian Sea province could contain up to 200 billion barrels of oil. By 2001, after ten years of intensive work on prime sites, far less than 20 billion barrels were produced, according to petroleum geologist Colin Campbell.

Everyone agrees that the increased production of unconventional oil and gas has delayed our blind date with disaster a bit. Is this delay years, decades, or centuries? Heinberg introduces us to petroleum geologists who believe that U.S. gas and oil production will begin its decline by 2020. "Production from shale gas wells typically declines 80 to 95 percent in the first 36 months of operation. Given steep shale gas well decline rates and low recovery efficiency, the United States may actually have fewer than 10 years of shale gas supply at the current rate of consumption." In the North Dakota oil fields, 1,400 new wells have to be drilled every year, just to maintain current production, according to a story in *Financial Times* (27 Aug 2014).

Today, everyone has spent their entire lives in an era of rising energy production and economic growth, just like our parents did. But economic growth is getting dodgy. It's being kept on life support by skyrocketing levels of debt. As energy production approaches its decline phase, prices are sure to rise. There will come a day when economic growth goes extinct. Without economic growth, our way of life will eventually become a hilarious story told by the campfires of our descendants.

Should we be making serious plans for the coming challenges? "Heck no," says the energy industry. Our treasure of unconventional energy is the equivalent of two Saudi Arabias! We now have a 100-year supply of gas, according Daniel Yergin. T. Boone Pickens says 160 years. Aubrey McClendon says 200 years. Even 100 years is daffy. How was it calculated? "Simply by taking the highest imaginable resource estimate for each play, then taking the very best imaginable recovery rate, then adding up the numbers." This results in projections that have no relationship to reality.

The Bakken and Eagle Ford deposits produce more than 80 percent of U.S. tight oil. David Hughes, author of *Drill, Baby, Drill*, estimated that the combined production of both deposits will end up being the equivalent of ten months of U.S. consumption. The U.S. Geological Service (USGS) estimated that Bakken contains 3.65 billion barrels of recoverable oil — about six weeks of current global consumption. The U.S. Energy Information Agency (EIA) predicted that Bakken oil will peak in 2017.

Tim Morgan is a consultant who does a lot of work for investment bankers. In his eye-opening 2013 report, *Perfect Storm*, he concluded that 200 years of growth is approaching the finish line, which may arrive in ten years or so.

Heinberg recommends that we shift to renewable energy with utmost speed. Hmmm. Solar panels and wind turbines have a limited lifespan. Using them, repairing them, and replacing them requires the existence of an extremely unsustainable industrial civilization. They are a Band-Aid, not a solution. This civilization will struggle to survive when it gets strangled by energy shortages. We'll be forced to make a painful transition to muscle-powered agriculture, which cannot feed seven billion.

Somewhere along the line, televisions, laptops, and refrigerators will become useless ballast. Even if scientists invented a way to extract affordable fossil energy for another 200 years, it would be a foolish thing to do. We've burned far too much carbon already. The climate is getting uppity.

I wonder if it might be more useful to voyage into the realm of unconventional thinking, on a sacred mission to explore big questions. Over and over, we are told that cool people work really hard, become really prosperous, and buy lots of really cool stuff. To me, that sounds like a tragic waste of the precious gift of life. It's causing lots of irreparable damage for no good reason. We weren't born to live like this. We were born for a life of wild freedom.

The book is short, full of helpful charts and graphs, well documented, and delightfully easy to read and understand.

Afterburn

Once upon a time, Richard Heinberg was a mild-mannered college professor in northern California. In 1998, he happened to read an article in *Scientific American* that revealed the Peak Oil theory. A small clan on the lunatic fringe had been discussing the notion, but it was now being yanked out of the closet by a number of retired petroleum geologists — respectable experts having front line experience with an increasingly ominous reality.

Peak Oil was terrifying. The geologists were telling us that our way of life was racing toward the cliff. Dignified ladies and gentlemen naturally swept it under the carpet, because the notion was certainly impossible in this age of techno-miracles. Anyway, the anticipated calamity was still 20 or 30 years away, so there was no need to think about it.

In 2003, Heinberg published *The Party's Over*, which explained Peak Oil to a general audience. Since then, he's made a career out of exposing the dark side of growth, progress, and other mischief. Eventually, he left the university and joined the Post Carbon Institute. His message is that resource depletion, climate change, and economic meltdown will blindside our way of life in this century. He suggests that now is a great time to pay closer attention to reality.

Decades of explosive economic growth were only possible because of cheap and abundant energy, abundant high quality mineral resources, and highly productive oil-powered agriculture. Today, the perpetual growth monster is kept on life support by pumping it up with trillions of dollars of debt. Back in the 1960s, a dollar of debt boosted the GDP by a dollar. By 2000, a dollar of debt boosted GDP by just 20 cents. Today, the tsunami of debt is creating a new stock market bubble, and its collapse may be worse than the crash of 2008. The notion that "growth is over" inspires the titans of finance leap from tall buildings.

It's already too late to cleverly pull the plug on climate change and live happily ever after. Our current strategy, ignoring the problem and denying it exists, is the preferred policy of our glorious leaders. It might be possible to soften the worst-case scenario if we reduced our fossil fuel consumption by 80 to 90 percent by 2050, a daunting challenge. The transition to renewable energy will be turbulent, because of its numerous shortcomings. For example, trucks, planes, and agriculture cannot run on electricity. Many uses of oil have no substitute.

Welcome to the subject matter of Heinberg's latest book, *Afterburn*. We're living in the final decades of a one-time freak-out in human history, the Great Burning. For two centuries, we've been extracting and burning staggering amounts of sequestered carbon, for no good reason. What were we thinking? It's nonrenewable, so using it as the core energy source for industrial civilization could only have a crappy ending. For thousands of years, Arab herders traveled across regions containing oceans of oil, left it alone, and enjoyed a good life. Self-destruction is not mandatory.

The book takes readers on an up-to-date tour of the unintended consequences of the Great Burning, and presents reasonable arguments for why it's moving into the sunset phase. The final chapters of *Afterburn* contemplate life after the burn. What can intelligent people do to prepare for a way of life that will be far smaller, simpler, and slower?

In the 1930s, a Nazi control freak named Joseph Goebbels revolutionized mind control via high-tech propaganda. This was made possible by the latest consumer fad, radio. One person spoke, and millions listened, day after day. Today, with the internet, and hundreds of TV channels, many millions are speaking at once, presenting a fantastic variety of viewpoints. Truth (if any) can become a needle in the haystack.

Many huge ideas have been born in the lunatic fringe, presented by heretics like Galileo and Darwin. At the same time, the fringe produces oceans of idiotic balderdash. At the opposite end of the spectrum is the mainstream world, where the one and only thing that matters is the idiotic quest for ongoing economic growth. Other issues, like climate change and resource depletion, are nothing more than annoying distractions that must be stepped around.

Heinberg is interesting because he camps in the no-man's-land between shameless mainstream disinformation and the wacko hysteria of the fringe. He's a likeable lad, and a clear writer who makes an effort to be respectful and fair-minded. Until recently, it's been compulsory for eco-writers to include hope and solutions, even if they're daffy, because bummer books gather dust. It's encouraging to see an emerging trend, in which the emphasis on hopium is becoming unhip, and readers are served larger doses of uncomfortable facts with no sugar coating.

Afterburn includes small servings of magical thinking, but overall it lays the cards on the table. A way of life can only be temporary if it is dependent on nonrenewable resources, or on consuming renewables at an unsustainable rate. An economy requiring perpetual growth is insane. Nature will fix our population excesses and eliminate overshoot. The lights will go out. All civilizations collapse. Ours will too. We won't be rescued by miraculous paradigm shifts. The biggest obstacle to intelligent change is human nature. Folks with food, money, and a roof don't worry about threats that are not immediate. There is a possibility that humankind will no longer exist by the end of this century. And so on.

Yes, things can look a little bleak, but don't surrender to cynicism and give up. We can't chase away the storm, but we can do many things that make a difference. Learn how to do practical stuff, like cook, sew, and garden. Become less reliant on purchased goods and services. Develop trusting relationships with your neighbors.

Today is a paradise for folks interested in changing the world. Imagine cool visions of a new and improved future where we could nurture cooperation, eliminate inequality, mindfully manage population, and minimize environmental injuries. Unfortunately, visioning is limited by the fact that the future is certain to be radically different. What can we say for sure about 2050? I remain stubbornly confident that there will be sun and moon, mountains and oceans, bacteria and insects. What else will make it?

When civilizations die, most or all of their cultural information also dies. Today, much of this information is stored in electronic media, or printed on acidic paper that has a short lifespan. Heinberg believes that it's essential to protect our books, because they are vital for cultural survival. He fears that the amazing achievements of the Great Burning will be forgotten. "Will it all have been for nothing?"

A far better question is, "What cultural achievements would we want to be remembered by?" During the Great Burning, we've learned so much about environmental history and human ecology. We are coming to understand why almost every aspect of our way of life is unsustainable. (Our schools should teach this!) The most valuable gift we could give to new generations is a thorough understanding of the many things we've learned from our mistakes, and the mistakes of our ancestors. They need a good map of the minefield.

The Essential Exponential

Galileo was a lad who had a powerful talent for thinking outside the box. He was capable of believing what he saw with his own eyes, and rejecting what society told him to believe, if it was nonsense. With his telescope, he could clearly perceive that the sun did not rotate around the Earth. He was alone in comprehending the truth, whilst the rest of society was completely wrong — not fun!

Later, as the nightmare of the Industrial Revolution was picking up steam, the mindset of the elite went manic, soaring in bizarre hallucinations of utopia and human supremacy. One of those wacky dreamers was the daddy of Thomas Malthus, and dad drove the lad mad. The lad could think outside the box. He commenced to write a book, which explained why perpetual growth was impossible (an atrocious heresy!). For 200 years, the dimwitted mainstream hordes have been tirelessly denouncing the lad who had an amazing ability to understand the obvious — there are limits!

Since World War II, a growing number of heretics have been preaching about limits, carrying capacity, overshoot, and the dangers of ignoring them — folks like Hubbert, Youngquist, Ehrlich, Hardin, and Catton. But few are listening. It's still a heresy. "Grow or die" remains the law of the land, and few other ideas disturb our foggy minds.

Today's sermon is about Albert Bartlett and his book, *The Essential Exponential*. Bartlett was a physics professor who was dumbfounded by the world's inability to comprehend the dangerous power of exponential growth. Virtually all high school graduates remain blissfully ignorant about the subject, just like most graduates of Ivy League schools.

You can see a tornado rip a town to smithereens. But as you bike to work each morning, you cannot see or hear the far more destructive force of exponential growth. It's like a thousand invisible hurricanes battering the planet, and pounding the future.

Linear growth is like adding one marble per week to your collection of ten marbles (10, 11, 12…). The rate of growth is steady. On a graph, linear growth is a straight line. Exponential growth occurs when something is increasing at a constantly growing rate, and the rate increases with each cycle — the way compound interest inflates the balance of your savings account.

For example, since 1950, world oil production has been growing exponentially, at about seven percent per year. At that rate, production doubles every ten years. Bartlett illustrated the scale of this doubling in the following diagram, showing the volume of oil consumed each decade. Children born after 1966 "will see the world consume most of its oil during their lifetime."

All Before 1950	1950 to 1960	

All
Before
1950

1950
to
1960

1970 to 1980

1960 to 1970

1990 to 2000

1980 to 1990

This amount of oil must be discovered if we wish to have oil consumption continue to grow 7 percent per year for the decade 2000-2010.

Population can also grow exponentially. In 1986, the world population grew 1.7 percent, a rate that would double our numbers in 41 years. In 1999, growth had slowed to 1.3 percent, doubling in 53 years — 80 million people were added in 1999.

Industrial society has been growing like crazy for 200 years. This was made possible by resources that were once so abundant that they seemed infinite. During the growth surge, few enterprises ran into limits that could not be worked around. This encouraged a mindset that paid little or no attention to limits. Nothing was impossible. Nothing!

Leap to full alert whenever you encounter a statement that begins with "At the current rate of consumption...." Bartlett saw an article claiming that, at the current rate of consumption, U.S. coal would last 500 years. While statements like this may technically be correct, they are meaningless when consumption is growing at an exponential rate.

He calculated that, at the actual growing rate of consumption, coal would last 46 years — which is far more meaningful information.

In 1956, Shell Oil geophysicist M. King Hubbert analyzed the trends in oil discoveries and production, and predicted that U.S. petroleum production would peak between 1966 and 1971. Experts called him a dolt. In fact, the peak occurred in 1970. People who understand numbers, like Hubbert and Bartlett, possess powerful magic.

When you understand the effects of exponential growth on finite nonrenewable resources, reality becomes spooky. Hubbert produced the following chart to illustrate the era of global fossil energy extraction on a 10,000-year timeline. The surge lasts about three centuries, and what follows is sure to be exciting and memorable.

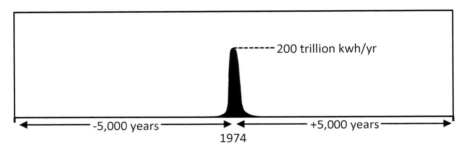

The above chart suggests a scenario in which a surge of incredible success is followed by a disastrous collapse. In *The Transition Handbook*, Rob Hopkins turned this chart upside down, suggesting a sharp plunge from stability into terrible chaos, hitting bottom, and a steep climb back to stability.

"Population growth is not sustainable," Bartlett insisted. "Can you think of any problem, on any scale, from microscopic to global, whose *long-term* solution is in any *demonstrable* way, aided, assisted, or advanced by having larger populations at the local, state, national, or global level?" The worst population deviant was the U.S., because our society consumes resources at an extreme rate.

Sustainable growth is an oxymoron. Bartlett carefully explained the original meaning of sustainability — a way of life that must remain stable for millennia. He presented 18 laws relating to sustainability, and 23 hypotheses. He devoted a great deal of thought to sustainability, because it's an incredibly important concept.

Today, genuine sustainability has been rudely pushed aside by the trendy and highly intoxicating silliness of ersatz sustainability, a masterpiece of magical thinking created by shameless marketing hucksters. Bartlett lamented that the herd is convinced "that the frequent use of the adjective 'sustainable' is all that is needed to create a sustainable society." He suffered from an amazing ability to understand the obvious.

Bartlett explained the basics of exponential growth in a lecture titled *Arithmetic, Population, and Energy*, which he gave over 1,500 times. YouTube carries a number of versions. It's an illuminating way to spend an hour of your life. Arithmetic can be fascinating, when the storyteller is a brilliant heretic.

The *Essential Exponential* is out of print. Some libraries and booksellers have copies. Much of the book is available free online, in an updated form (albarlett.org). Some sections present calculus equations for understanding the mechanics (which go way over my head), but many others are good old-fashioned writing, and present important ideas in a manner that's easy to understand.

One-Straw Revolutionary

Long, long ago, hip folks in the Beatles era were jabbering about Masanobu Fukuoka's book, *The One-Straw Revolution*. It explained how he grew healthy food via *natural farming*, a low budget, low impact approach. On his farm in Japan, Fukuoka was growing grain, fruit, and vegetables without plowing, cultivating, chemicals, compost, fertilizer, fossil energy, erosion, pruning, or regular weeding. He farmed like this for more than 25 years, and his yields were comparable to those at conventional farms.

The Japanese edition of his book was published in 1975, at a time when oil shocks had spurred interest in energy efficiency. When the English version was published in 1978, it was an international smash hit, and Fukuoka became a celebrity. Larry Korn was the book's translator. He's a California lad who worked on Fukuoka's farm for more than two years. Now, in 2015, Korn has published *One-Straw Revolutionary*, which is the subject of this review. It describes Fukuoka the man, and his philosophy, with glowing praise.

Korn detests conventional industrial farming, because it has so many drawbacks. A bit less troublesome is organic farming done on an industrial scale. At the positive end of the spectrum, he sees Fukuoka's natural farming as very close to the ideal, both environmentally and philosophically. A bit less wonderful than natural farming are perma- culture and old-fashioned small-scale organic farming.

The ideal is something like the California Indians that were fondly described in M. Kat Anderson's book, *Tending the Wild*. They were wild hunter-gatherers who included wild plant seeds in their diet. They de- voted special care to the wild plant species that were important to their way of life. Most folks would consider this to be mindful foraging — tending, not farming.

These Indians did not till the soil, and were not warlike. Nobody owned the land. There were no masters or servants. There was no market system or tax collectors. They had a time-proven method for living, and this knowledge was carefully passed from generation to gen- eration. The Indians were wild, free, and living sustainably — in the original meaning of the word. When the Spanish invaders arrived, they saw these Indians as lazy, because they worked so little.

Fukuoka, on the other hand, resided in a densely populated indus- trial civilization, which was eagerly adapting American style industrial agriculture. While the Indians foraged in a healthy wild ecosystem, Fu- kuoka worked on an ecosystem that had been heavily altered by centu- ries of agriculture. He raised domesticated plants and animals. Fukuo- ka was experimenting with radically unconventional methods, and had no traditions or mentors to guide him.

He practiced natural farming on one acre (0.4 ha) of grain field, and ten acres (4 ha) devoted to a mix of fruit trees and vegetables. When Korn arrived in 1974, Fukuoka was assisted by five apprentices, who were not at all lazy, and rarely had a day off. Cash had to be gen- erated to purchase necessities and pay taxes, so surplus food had to be produced. Food shipped off to cities carried away phosphorus, potas- sium, and other minerals that never returned to the farm's soil. Thus, his natural farming was quite different from California tending.

On the plus side, Fukuoka's experiment benefitted from rich soil and generous rainfall — especially during the growing season. Vegeta- bles could be grown year round in the mild climate, and two crops of grain could be harvested each year. On the down side, few succeeded in duplicating his success, even in Japan. It took years to get the operation working, requiring extra servings of intuition and good luck. Korn warned, "In most parts of North America and the world the specific method Mr. Fukuoka uses would be impractical."

In the natural farming mindset, the strategy should not be guided by intellect; nature should run the show. Fukuoka talked to plants, asking them for guidance. When he planted the orchard, he added a mixture of 100 types of seeds to wet clay, made seed balls, and tossed the balls on the land. Seeds included grains, vegetables, flowers, clover, shrubs, and trees. Nature decided what thrived and what didn't. Within a few years, a jungle of dense growth sorted itself out. But sometimes nature gave him a dope slap. In the early days, Fukuoka allowed nature to manage an existing orchard, and he was horrified to watch 400 trees die from insects and disease.

My work focuses on ecological sustainability, at a time when the original meaning of sustainability has largely been abandoned, and replaced by sparkly marketing hype. I go on full alert when I see "sustainable agriculture." In my book, *What is Sustainable*, I took a look at what Korn calls "indigenous agriculture," which is often imagined to be sustainable.

California tending was far different from the intensive corn farming on the other side of the Rockies, which led to soil depletion, erosion, population growth, health problems, warfare, and temporary civilizations like Cahokia. In his book, *Indians of North America*, Harold E. Driver estimated that less than half of North America was inhabited by farmers, but 90 to 95 percent of Native Americans ate crop foods, indicating that farm country was densely populated. In corn country, defensive palisades surrounded many villages.

In 2015, humankind is temporarily in extreme overshoot, as the cheap energy bubble glides toward its sunset years, and the climate change storms are moving in. Obviously, feeding seven billion sustainably is impossible. At the same time, highly unsustainable industrial farming cannot continue feeding billions indefinitely. It's essential that young folks have a good understanding of ecological sustainability, and our education system is doing a terrible job of informing them.

The California Indians provide an important example of a vital truth. When voluntary self-restraint was used to keep population below carrying capacity, people could live sustainably in a wild ecosystem via nothing more complex than hunting and foraging. They had no need for farming, with its many headaches, backaches, and heartaches.

Korn's book got exciting near the end. Farming was just one facet of Fukuoka's dream. As a young man, he attended an agriculture college, and then endured a dreary job as a plant inspector. His mind overloaded, his health fell apart, and he nearly died. In 1937, he had a beautiful vision, quit his job, and went back home to the farm.

In his vision, he suddenly realized that all life was one, and sacred. Nature was whole, healthy, and perfect — and nothing our ambitious intellects imagined could improve this harmonious unity in any way. Humans do not exist in a realm outside of nature, no matter what our teachers tell us. Heaven is where your feet are standing.

The world of 1937 was a filthy, crazy, overpopulated train wreck, and this was largely thanks to science, dogmas, and philosophies. Intellect alienated us from our "big life" home. Civilization had created a dysfunctional world that was far too complex. The lives of most people were no longer intimately connected to the natural world.

In agriculture, the herd of experts insisted that plowing, pruning, cultivating, chemicals, and weeding were mandatory for success. One after another, Fukuoka abandoned these required tasks, made some needed adjustments, and didn't crash. His farm got simpler and healthier.

No other animals harm themselves by pursuing science. Fukuoka realized that people should be like birds. "Birds don't run around carefully preparing fields, planting seeds, and harvesting food. They don't create anything… they just receive what is there for them with a humble and grateful heart." Bingo!

How can we reorient to nature? Korn says, "For most of us, that process begins by unlearning most of the things we were taught when we were young." The healing process requires abandoning many, many beliefs and behaviors that our culture encourages. We need to waste less, spend less, and earn less, take only what we need, and nothing more. "Wearing simple clothing, eating simple food, and living a humble, ordinary life elevates the human spirit by bringing us closer to the source of life."

Who Will Feed China?

Lester Brown is an environmental analyst, and founder of the Worldwatch Institute, and the Earth Policy Institute. His grand plan was to observe global trends, and produce objective information. Brown's many books and reports have provided rational advice for the world's irrational policymakers. He has not sold his soul to corporate interests.

In 1994, Brown wrote an essay, *Who Will Feed China?* It triggered an explosive response. Chinese leaders angrily denounced him. But behind the scenes, they realized that their nation was vulnerable, because they had not perceived the big picture clearly. Brown expanded his essay into a book with the same title, published in 1995. It became a classic. Reading it 20 years later is eerie, because many of his warnings now sound like the daily news.

Before they industrialized, Japan, South Korea, and Taiwan were already densely populated. Then, the growth of industry gobbled up a lot of cropland, which reduced food production, and forced all three to become dependent on imported grain. In 1994, Japan imported 72 percent of its grain, South Korea 66 percent, and Taiwan 76 percent.

Brown saw that China was on a similar trajectory. Cropland was limited, and it was rapidly being lost to sprawl, industry, and highways. They were likely to lose half of their cropland by 2030. They were also likely to add another 500 million people by 2030. As incomes rose, people were eager to enjoy a richer diet, including more meat and beer. This required even more cropland per person.

Freshwater for agriculture was also limited, and much of it was being diverted to growing cities and factories. About 300 cities were already short of water. China's capitol, Beijing, was among 100 cities with severe water shortages. Demand for water was sure to rise. Only a few Chinese had indoor plumbing, and everyone wanted it.

Many farmers were forced to drill wells and pump irrigation water from aquifers, often at rates in excess of natural recharge — water mining. As enormous amounts of water were removed underground, subsidence occurs. The ground sinks, filling the void below, making it impossible for the aquifer to recharge in the future. In northern China, subsidence affects a region the size of Hungary. Irrigated fields produce the most food, but water mining will eventually force a reduction in irrigation. Some regions may be forced to stop growing rice, a water-guzzling crop, and replace it with less productive millet or sorghum.

Between 1977 and 1984, grain productivity (yield per hectare) annually increased at an average rate of 7.1 percent. The annual increase was less than 2 percent between 1984 and 1990, and just 0.7 percent between 1990 and 1994. There were great hopes for biotechnology, but 20 years of efforts led to no significant increase in grain yields. Meanwhile, the Yellow River moved 1.6 billion tons of topsoil to the ocean every year.

Now, assemble the pieces. Population was likely to grow from 1.2 billion in 1995 to 1.66 billion in 2045. Grain consumption per person was growing, likely to increase 33 percent by 2030. Cropland area was likely to decrease 50 percent by 2030. Water for irrigation was limited, and certain to diminish. Annual grain harvests may have been close to, or beyond, their historic peak. The effects of climate change cannot be predicted, but might be severe. In 1995, the notion of Peak Oil had not yet spread beyond the lunatic fringe, and Brown didn't mention it, but at some point, it will make modern agriculture impossible.

Demand for grain was rising at a rate that would sharply exceed China's harvests. If their economy remained strong, they would have the money to import food. But, would the food they need be available on the world market? Following a century of catastrophic population growth, many nations were dependent on imported food.

As world population continued to grow, the ability to further increase food production was wheezing. World grain stocks fell from 465 million tons in 1987, to 298 million tons in 1994. At some point, surging demand for grain would exceed the surpluses of the exporters. This would drive up the price of food.

Brown selected ten large developing nations where population growth remained extreme, and projected how much food they would need to import by 2030. "By 2030, these countries — assuming no improvement in diet — will need to import 190 million tons of grain.

This is six times the amount they import today and nearly equal to total world grain exports in 1994."

We were moving into an era of food instability. "For the first time, an environmental event — the collision of expanding human demand with some of the earth's natural limits — will have an economic impact that affects the entire world." Annual economic growth for the world was falling. The global economy grew 5.2 percent in the '60s, 3.4 percent in the '70s, 2.9 percent in the '80s, and 1.4 percent in 1990-94. Slower growth, plus rising food prices, plus falling incomes, sets the stage for trouble. "It could lead to political unrest and a swelling flow of hungry migrants across national borders."

Agriculture was running out of steam. The wizards of industrial civilization insisted that perpetual growth was possible, because our miraculous technology could overcome all challenges. They were wrong. Brown concludes, "The bottom line is that achieving a humane balance between food and people is now more in the hands of family planners than farmers." When Brown wrote, there were 5.6 billion of us. Irrational policymakers disregarded the urgent need for family planning. And so, today, at 7.3 billion, the world is a far more unstable place, with no light at the end of the tunnel.

Twenty years before Brown's book, China realized that population growth was a problem. They were adding 13 million every year, and emigration was not a real option. Their one-child policy was launched in 1979, and the transition was bumpy. The birthrate fell from 2.7 percent in 1970 to 1.1 percent in 1994. It succeeded in preventing much misery, but it didn't stop growth. Brown praised them for actually taking action, forcing the present generation to sacrifice for the benefit of future generations — a concept unimaginable to Americans.

Changes in the Land

Historian William Cronon was one of a group of scholars that pioneered a new and improved way of understanding the past. Environmental history put the spotlight on many essential issues that were ignored by traditional history, and this made the sagas far more potent and illuminating.

His book, *Changes in the Land*, is an environmental history of colonial New England. It documents the clash of two cultures that could not have been more different, the Indians and the settlers. It describes the horrific mortality of imported diseases, and two centuries of senseless warfare on the fish, forests, soils, and wildlife.

The prize at the bottom of the box is a mirror. The patterns of thinking that the colonists brought to America are essentially our modern insanity in its adolescent form. We are the unfortunate inheritors of a dysfunctional culture. It helps to know this. It helps to be able to perceive the glaring defects, things we have been taught to believe are perfectly normal.

Cronon was the son of a history professor, and his father gave him the key for understanding the world. He told his son to carry one question on his journey through life: "How did things get to be this way?" Schoolbook history does a poor job of answering this question, because it often puts haloes on people who caused much harm, folks who faithfully obeyed the expectations of their loony culture and peers.

In Cronon's book, alert readers will discover uncomfortable answers to how things got to be this way. We have inherited a dead end way of life. In the coming decades, big challenges like climate change, population growth, and the end of the cheap energy bubble seem certain to disrupt industrial civilization, as we know it.

We can't return to hunting and gathering anytime soon, nor can we remain on our sinking ship. To continue our existence on Earth, big changes are needed, new ideas. This presents a fabulous opportunity to learn from our mistakes, to live slower, lighter, and better. Cronon's book reveals important lessons — what worked well, and what failed.

In the 5,000 years before the Pilgrims landed at Plymouth Rock, Europe had been transformed from a thriving wilderness to a scarred and battered land, thanks to soil mining, forest mining, fish mining, mineral mining, and a lot of crazy thinking. During the same 5,000 years, the Indians of northern New England kept their numbers low, and didn't thrash their ecosystem, because it was a sacred place, and they were well adapted to living in it.

In southern New England, the Indians regularly cleared the land by setting fires. This created open, park-like forests, which provided habitat attractive to game. Burning altered the ecosystem. One early settler noted a hill near Boston, from which you could observe thousands of treeless acres below. This was not a pristine ecosystem in its climax state.

In the north, the Indians did not clear the land with fire. The trees in that region were too flammable, so the forests were allowed to live wild and free. Indians travelled more by canoe.

In the south, where the climate was warmer, Indians practiced slash and burn agriculture. Forests were killed and fields were planted with corn, beans, and squash. Corn is a highly productive crop that is also a heavy feeder on soil nutrients. After five to ten seasons, the soil was depleted, and the field was abandoned. The Indians had no livestock to provide manure for fertilizer. Few used fish for fertilizer, because they had no carts for hauling them.

This digging stick agriculture was soil mining, unsustainable. Corn had arrived in New England just a few hundred years prior to colonization, too recently to produce civilization and meltdown, as it had in Cahokia on the Mississippi. Corn spurred population growth, which increased the toll on forests and soils. (Other writers have noted that corn country was not a land of love, peace, and happiness. Most Iroquois villages were surrounded by defensive palisades, because more people led to more stress and more conflict.)

The colonists imported an agricultural system that rocked the ecological boat much harder. Their plows loosened the soil more deeply, encouraging erosion. Their pastures were often overgrazed, which encouraged erosion. They aggressively cut forests to expand pastures, cropland, and settlements, and this encouraged erosion. Harbors were clogged with eroded soil. Their cattle roamed the countryside, so little manure was collected for fertilizer. They planted corn alone, so the soil did not benefit from the nitrogen that beans could add. They burned trees to make ash for fertilizer.

Cronon devotes much attention to the eco-blunders of the settlers. A key factor here is that their objective was not simple subsistence. They had great interest in accumulating wealth and status, and this was achieved by taking commodities to market, like lumber and livestock. The more land they cleared, the more cattle they could raise. It was impossible to be too rich.

This silly hunger for status has a long history of inspiring reckless behavior. When a colonist gazed on the land, his mind focused on the commodities, the stuff he could loot and sell. He noticed the enormous numbers of fish, the millions of waterfowl, the unbelievable old growth forests, the furbearing animals — all the things that his kinfolk in Europe had nearly wiped out.

Indians hunted for dinner, not for the market. They did not own the deer, elk, and moose that they hunted, so nobody freaked out if a wolf ate one. These wild animals had coevolved with wolves, so a balance was maintained. Colonists introduced domesticated animals that had not coevolved with wolves. The slow, dimwitted livestock were sitting ducks for predators, which boosted wolf populations, which led infuriated settlers to launch wolf extermination programs.

Indians were not chained to private property. When their fields wore out, they cleared new fields. Colonists owned a fixed piece of land, which narrowed their options. In the winter months, Indians moved to hunting camps, selecting sites with adequate firewood available. They had nice fires and stayed warm, while the colonists shivered in their fixed villages, where firewood was scarce.

Colonists suffered from an insatiable hunger for wealth and status, which drove them to spend their lives working like madmen. Instead of belongings, the Indians had a leisurely way of life, and this was their source of wealth. They thought that the workaholic settlers were out of their minds. Indians were mobile, so hoarding stuff made no sense. By having few wants, the path to abundance was a short one. Even the least industrious wanted nothing.

Liebig's Law says, "Populations are not limited by the total annual resources available, but by the minimum amount available at the scarcest time of the year." So, despite the seasonal fish runs and bird migrations, life was not easy in February and March, when the game was lean and hard to hunt. Indians stored little fish and meat. In rough winters, they could go ten days without food.

In the south, the Indians were engaged in a high-risk experiment by growing corn, because agriculture is almost never harmless, and it often opens the floodgates to numerous troublesome consequences.

In the north, the Indians were lucky that their home was unsuitable for farming. They didn't breed like colonists. They adapted to their ecosystem and lived like genuine conservatives, not looters. This was a path with a future, until the looters arrived.

The Dying of the Trees

Long, long ago, before the 1970s, thousands of people would make a springtime pilgrimage to the Catoctin woods of Maryland to enjoy the flowering dogwood trees. Today, the tourists no longer come, because 79 percent of the dogwoods are dead, and the rest are dying. A mystery fungus created a rapidly spreading blight, which penetrated the bark and blocked the flow of water and nutrients. It killed new dogwood seedlings. The experts were puzzled. Could the trees have been weakened by acid rain, smog, increased UV radiation, or a changing climate?

The dogwood die-off captured the attention of Maryland resident Charles Little, a conservationist and writer. It inspired him to spend three years visiting 13 states, observe dying trees, interview experts, and read papers and reports. Then he wrote *The Dying of the Trees*. It was a heartbreaking project, because everything he learned was grim, and worsening.

On one trip, he visited Hub Vogelmann, in the Green Mountains of Vermont, a region downwind from the industrial Midwest. Three-quarters of the spruce trees were dead, and there was no evidence of insects or disease. In tree ring studies, vanadium, arsenic, and barium began appearing in the wood around 1920. Following World War II, the wood also contained copper, lead, zinc, and cadmium. Aluminum is commonly found in forest soils, but acid rain breaks down aluminum silicates, enabling the metal to be absorbed by plants. It kills the roots. Vogelmann was sharply criticized for suggesting that the problem was related to acid rain, an emerging issue by 1979.

Acid rain was killing forests in Germany and Eastern Europe. It was killing the sugar maples in New England, Ontario, and Quebec. In the Appalachian region of Quebec, 91 percent of the maples were in decline by 1988. The rain was ten times more acidic than normal. It was leaching the phosphorus, potassium, and magnesium out of the soil — essential nutrients. In some places, the livers and kidneys of moose and deer contained so much cadmium that the Canadian government issued health warnings. In glaring defiance of the evidence, the U.S. Forest Service reported that the maples were healthy and improving.

Little visited Rock Creek, near Beckley, West Virginia. It was home to a remnant of the mesophytic forest, bits of which are spread across several states. This ecosystem may be 100 million years old. It was never submerged by rising seas, or erased by glaciers. It was the mother forest for the trees now living in eastern North America.

Sadly, mature trees at Rock Creek, in full foliage, were falling over, their trunks hollowed out by rot. Fungi, supercharged by excess nitrogen, were now able to penetrate the bark. Trees were producing up to 80 percent fewer seeds. John Flynn was among the pioneers in reporting the acid rain story to the national media. He was harshly criticized by both industry and the U.S. Forest Service.

Once, on a visit to England, Little met an elderly sailor who had visited Oregon as a young man. The immense virgin forests had amazed him. Little did not tell the old fellow that those ancient forests were mostly gone now, and that industry was eager to destroy the ten percent that remained. It took the Brits a thousand years to exterminate their ancient forest. Americans largely did it in one generation, thanks to better technology and mass hysteria.

The vast white pine forests that once stretched from Maine to Minnesota never recovered. Deciduous trees took their place. Ancient forests are not renewable resources. "In clear-cutting such forests, then, we not only kill the trees that are cut, but we annihilate the possibility of such trees for all time." Forests are incredibly complex ecosystems, and logging disrupts a state of balance that took eons to develop. Many wildlife species cannot survive on cutover lands. A monoculture tree plantation is not a forest, and is more vulnerable to cold, drought, pests, and diseases.

Little visited Colorado, where many forests were brown and dead. The original forest was exterminated about 100 years ago. The second growth that replaced it was a different mix of species, mostly shade-tolerant, which were more vulnerable to spruce budworms. These trees were densely packed together, thanks to a strategy of fire suppression, which aggressively extinguished every wildfire. The dense growth was attractive to budworms, which weakened the trees. Then the bark beetles were able to finish them off. Dead forests loaded with fuel invite fire.

Native Americans controlled fuel buildup with periodic low-level burns, but this is impossible today, because of the massive accumulations of fuel. There is no undo button for a century of mistakes. The government cannot afford to thin overgrown forests and remove the excess fuel from many millions of acres, so the stage is set for catastrophic fires. There will come a day when the cost and availability of oil makes modern high-tech firefighting impossible.

Forests often die in slow motion. A speedy decline might take 25 years, and be invisible to casual observers. Forest death increased in the twentieth century, following the extermination of ancient forests. It worsened after World War II, as pollution levels increased. Climate change is likely to cause additional harm.

A vital lesson in this book is to never automatically believe anything. Master the art of critical thinking, and always question authority. Our culture is out of its mind, and many of its deeply held beliefs are bull excrement. Each generation innocently passes this load of excrement to the next, because it's all they know.

Here's my favorite passage: "A hand will be raised at the back of the room. 'But what can we do?' the petitioner will ask. Do? What can we *do*? What a question that is when we scarcely understand what we have already done!"

In a series of stories, Little's book informs readers that industrial civilization and healthy forests do not mix. But it barely scratches the surface of the harms caused by the logging industry, or the many other industries. When I proudly received my golden meal ticket from the university, I was dumber than a box of rocks. I was well trained to spend the rest of my days striving for respect and status by shopping the planet to pieces.

Today, as the clock is running out on industrial civilization, it's essential to better understand what we have already done. We won't discover every fatal defect, because our way of life is overloaded with them, but the ones that we can see are more likely to be addressed. We are on a dead end path. We would be wise to outgrow our habits and illusions, and remember how to live.

Little recommends the obvious — sharply reverse population growth, end the extermination of forests, plant billions of trees, and stop industrial pollution. He cautions readers that we're well beyond the point where the damage can be repaired. Our task today is damage control — learning, growing, teaching, and mindfully reducing the harm we cause each day. The book does not conclude with the traditional slop bucket of magical thinking. His straight talk is refreshing.

The Ostrich Factor

Garrett Hardin was a lad who not only thought a lot, but could also think well. I recently discovered a Hardin book I had not heard of, *The Ostrich Factor — Our Population Myopia* (1998). Hardin was an interesting blend of an ecological conservative, and a growth-hating political conservative who detested economists. I hoped that this book would provide fresh insights on the huge and difficult problem of overpopulation.

After *Living Within Limits* was published in 1993, critics noted that Hardin complained about overpopulation, but failed to provide a remedy. Hardin admitted that he had been intimidated by the explosive taboo on the subject, which incinerates every dreamer who blunders into it, foolishly preaching common sense. Hence, the ostrich factor — never touch 800-volt issues that are surrounded by large piles of scorched skeletons. You can't win, so bury your head in the sand, and have a nice day!

Modern society is focused on the individual, not the community or ecosystem. I am all that matters. If I can gain status and respect by wiping out forests or fisheries, or throwing the planet's climate out of balance, I will. I don't care that I'm leaving behind a wasteland for future generations. If future generations were able to vote right now, or if we were raised in a sane culture, our world would be radically different and far healthier.

Hardin was fascinated by the power of taboos, and he invited an imaginary Martian into his book, to observe our society as an objective outsider. The two of them explored uncomfortable notions that will make some readers squirm and snarl. Taboos put a powerful headlock on our ability to think. They push many commonsense ideas off limits, severely handicapping our freedom to contemplate, forcing many to live like two-year olds, ecological psychopaths, or chronically depressed shoppers.

Taboos vary from place to place and time to time. I was surprised to see that Hardin only mentioned abortion once, with regard to a quote from 1886, describing a situation where abortion was legal, but contraception was not. In that scenario, many physicians chose to break the law against providing contraception.

It is important to understand that many wild cultures had customs that encouraged population stability. Their ongoing survival depended entirely on food from the surrounding ecosystem, and too many mouths led to painful problems. Their utmost concern was the health and stability of the community, not the whims of individuals. They shared and cooperated. It was obvious to them that the carrying capacity of their ecosystem had genuine limits. For us, living in a temporary wonderland of supermarkets and credit cards, limits are hard to imagine — until we crash into them.

The emergence of agriculture boosted carrying capacity during periods of good harvests and adequate food reserves. Limits on breeding weakened or vanished. Hardin quoted Tertullian, a third century Christian thinker from Tunisia, who was spooked by the misery of overpopulation (when the global population was 150 million). Tertullian wrote, "As our demands grow greater, our complaints against nature's inadequacy are heard by all. The scourges of pestilence, famine, wars, and earthquakes have come to be regarded as a blessing to overcrowded nations, since they serve to prune away the luxuriant growth of the human race."

Perpetual growth on a finite planet is obviously impossible, obviously insane, and insanely destructive. *Sustainable growth* is an oxymoron. But few goofy myths are more powerful. We are constantly reminded that perpetual growth is the purpose of life. Grow or die! Our official religion is Growth Forever. Fanatical believers are called optimistic, and optimism is "good." Hardin disagreed, "At the present rate of population growth, it's difficult to be optimistic about the future."

With regard to population, our culture asserts two rights simultaneously. (1) Right to life. The UN decrees that "every man, woman, and child has the inalienable right to be free from hunger and malnutrition." (2) Right to limitless reproductive freedom. "Every woman has the right — perhaps with the agreement of her mate(s) — to determine how many children she shall produce."

Rights are legal inventions. Note that the two *rights* above are not accompanied by any required *responsibilities*. Hardin concluded that overpopulation would not be resolved by the voluntary choices of individual families. In an overcrowded finite world, unrestricted freedom is intolerable. Responsibilities should be based on community-sensitive rules, ideally produced by a policy of "mutual coercion, mutually agreed upon." Our wild ancestors generally succeeded in doing this, because their cultures saw limits as being perfectly normal and beneficial, not draconian.

Hardin knew that "coercion" is an obscene word in a culture that worships individualism, but he noted that we submit to coercion when we stop for red lights, or when we bike on the right side of the road. Coercion is often reciprocal. Money is coercion. There are many things we will eagerly do for money that we would never do for free. We are often coerced by nothing more than a sweet "pretty please."

Hardin thought that one world government was impossible, because there is not a single world culture. Trying to get different cultures to agree on anything is a challenge for advocates of multiculturalism. Because of this, Hardin offered no silver bullet solution for the world. Each culture will have to design its own method for limiting population.

Predicaments have no solutions, but problems do. Overpopulation is merely a temporary problem, and there are two solutions. (1) We can make a difficult commonsense effort to live below carrying capacity. (2) We can bury our heads in the sand, make no effort to influence the future, and let Big Mama Nature mercilessly do the dirty work. The commonsense approach saves a lot of wear and tear on the ecosystem, and makes life far less hellish. It is enthusiastically endorsed by the spirits of future generations.

Where We Belong

Where We Belong is a collection of Paul Shepard essays that discuss how we perceive the natural world, and how this influences the way we treat it. Most of the essays were written between the 1950s and 1970s. They include some ideas that evolved into major components of his classics. Almost half of this book is devoted to provocative discussions of pioneer diaries, a special treat.

Humans evolved as hunters and scavengers on tropical savannahs. Today, our genes are still those of Pleistocene hunter-gatherers. Shepard believed that the process of normal human development depended on experiences best provided by living close to wild nature. Children need to be surrounded by a variety of wild species, to observe them, and learn from them. They need to be outdoors, and experience how everything in their land is alive.

They need a culture that guides them through the transition from adolescence to adulthood, via rituals of initiation. When this is not provided, "Self-generated substitutes created by adolescents are a virtual catalog of delinquency and neurosis... adolescents cannot discover their maturity in a city." They don't understand that the all-natural dance of creatures eating creatures is normal and good. They think that food comes from stores.

Some of the damage can be healed by spending more time with nature. Emotionally impoverished city folks can "recover elements of human ecology warped by millennia of immersion in domesticated landscapes. Paramount among these is the opportunity to be free of domestic animals both as social partners and as models of the nonhuman." We have a powerful desire to live in a wild landscape that is inhabited by wild animals — and parks and pets are a poor substitute.

Shepard was never a cheerleader for the domestication of plants and animals, because it spawned a way of living that was harmful to everything. The relationship between the human and the more-than-human shifted from one of freedom to one of human domination and control. This led to profound changes in the way we perceived the world, and to destructive changes in behavior.

From the first civilizations, growing population fueled ongoing deforestation. Sheep, goats, and cattle were then turned loose on the former forest. These "hoofed locusts" gobbled up young seedlings, and ensured that the forest would never recover. The exposed soil was then washed away by the rains, creating vast wastelands that modern visitors now perceive as natural and picturesque. This resulted in a "lobotomy on the land, done not with a scalpel but with teeth and hooves."

The Minoan community of Jerash, a dusty village of 3,000, was once home to 250,000. The original streets are now buried under 13 feet (4 m) of soil. "No wonder Western consciousness is an overheated drama of God's vengeance and catastrophe, preoccupation with sacrifice, portents, and omens of punishment by a heavy-handed Jehovah. Like the dinosaurs, which are known mainly for their vanishing, the ancestors we know best, and from whom we take our style, are those who seem to have lived mainly to call down calamity upon themselves."

Much of the book is devoted to Shepard's discussion of pioneer diaries from New Zealand and the Oregon Trail. These essays are illuminating and disturbing. In New Zealand, the English observed a gloomy, desolate, terrifying wildness, like "Caesar's Britain," that was dreadfully unimproved. To their fundamentalist minds, wilderness was immoral and sinful. The solution, of course, was to erase the existing ecosystem, and turn the land into a proper English countryside. Settler Richard Taylor wrote, "The fern is like the savage; both are going down before civilization."

On the Oregon Trail, early travelers from New England and the Midwest experienced landscapes that were beyond their imagination — vast wide-open spaces, and dark skies with billions of twinkling stars. Their wagons were prairie schooners, sailing across the seas of waving grass. At night, they sat around fires, fiddling and singing, listening to the hoots of owls, bellowing bison, and the music of the wind. They were serenaded by enthusiastic choirs of wolves, howling and shrieking their ancient wild music.

Folks used to existing in the bowels of civilization were jarred by feelings of isolation, solitude, and emptiness. At times, the land was absolutely silent. Then there were deluges, prairie fires, and tornados. Humming clouds of the native mosquitoes were exceedingly friendly to the smelly travelers in funny attire. "Everyone was deeply moved by the immense herds of buffalo as they roamed beside, toward, and even through the wagon trains."

In hotter and drier regions, travelers found buffalo trails that looked like old roads, because of frequent use. They saw rock formations that resembled castles, lighthouses, churches, palaces, and so on. From a distance, they looked like manmade ancient ruins, ghost towns. They wondered if the treeless landscape had once been cleared.

It was spooky to experience a vast region showing no signs of being bludgeoned by civilization, except along the trail, which was strewn with litter. Many began the pilgrimage overloaded with stuff, dumping ballast along the way, to make the journey less challenging. Everywhere along the trail, people carved their names on rocks, stumps, skulls, and trees.

Readers get two impressions from these pioneer stories. One is that the experience was precious and sacred, a very long trek through a healthy wild land. Imagine how much people would pay today to experience a wild Nebraska where there were far more buffalo and wolves than humans — no highways, beer cans, motels, or fences. The tales call up deep ancestral memories of how we all once lived, pleasant memories.

The other impression was that these travelers had not come to abandon civilization and return to wildness and freedom. If the western plains had water, good soil, and forests, the travelers on the Oregon Trail would have stopped in their tracks, built cabins, and destroyed it. But they knew that they could not survive on the plains, so they kept moving toward the promised land of salmon and forests, where their descendants would build Portland and Eugene, and create the ancient ruins of the future — enduring monuments to our experiment in civilization, warning signs to the generations yet-to-be-born.

The essays in this book discuss aspects of how civilized Western people interpret the natural world. Their perspective is strongly influenced by our culture of wealth, alienation, and destruction. What's missing in this book is the perspective of people rooted in place, who have reverence and respect for the land they inhabit.

Okanagan elder Jeanette Armstrong is one of many who eloquently discuss the vital importance of having a healthy connection to place, community, and family. She sees that our world is being wrecked by alienated people who have no connection to place, people who have no hearts, because they are "dis-placed." Shepard put it like this, "Knowing who you are is impossible without knowing where you are."

Greenland Dreams

I recently took a mental voyage to Greenland, which began when I read Knud Rasmussen's book, *The People of the Polar North*, published in 1908. Rasmussen was born and raised in Greenland, the son of a Danish minister and his Danish-Eskimo wife. Most of Knud's buddies were Eskimos (Inuit), and he fluently spoke both languages. The family moved to Denmark when Knud was 14, and he soon realized that the wild frontier was far more healthy and alive than the noisy crazy crowds of civilization.

At the age of 23, he eagerly returned to Greenland. His mission was to document the little known culture and history of his people, before they were overwhelmed by the madness of modernity, or driven to extinction by disease. He had absolute respect for the indigenous culture, and he excelled at getting the wild people to trust him with their stories. Reading this book struck some deep ancestral chords. It was a magic portal into a saner and healthier world. Stories like this are good medicine. They put things in a clear perspective.

In those days, Greenland was intensely alive — birds, fish, whales, seals, walruses, reindeer, bears — a precious treasure of abundance and vitality that is beyond the imagination of modern minds. The spiritual realm of the Eskimos embraced the entire family of life, a realm in which humans were no more significant than lemmings or lice. Humans were not the dominant animal, and Eskimo culture had no self-important gods and goddesses. Everything was alive, and all were related.

In the old days, all things animate and inanimate were alive, and all beings were able to communicate with each other. People could change into bears, and bears could change into people. There were far fewer boundaries. Every community had at least one shaman, and he or she was kept busy attending to the affairs of the spirit world. They understood the mysteries of hidden things, and had power over the destinies of men. Rasmussen always sought out the shamans in his travels.

The Eskimos did not have permanent homes; they followed the food. One group regularly waited for the walruses to come ashore at Taseralik, usually in September. The huge slow-moving animals were sitting ducks on the rocks, and up to 50 were killed per hour. The clan spent the long dark winters there, hunting for seals, and dining on the meat and fish they had stored. In April, when the ice began breaking up, they moved to the mouth of the Ström Fjord, and hunted seal and walrus. In June, they moved to Iginiarfik and caught capelin, small fish like smelt. Then they returned to Taseralik to catch halibut.

Living near the Arctic was challenging for two-legged animals that evolution had fine-tuned for living in the tropics. By far, Eskimos were the most high-tech subsistence hunters that ever lived. In open waters, they hunted and fished in kayaks and umiaqs. When it was time to move camp or visit other villages, they traveled across the ice on dog-sleds, which required thick ice. There were many times when thin ice appeared to be thick ice, and this illusion shortened many lives. During the long, dark winters, the average temperature was -25°F (-31°C).

Sila, the weather, was a power that dominated Eskimo life. Green-landers did not spend their days staring at cell phones, because Sila would blow them away with 150 mph (240 kph) winds, bury them in sudden avalanches, wash them away with flash floods, drown them in stormy seas, or melt the ice they were sledding across.

There was also Nerrivik ("the food dish"), a woman at the bottom of the sea, who ruled the beings of the water world. She was a moody power, and she often withheld the seals from hungry hunters. When this happened, shamans were required to journey into her world, tidy her hair, and calm her down.

Rasmussen's buddy, Peter Freuchen, took a nap during a storm when the temperature was -60°F (-51°C). When he awoke, his feet were frozen. This cost him a leg. Rasmussen told the story of Qumangâpik, who had four wives and 15 children. The first wife froze to death, the second was buried by an avalanche, the third died of ill-ness, and the fourth froze to death. Of his 15 children, one starved, four were frozen, and five died of illness. Qumangâpik froze to death, with his wife and two little children. Three of his kids outlived him.

In Greenland, it was ridiculously easy to die from brief lapses of attention or the fickle whims of luck. When they ran out of meat, they ate their dogs. Then they ate corpses. Sometimes they killed and ate the weak. Many times, everyone died. They did not rot away in nurs-ing homes. For those who became a burden on the clan, the ride was soon over. You were either strong and healthy, or you found enjoyment in the afterlife, which was a good place. There was no hell for heathen Eskimos.

There was no television, radio, internet, or cell phones. There were no malls, roads, or cities. There was no money. There were no rich or poor. Nobody starved unless everyone starved. There were no lawyers, soldiers, farmers, herders, police, politicians, pimps, prostitutes, salespersons, miners, loggers, fashion models, or recreational shoppers. Eskimos were purely wild and free people, living in a wild and free land, like undamaged human beings.

Eskimos pitied (and giggled at) the Danes, because they suffered from hurricane minds — they never stopped thinking. Rasmussen once observed an Eskimo who appeared to be deep in thought. Knud asked him what he was thinking about, and the man laughed. The only time we think is when we're running low on meat. Their language included no tools for discussing abstractions or ideas. They rarely made plans for tomorrow. They warmly glowed with "an irresponsible happiness at merely being alive…."

I also read Gretel Ehrlich's book, *This Cold Heaven*, published in 2001. She was an American who had made several extended visits to Greenland between 1993 and 1999. She was fascinated by Rasmussen's stories, and had read the 6,000 pages of his expedition notes. The chapters of her book flip-flop between discussions of Knud's life, and descriptions of the folks she met while visiting Greenland.

The recent decades had not been kind for Greenland. As the cancer of a cash economy spread, it took a heavy toll on the remaining wildlife. But compared to her California home, it seemed like paradise. Her friend Maria told her, "It's too bad for you when you visit Greenland, because then you have to keep going back. When you have been with those people — with the Inuit — you know that you have been with human beings."

Robert Peary went to the North Pole in 1909. Like many white lads, the incredible beauty of Inuit women inspired him, with immense throbbing excitement, to toss his Christian virtues to the wind. In 1997, Ehrlich met two of his granddaughters at Thule. They lamented that when the Europeans stomped ashore in 1721, there were 16,000 wild heathen souls in all of Greenland. It wasn't long before the population fell to just 110, thanks to smallpox. Now there are 60,000, thanks to the industrial food system.

When Rasmussen traveled across northern Canada in the 1920s, he reported a vast herd of migrating caribou that took three days to pass. During the warm months, the skies of Greenland were filled with millions of migrating birds that came to nest on rocky islands. Happy people harvested many birds and eggs. In 1933, the birds got their revenge. *Kivioq* was an Arctic delicacy, consisting of dead auks stuffed into seal gut and allowed to rot for two months. Rasmussen died from salmonella poisoning after gobbling down a bowl of it. Urp!

Today, the era of nomadic living is over. In 1995, the village of Uummannaq was home to 1,400 people and 6,000 dogs. All settlements reeked of "dog shit, seal guts, and unwashed bodies." Epidemics of distemper periodically hammered down canine overpopulation. Dogs were kept chained all the time, except on hunting trips. Male dogs that broke free were a public nuisance, and it was the village dog-catcher's job to simply shoot them on sight.

Ehrlich went on a few hunting trips, riding on a dogsled across the ice. It felt like a prehistoric experience, but there was one huge difference. The harpoons and bows had been replaced by high-powered rifles. It was now far easier to kill seals and polar bears from a distance.

People no longer hunted and fished for subsistence alone. In addition to food and furs for their family, they also needed surplus, to pay for electricity, phones, ammunition, heating oil, groceries, computers, cigarettes, alcohol, etc. The more wildlife they destroyed, the more money they could make, and the more cool stuff they could buy. This vicious cycle grew. Many people were hunting and fishing as if they were the last generation.

Trouble was born when the Danes first laid eyes on a thriving ecosystem. Their civilized brains began spinning with excitement, calculating how much wealth could be reaped by exterminating Greenland's wildlife. It was impossible for their minds to contemplate the notion of turning around, going home, and leaving the Eskimos in peace.

Even if the Eskimos had promptly hacked the first missionaries and traders into dog food, they were powerless to prevent the heavily armed Danes from gang raping their paradise, and poisoning their ancient culture. When guns, knives, pots, and matches became available at trading posts, few wild folks anywhere rejected them. We have a weakness for useful tools.

Shortly after Ehrlich's book was published, a mob of wildlife advocates discovered Greenland's disinterest in wildlife conservation, and commenced to yowl and bellow. Greenland shrugged. It is, after all, the twenty-first century. Greenland has the highest suicide rate in the world.

A Country Called Childhood

Jay Griffiths soared away on a seven-year pilgrimage to forage for the knowledge that illuminated her previous book on wildness. She spent a lot of time with wild tribes, and with conquered people who still had beautiful memories of wildness and freedom. As she bounced from place to place, both modern and indigenous, she became aware of a glaring difference between wild people and the dominant culture — the way they raised their children.

This presented her with a perplexing riddle. "Why are so many children in Euro-American cultures unhappy? Why is it that children in many traditional cultures seem happier, fluent in their child-nature?" Her dance with this riddle gave birth to her book, *A Country Called Childhood*. (I read the U.K. version, titled *Kith*.)

Griffiths is English, and the book's title refers to the old phrase, "kith and kin." Kin means close family. Kith originally meant knowledge or native land, the home outside the house. When peasants lived on the land, their knowledge was rooted in the living place around them, not in exotic stuff like philosophy or literature. In recent centuries, most peasants have been driven out of their rural homes, and their traditional knowledge has been forgotten.

Today, the meaning of kith has been reduced to extended family and neighbors. Like "sustainable," kith was once a beautiful word of great importance. Both words are lifesavers, if we could just remember them. They are not forever lost. Griffiths reminds us that "the past is not behind us, but within us."

In this book, kith is used in its ancient form, a sacred word of power. Why are kids so unhappy? They have no kith. They are dreadfully impoverished. In our society, kids (and adults) are unwell because they have largely been exiled from nature. They live indoors in manmade environments. Nature is an essential nutrient for health and sanity. Kith is life.

Griffiths and her brothers spent much of their youth playing outdoors, wandering across the land, getting wet and dirty, without adult supervision. They rarely watched television. She fears that her generation may be the last to experience the remaining vestiges of a normal childhood. But the game will change radically as the lights blink out, and the healing process begins.

Being surrounded by nature is what all animals require for a normal and healthy life. Like all other animals, young humans need to explore, play, learn. Children need nature like fish need water. They need a place where they belong, a home, a land that will be "mentor, teacher, and parent."

They need to grow up in lands that still have some original parts — deer, birds, snakes, frogs, coyotes — our relatives who have not forgotten how to live. They have so much to teach us. Pets are unacceptable replacements for our wild and free relatives. Cities are unacceptable substitutes for healthy places to live.

Several centuries back, Griffiths' ancestors lived in villages near commons. The commons were open lands where the people could hunt, fish, pick berries, gather wood, and graze livestock. Today, the commons are nearly extinct. They have been eliminated by a process called enclosure, whereby wealthy lords fenced off the commons, replaced forests with sheep pastures, evicted most peasants, and burned down their humble cottages.

Enclosure is the diabolical anti-kith. Modern kids no longer have abundant open spaces in which they can mature in a healthy manner. Space has been enclosed and denatured. So has freedom, the essence of childhood. They are no longer free to spend their days wandering where whimsy leads them. Modern childhood is now rigidly scheduled.

Community has also been enclosed. Kids used to be raised in villages where there were no strangers. Kids were mentored and parented by neighbors and extended family. Modern kids grow up in a world of automobiles, strangers, and nuclear families. Outdoors, behind every bush, are tweakers, psychopaths, perverts, and predators. Kids spend much of their lives under house arrest.

Kids have immense interest in learning, but we give them "a school system that is half factory, half prison, and too easily ignores the very education which children crave." They major in obedience, punctuality, self-centeredness, and the myths of civilization. They spend their childhood years indoors, in classrooms, and graduate knowing nearly nothing about the ecosystem they inhabit, their kith.

This is quite different from how children in traditional societies are raised. Wild children are in constant human contact until they learn to walk, some sleep with their parents for the first five years or so. They are never left alone to cry themselves to sleep. They are never scolded, beaten, or given commands. They are socialized, respected, treated like adults. Socialization teaches them to be respectful of others, and nurture good relationships. They develop confidence and self-reliance.

Importantly, wild cultures do an excellent job of guiding youths through a healthy transition into adulthood. Every person is born with a unique personality. We all have different gifts, interests, and destinies. Elders carefully help youths find their path in life. "Every child needs their time in the woods, to find their vision or their dream. Yet most children today have no such rite, no way of negotiating that difficult transition into adulthood." Most of them want to become famous celebrities.

The first generation of enclosure victims was painfully aware of all they had lost. Their city born descendants have little or no awareness of the lost treasure of kith, and the harsh poverty of their consumer prosperity. They are "denied their role as part of the wildlife." Many may go to their graves without ever experiencing the beauty that is the sacred birthright of tropical primates, and every other living being.

Griffiths learned to talk and read at a very early age. She has a great passion for words and learning. You get the impression that she has read 10 or 20 books a week since she was crawling around in nappies. She writes with flourish and flamboyance. This book is not an instruction manual for childrearing, but it provides a wealth of important insights for tropical primates who live in modern society. It's an excellent companion to Jean Liedloff's masterpiece, *The Continuum Concept*.

Feral

Beneath the pavement in London, archaeologists have found the bones of hippos, elephants, giant deer, aurochs, and lions. The Thames watershed was once a gorgeous, thriving, wild paradise. In the early Mesolithic, the western seaboard of Europe, from Scotland to Spain, was covered by a magnificent rainforest. Indeed, the entire planet was once a thriving wild paradise.

Evolution created utterly fantastic masterpieces. The megafauna of the Americas grew to enormous size, in the absence of too-clever two-legged tool addicts. Ground sloths weighed as much as elephants. Beavers were the size of bears. The Argentine roc had a 26-foot wingspan (8 m). All of them vanished between 15,000 and 10,000 years ago, about the time you-know-who arrived, with their state of the art hunting technology.

On a damp gray dawn, the English writer George Monbiot woke up screaming once again. He suffers from a chronic spiritual disease called ecological boredom. Living amidst endless crowds of two-legged strangers can become unbearably unpleasant for sensitive people with minds. Human souls can only thrive in unmolested wildness (the opposite of modern England). He leaped out of bed, packed his things, and moved to the coast of Wales, where there was more grass than concrete. He hoped that this would exorcise his demons.

They weren't demons. Obviously, ecological boredom is a perfectly normal response to the fierce madness of twenty-first century life, and it's curable. What's needed to break this curse is a holy ceremony called rewilding. During five years of country living in Wales, Monbiot wrote *Feral*, to explain his voyage and vision. It's a 500-decibel alarm clock.

Our hominid ancestors were wild animals for millions of years. In the last few thousand years, we've declared war on wild ecosystems, in our whacked out crusade to domesticate everything everywhere, and lock Big Mama Nature in a maximum-security prison. Rewilding is about throwing this sick, suicidal process into reverse.

It's about allowing extinct woodlands to become healthy thriving forests once again. It's about reintroducing the wild beings that have been driven off the land — bear, bison, beavers — a sacred homecoming. It's about creating marine reserves so aquatic species have places

161

of refuge from the insane gang rape of industrial fish mining. Importantly, it's about introducing our children to the living planet of their birth.

Wales was a land of lush forests 2,100 years ago. Today, it's largely a mix of sheep pasture and other assorted wastelands. One day, Monbiot climbed to a hilltop in the Cambrian Mountains, where he could see for miles. He noted a few distant Sitka spruce tree farms, and a bit of scrubby brush, but otherwise, "across that whole, huge view, there were no trees. The land had been flayed. The fur had been peeled off, and every contoured muscle and nub of bone was exposed."

Some folks now call it the Cambrian Desert, whilst tourism hucksters refer to it as one of the largest wilderness areas in the U.K. To Monbiot, rural Wales is a heartbreaking sheepwreck, reduced to ecological ruins by the white plague — countless dimwitted furry freaks from Mesopotamia that gobble the vegetation down to the roots, and prevent forest recovery.

One day, Monbiot met a brilliant young sheep rancher, Dafydd Morris-Jones, who had no sympathy for rewilding at all. His family had been raising sheep on this land for ages. Every rock in the valley had a name, and his uncle remembered all of them. Allowing the forest to return would amount to cultural genocide, snuffing out the traditional indigenous way of life, and erasing it forever.

I had great sympathy for Dafydd's view. In 1843, my great-grandfather, Richard E. Rees, was born in the parish of Llangurig, Wales — deep in the heart of sheep country. His mother was a hand-loom weaver. They lived down the road from the wool mill in Cwmbelan. My ancestors survived for many generations by preventing the return of the forest, deer, and boars, by preventing an injured land from healing. Of course, for the last several thousand years, none of my ancestors had been wild people — they suffered from the tremendous misfortune of having been born in captivity.

Every generation perceives the world of their childhood as the normal state, the ideal. Many don't comprehend that the ecosystem was badly damaged long before they were born. What they accept as normal might give their grandparents nightmares. Monbiot refers to this shortsightedness as *shifting baseline syndrome*. The past is erased by mental blinders. Each generation adapts to an ongoing pattern of decline. Humans have an amazing tolerance for crowding, filth, and stress.

Monbiot gushes with excitement when describing the amazing changes that followed the reintroduction of wolves to Yellowstone Park. They promptly corrected deer overpopulation, which led to forest regeneration, which led to healthier streams, which led to more fish. As wolves reduced the coyotes, the result was more rabbits, mice, hawks, weasels, boxes, badgers, eagles, and ravens.

A number of European organizations are promoting rewilding. Pan Parks has protected 240,000 hectares (593,000 acres), and is working on a million more. Wild Europe is working to create wildlife corridors across the continent. Rewilding Europe promotes the reintroduction of missing species. Pleistocene Park in Siberia is reintroducing many species in a 160 km^2 park (62 sq. mi.), which it plans to expand to 600 km^2 (232 sq. mi.).

In continental Europe, the rewilding movement is building momentum. Wolves, bears, bison, and beavers have begun the path to recovery. Not every effort succeeds — Italy reintroduced two male lynx, and the cute couple mysteriously failed to produce offspring. Britain and Ireland remain out to lunch. Most of the land is owned by wealthy elites who are obsessed with preserving a "tidy" looking countryside — treeless and profoundly dreary. They enjoy recreational hunting, and wolves would spoil their fun.

Monbiot delights in goosing every sacred cow along his path, and readers of many varieties are sure to foam at the mouth and mutter naughty obscenities. For me, *Feral* had a few zits, but they don't sink the book. He leads us to the mountaintop and allows us to view the world from above the haze of assumptions, illusions, and fantasies. Who are we? Where is our home? Where are we going?

He rubs our noses in the foul messes we've made, hoping we'll learn from our accidents and grow. He confronts us with big important issues that we've avoided for far too long — the yucky stuff we're doing for no good reason. I like that. This is important. He recommends intriguing alternatives to stoopid. It's about time.

The Once and Future World

J. B. MacKinnon grew up on the edge of a Canadian prairie. "I knew the prairie in the hands-in-every-crevice detail that only a child can, and it was, for me, a place of magic." He developed a healthy relationship with the living ecosystem, an experience that is no longer ordinary. Years later, as an adult, he returned to visit home, and his sacred prairie had been erased by the Royal Heights subdivision. He could find no trace of the red foxes that he had loved so much. It hurt.

By and by, curiosity inspired him to spend some time studying books about the days of yesteryear. To his surprise, he learned that the foxes of his region were not indigenous, nor was much of the prairie vegetation. His childhood home bore little resemblance to the wild prairie that existed several centuries earlier. Before he was born, the land was home to caribou, elk, wolves, and buffalo, all absent in his lifetime. What happened? Could the damage be repaired? MacKinnon explored these questions in *The Once and Future World*.

The world we experience in childhood is typically perceived as being the normal, unspoiled state. We can comprehend the damage that has occurred during our lifetime, but not all that has been lost since grandma was little, or grandma's grandma. This ecological amnesia is called *shifting baseline syndrome*.

Thank goodness for the venerable grandmothers of the temple of environmental history. They can take us to sacred mountains offering views of eons past, and help us remember who we are, where we came from, and how much has been lost. We can see the Pleistocene cave paintings, aglow with reverence and respect for the family of life, created by a culture in which humans were "just another species on the landscape." Later paintings by civilized Greeks illustrate a culture of total disconnection — human gods, goddesses, warriors, lion killers — starring the one and only species that mattered.

Like MacKinnon, the world of my childhood has been erased. Three hundred years earlier, it had been a paradise of forests dotted with many pristine lakes, home to unimaginable numbers of fish, turtles, waterfowl, and assorted woodland critters. Thousands of years earlier, in the wake of the melting glaciers, Pleistocene Michigan had been home to giant beavers, walruses, whales, mastodons, mammoths, peccaries, elk, moose, caribou, musk oxen, and bison. I had been completely unaware that they belonged in this ecosystem, and that their absence was abnormal. I did not dream of their return, since I didn't know they were missing.

MacKinnon says that we have inherited a 10 percent world, because 90 percent of the planet's wildness is largely gone. We can't begin to comprehend all that has been lost in the last century or three. But the tragedy can also be medicinal. "The history of nature is not always a lament. It is also an invitation to envision another world." Indeed! Our current vision is suicidal. His mantra is remember, reconnect, and rewild. "We need to remember what nature can be; reconnect to it as something meaningful in our lives; and start to remake a wilder world." Great!

The rewilding bandwagon is picking up momentum now. Twenty years ago, it meant reintroducing missing species, like elephants, mountain lions, and wolves, acts that would spark firestorms of opposition. Lately, it has expanded to include smaller, doable tweaks that can be done right now, around the neighborhood, to make the ecosystem a bit more wild — reconnection. Tiny successes are likely to feed the soul, and inspire bolder acts of healing. It all adds up.

Importantly, rewilding directs some of our attention to the ecosystem that we inhabit, a form of awareness that's getting close to extinction in consumer societies. MacKinnon doesn't fetch his paddle to spank capitalism, greedy corporations, corrupt politicians, unsuccessful activists, or the consumer hordes that live high impact lives whilst brushing off any responsibility. Instead, he suggests that most people simply don't get it. Industrial strength cultural programming makes it difficult or impossible for most people to wander beyond the mall parking lot. Listen to this:

"Standing on the globe as we know it today, among people who are predominantly urban, who often spend more time in virtual landscapes than in natural ones, and who in large part have never known — do not have a single personal memory — of anything approaching nature in its full potential, it is hard to even wrap one's head around where to begin."

Most people are focused on short-term human interests, and nothing else. They have been taught to inhabit a world of pure fantasy. On the walls of their caves are paintings of trophy homes, SUVs, smart phones, tablet computers, big TVs, and on and on. Most of them will never find their way home, or fully experience their core animal essence.

The tiny minority of folks who have developed the ability to think outside the box, like biologist Michael Soulé, feel "profoundly alienated from mainstream society." Communication is nearly impossible. He says, "We are different. We're wired to love different things than other people are." I know what he means. We don't feel at home in this society. Maybe we're pioneers, scouting a new and safer path.

Mark Fisher is one of the different folks, an advocate for rewilding. He works with the Wildland Research Institute in northern England, a devastated nation where people sometimes strongly oppose even the reintroduction of trees (let alone vicious man-eating beavers). On a visit to America, he was overcome with emotion when he saw wolves running wild in Yellowstone. When he stood on an overlook at White Mountain National Forest, and observed 800,000 acres of woodland, "I just cried my eyes out." Ancestral memories returned with great beauty.

Once upon a time, MacKinnon met a mother and daughter who had lived for 30 years in a remote region of British Columbia, in grizzly bear country. The mother had had two brushes with the bears, and perceived them as "highly spiritual experiences." Being reminded that humans were not the Master Species helped her remember who she was. "It was just like coming home." The daughter had no notion that living near grizzlies was unusual. MacKinnon found hope in this, "We are always only a single generation away from a new sense of what is normal."

Finally, I was fascinated to learn about our olive baboon relatives who live in Ghana. Like us, their diet is omnivorous. Like us, they evolved in a tropical climate, where they needed no clothes, fire, or shelter. Like us, they can inhabit rainforests, deserts, and savannahs, but prefer savannah. On average, males weigh 53 pounds (24 kg), and females weigh 32 pounds (14.5 kg). Despite their size, they have been able to survive for millions of years in a world of powerful carnivores — without tools — without becoming hopelessly stuck in the toxic tar baby of innovation and technology, with its enormous bloody costs.

Instead of chasing large herbivores with spears, baboons hunt a wide variety of small critters with their bare hands and teamwork. Hunting provides a third of their food. Unlike us, they never migrated out of Africa, into chilly climates where they could not survive without techno-crutches. Unlike us, they didn't exterminate the predators that kept their numbers in balance. They have never had any need for fire, psych meds, or cell phones. Might there be a lesson here?

The Future Eaters

After spending more than 20 years reading hundreds of books describing various aspects of the Earth Crisis, *The Future Eaters* by Tim Flannery stands out. It provides a sliver of hope for the future that is not built on magical thinking. Flannery is a lad who is madly in love with the Australian region, and he dreams that it will eventually heal, far down the road someday.

Here's the story. Hominids evolved in Africa, and later migrated into Eurasia, where they lived in some regions for a million years before *Homo sapiens* drifted in. In ecosystems where the fauna coevolved with hominids, the critters clearly understood that two-legs were predators, and they behaved accordingly. But when *Homo sapiens* first appeared in Australia, none of the critters had ever seen a two-leg before, so they had no fear.

The fearless elephant seals on King Island weighed up to four tons. They would calmly sun themselves while humans killed the animal sitting beside them. On Kangaroo Island, men could walk up to fearless kangaroos and dispatch them with clubs. Countless birds were killed with sticks. Flannery referred to these hunters as future eaters. Future eaters were *Homo sapiens* that migrated into lands where the ecosystem had not coevolved with hominids.

The first phase of future eating was to hunt like there's no tomorrow. For example, New Zealand was loaded with birds. Moas were ostrich-like birds that could grow to 10 feet (3 m) tall, and weigh 550 pounds (250 kg). Future eaters arrived between 800 and 1,000 years ago, and by 400 years ago, the moas were extinct. Today we have found many collections of moa bones, some containing the remains of up to 90,000 birds. Evidence suggests that a third of the meat was tossed away to rot. Obviously, the birds were super-abundant and super-easy to kill.

Meanwhile, well-fed future eaters gave birth to growing numbers of baby future eaters. More predators + less prey = trouble. The party got ugly. Friendly neighbors became mortal enemies. Moas disappeared from the menu, and were replaced with Moe and Mona from a nearby village. Cannibalism beats starvation. Overhunting and overbreeding, followed by bloody social breakdown, was a common pattern in the world of the future eaters.

Following the crash, the survivors had two options: learn from their mistakes, or fool around with new mistakes. The New Zealanders didn't have time to get their act together before they were discovered by palefaces. It was a different story in New Caledonia, where the future eaters arrived 3,500 years ago. They partied hard, crashed, did the warfare thing, adapted to their damaged ecosystem, and were having a nice time when Captain Cook washed up on shore.

Future eating contributed to extinctions. In Australia, large animals were going extinct by 35,000 years ago. Most megafauna in the Americas vanished 11,000 years ago. In New Caledonia, it was 3,500 years ago. In recently settled New Zealand, big animals went extinct 500 to 800 years ago.

In Africa, Asia, and Europe, some megafauna managed to survive. The unlucky ones were domesticated, which led to radical changes in our way of life. Enslaved horses facilitated the bloody spread of the Indo-European culture from Ireland to India. Along with oxen, horses enabled the expansion of soil mining. Vast forests were eliminated to make room for growing herds of hungry hooved locusts.

Australia is an unusual continent. It has been geologically static for 60 million years. Most of the soil is extremely old, and very low in nutrients. Consequently, the fauna that won the evolution sweepstakes were energy efficient, majoring in marsupials and reptiles.

On other continents, soils often contain twice as much phosphate and nitrates. Lands having rich soils produced energy-guzzling ecosystems, including large numbers of megafauna. The most energy-intensive species of all are warm-blooded meat eaters like us. Europe has 660 million people, and Australia has 17 million.

In addition to feeble soils, Australia has spooky weather, driven by the El Niño Southern Oscillation (ENSO). The climate unpredictably swings between droughts and floods. Droughts can last for many years, and then be washed away with a deluge. These freaky swings encourage cautious lifestyles, weed out energy-guzzling species, and make agriculture especially unreliable.

Flannery wonders if it's moral to "live as a vegetarian in Australia, destroying seven kilograms of irreplaceable soil, upon which everything depends, for each kilogram of bread we consume?" This question is relevant in all lands. There is no free lunch in farm country.

Anyway, before humans arrived in the Australian region, the ecosystems were self-sustaining. Then the future eaters appeared. Extinctions included species that had performed essential ecosystem functions, like controlling woody brush. When brush got out of control, it reduced grazing land for herbivores, and encouraged devastating wildfires.

To reduce this new imbalance, Aborigines periodically lit fires to keep the fuel from accumulating. Unfortunately, during burns, soil nutrients went up in smoke, especially nitrogen. Exposed soils were vulnerable to wind erosion. The land got drier. Centuries of burning produced a downward spiral that was largely irreversible. There was no undo command.

The hunters must have had turbulent times as the initial era of plenty and prosperity dissolved into scarcity. Then, "for 60,000 years Aborigines managed the crippled ecosystems, preventing them from degenerating further." For the last 12,000 years, surviving evidence suggests that they lived in a stable and sustainable manner. They succeeded at this by learning the most important trick of all — adapting to their ecosystem. They were forced to return their future eater badges and uniforms, and they were glad to do so.

Meanwhile, back in Eurasia, the nutrient rich soils were sprouting the biggest and craziest mob of future eaters to ever walk the Earth. For the last 12,000 years, they have exploded in number, exterminated the megafauna, laid waste to forests and fisheries, and spilled oceans of blood. Then, they discovered Australia, and imported the future eater mindset, with predictable results.

Today, the human population of the planet is almost entirely future eaters. Our binge of plenty and prosperity is wheezing, bleeding, and staggering. Climate change and the end of cheap and abundant energy will derail civilization as we know it. We are proceeding into an era of scarcity and conflict. We would be wise to remember the most important trick of all.

On the plus side, we are the first future eaters to comprehend the catastrophic effects of our future eating lifestyle. It's never too late to learn, think, and grow. There's never been a better time to question everything. In a few centuries, if we make it, we may be asked to return our badges and uniforms. There is hope! Hooray!

Straw Dogs

When the philosopher John Gray looks out over the world, he sees a bloody madhouse, a hell broth of deranged magical thinking. In his bestselling book, *Straw Dogs*, he turns into a ruthless vigilante who tirelessly pounds the crap out of ridiculous ideas that condemn us to mindless self-destruction. What might happen if we ever succeeded at clearing the decks of loony whims? Would this make it easier to think clearly, and move onto a path with a future?

By the time you get to the end of the book, not one sacred cow is left standing. He rubbishes our entire belief system. Readers who are thoroughbred critical thinkers may not find much to disagree with, but those who uncritically accept everything they are told by society will foam at the mouth and scream obscenities. To some, he is an honorable and dignified iconoclast, and to others he is a super-pessimistic misanthrope. Reader comments at Amazon are all over the place, and quite interesting.

Gray's thinking is an unusual swirl of intellect and animism. In his analysis of our current predicament, the two primary culprits are humanism and progress.

Humanism is the illusion that humans are apart from, and superior to, all other beings in the family of life. We feel no obligation to obey the laws of nature, because they don't apply to us. Our sacred species does not really belong in the natural world, because we are so much better than filthy wild animals. Humanism is a notion that we picked up somewhere on the path to civilization. It has been passed from the Platonists, to the Christians, to the Enlightenment, and to modern secular humanists.

Progress is the belief that life never stops getting better and better. As long as we can maintain a fervent blind faith in scientific progress, there is little need for us to exercise our thinkers. Witness the fact that nearly all of those who graduate from the most prestigious institutions of higher learning — and most other people, too — are entranced by a ridiculously irrational belief in perpetual economic growth.

Darwin drove a stake through the heart of the humanist fantasy, demonstrating that humans were simply animals, like all the rest, and we have survived by luck alone. The humanists were not amused. They jerked out the stake, seized Darwin's notion of the survival of the fittest, and proclaimed that our remarkable success was indisputable proof that we are, without a doubt, the greatest!

Gray looks outside his window, perceives thousands of serious problems, and concludes that catastrophes are on the way. Humanists look out the window, disregard thousands of serious problems, and see reality as an unfinished masterpiece — our amazing species will be saved once we are all fully illuminated by precious reason.

He acknowledges that there has been real progress in science and technology, but sees little progress in morals and ethics. While progress does reduce human suffering in some ways, it is simultaneously inventing bigger and better weapons for killing people and ecosystems.

In 1543, Japan had more guns than any other nation. In that year, they banned firearms, and the nation was gun-free until 1879, when Commodore Perry arrived from the modern world, and frightened Japan into a process of rapid industrialization. Their era of isolation was over, and they understood the diabolical law of civilization: "Any country that renounces technology will become the prey to those who do not. There is no escape from a world of predatory states."

The greatest atrocities in human history have been enabled by advances in modern technology. Innovation is impossible to control. Horrid inventions that are banned in many countries will be eagerly produced by others. Some technology, like biological weapons or cyber warfare can be pursued in the shadow world, unknown to governments or corporate entities.

At the same time, the traditional concept of warfare as being nation versus nation is dissolving. With the rise of movements like Al Qaeda and the Taliban that exist entirely beyond government control, we're seeing a revival of religious warfare, where there are no standing armies or front lines. The woman standing beside you might be a bomb.

Humanists envision a secular world that is educated, rational, and ethical, but few societies are secular today. In primitive countries, like the U.S., millions of educated people reject the notion of evolution. Millions of fundamentalists, of every variety, insist that their specific interpretation of sacred texts and visions is the one and only correct way to live, and that the rest of humankind must be converted to their beliefs — or else!

With regard to the Earth Crisis, Gray does not assign all blame to agriculture and civilization. He believes that our problems began far earlier. "There was never a Golden Age of harmony with the Earth. Most hunter-gatherers were fully as rapacious as later humans. But they were few, and they lived better than most who came after them." Throughout our long journey, the cost of every "advance" has been ecological injury.

He acknowledges that some cultures did manage to live sustainably for long stretches of time. An essential component of their success was restraint. They used practices like infanticide, geronticide, and sexual abstinence to limit the size of their clans — no crowding, no scarcity, no conflict. These brilliant hunters clearly understood that, in a world of finite food sources, perpetual growth was dumber than dog poop.

Unfortunately, farmers threw restraint out the window. Growing population forced us become deeply addicted to agriculture, and we burned our bridges behind us. Today, a return to living in balance is obstructed by our enormous population. We could greatly reduce our misery by reducing our numbers, but this will never be done voluntarily on a global scale. We've entrusted the remedy to Big Mama Nature, who will effectively clean up the mess without mercy. The human herd might shrink at a rate as rapid as its explosion.

Throughout the book, Gray is a tireless fire hose of criticism. He tells us that consciousness, reason, and self-awareness are highly overrated; *Homo rapiens* bears a striking resemblance to cancer, and so on. This does get tiresome. Is he a dark man with an unhealthy mind, or is he a sane man who is clearly and competently describing a dark reality? He encourages us to turn on our thinkers and reexamine our beliefs, a pastime that can often be quite profitable. The book has been a best seller. It's short and easy to read.

Here's a line that intrigued me: "It is not of becoming the planet's wise stewards that Earth-lovers dream, but of a time when humans have ceased to matter." Gray bets that humankind will succeed in our crusade of self-destruction, at which point the healing process can begin. Earth will forget us, and life will move on. On the other hand, modern folks spend their lives wearing their freaky Master of the Universe masks, which conceal their ordinary animal faces. In theory, humans could "cease to matter" by taking off our masks, abandoning our achievements, humbly returning to the family of life, and disappearing into the crowd.

Apocalyptic Planet

Craig Childs is a nature writer and globetrotting adventure hog. He's been thinking a lot about apocalypse lately. It's hard not to. The jungle drums are pounding out a growing stream of warnings — attention! — big trouble ahead.

The Christian currents in our culture encourage us to perceive time as being something like a drag strip. At one end is the starting line (creation), and at the other end is the finish line (judgment day). We're speeding closer and closer to the end, which some perceive to be the final Game Over for everything everywhere. Childs disagrees. "We are not on a one-way trip to a brown and sandblasted planet."

He was lucky to survive into adulthood still possessing an unfettered imagination, and he can zoom right over the snarling snapping dogmas that impede most folks who attempt to think outside the box. In his book *Apocalyptic Planet*, he gives readers a helpful primer on eco-catastrophe. The bottom line is that Earth is constantly changing, and it's not uncommon for change events to be sudden and catastrophic.

He believes that the big storm on the horizon today is not "The Apocalypse." It's just one more turbulent era in a four billion year story. Out of the pile of planetary disasters, he selects nine examples, travels to locations that illustrate each one, and then spins stories. Each tale cuts back and forth between his adventures at the site, and background information from assorted sources. It's a catastrophe buffet.

Deserts are a quarter of all land, and many are growing now. History tells us that they can expand and contract rapidly, taking out societies in the process. Four out of ten people live in regions prone to drying up. New Mexico once experienced a drought that lasted 1,000 years. Beneath the driest regions of the Sahara, pollen samples indicate that the land was once tropical savannah and woodlands. A few years ago, Atlanta, Georgia (not an arid region) came close to draining its water supply during a long drought.

Glaciers are melting at a rate that alarms people who think. Childs visited the Northern Patagonia Ice Field, where hunks the size of buildings were crashing down off the edge of the dying glacier. Enormous volumes of melt water are raising the global sea level. He also visited the Bering Sea, where the old land bridge from Asia to America is now 340 feet (103 m) underwater. Beringia was once a broad treeless steppe, home to an amazing community of megafauna. If climate change eliminates all ice, the seas could rise another 120 feet (36 m) or so, and some major rivers will run dry from lack of melt water. About 40 percent of humankind resides near coasts. Nobody knows how fast the seas will rise, or how much.

The planet has been smacked countless times by asteroids. Many believe that the dinosaur era was terminated by the Chicxubal impact on the Yucatan Peninsula. There are many, many objects zooming around in space that could hit us, but Childs recommends that our time would be better spent worrying about catastrophic volcanic eruptions. There are daily eruptions from 200 active volcanoes. Extreme eruptions have loaded the atmosphere with dust, blocking out sunlight, leading to winters that lasted for years.

Climate change is likely to affect the movement of the planet's tectonic plates. As glaciers melt and dam reservoirs evaporate, there will be less weight on the land below, allowing it to rise. Tectonic shifts can lead to earthquakes, tsunamis, volcanic eruptions, and altered ocean currents and weather patterns.

All civilizations are temporary outbursts of overbreeding and harmful lifestyles. On a visit to Mayan ruins in Guatemala, Childs discussed their collapse, the result of a combination of factors. "The issue, ultimately, was carrying capacity." Over the years, I've often seen people sharing their opinions of the Earth's carrying capacity for humans. Estimates usually range between 100 million and 15 billion, as if there is one correct answer.

Actually, the long-term carrying capacity is constantly changing, and these days it's getting smaller and smaller. Ocean acidification, chronic overfishing, and other harms have sharply reduced the vitality of marine ecosystems. Chronic forest mining, soil mining, and industrialization have sharply reduced the vitality of terrestrial ecosystems.

The fossil energy bubble enabled a huge temporary spike in carrying capacity, but as the bubble passes, we'll discover that the long-term carrying capacity is far less than it was 10,000 years ago, when the ecosystem enjoyed excellent health. Climate change is likely to reduce it further still, as large numbers of plant and animal species are blind-sided.

There have been five mass extinction events in ages past, and we are now in the sixth. Childs takes us on an amusing visit to the site of a catastrophic mass extinction, the state of Iowa, where 90 percent of the ecosystem has been reduced to agriculture. He and a buddy spent two days hiking through fields, dwarfed by tall stalks of corn (maize), during a week of blast furnace heat.

They were looking for signs of life besides corn, and they found almost none. The ecosystem was once home to 300 species of plants, 60 mammals, 300 birds, and over 1,000 insects. "This had historically been tallgrass prairie, one of the largest and most diverse biomasses in North America where a person on horseback could not be seen for the height of the grass." The sixth mass extinction is unlike the previous five, in that it is the result of human activities, an embarrassing accomplishment.

Yeast devours sugar and converts it into alcohol and carbon dioxide. When yeast are added to a vat of freshly pressed grape juice, they plunge into a sweet paradise, and promptly produce a bubbly population explosion. The alcohol in the vat will keep increasing until it reaches toxic levels, at which point the yeast experience a mass extinction event, the tragic consequence of living in an artificial environment constructed by thirsty alcoholics.

Humans evolved in a tropical climate. Eventually, we migrated into non-tropical climates, and developed the skills and technology necessary for surviving in chilly weather, but the ice ages were a time of struggle, not a sweet paradise. Then, a freak thing happened. The weather got warm, and stayed warm, for 10,000 years. Suddenly, we were like yeast in grape juice. Yippee! The unusually long warm era enabled the emergence of steamroller civilization and the human domination of the planet.

The 800-pound gorilla in this book is climate change, and concern about the decades that lie before us. Childs cites the views of a number of scientists, and they are all over the place. A loose cannon at the EPA says that global warming is a hoax, but the others agree that the climate is warming, and humans are the primary culprits. Some think that we've passed the tipping point, and all ice will soon be gone. Others think that if emissions are reduced, disaster might be avoided. One is sure that technology will fix everything — geoengineering will allow us to control the planet's climate like a thermostat. Another says that humankind will be gone in 100 years.

The long-term history of climate trends tells us that global temperatures commonly swing up and down, sometimes as much as 10°C to 12°C. Huge temperature swings lead to extinctions, but life on Earth has persisted. The current jump in temperature is unlike the previous ones in that it is the outcome of human activities. It is the result of a unique combination of factors, with no historical precedent. Humans are unique in being able to adapt to a wide variety of ecosystems, but ecosystems are far less adaptable to sudden climate shifts. Agriculture is on thin ice, as are seven billion people.

In a hut on the Greenland ice sheet, Childs had a long chat with José Rial, a chaos researcher and climate change scholar. Rial understands that nature is highly unstable, and quite capable of rapid and unpredictable changes. "What we study doesn't always help us predict very much, but it helps us to understand what is possible." Childs added, "He knows that the actual future is the one we never expect."

Windfall

McKenzie Funk's book, *Windfall*, explores the question, "What are we doing about climate change?" Readers are introduced to ambitious speculators who are eager to make enormous profits on new opportunities resulting from a warming planet. They are not investing in research for sharply reducing carbon emissions. They are obsessed with keeping the economic growth monster on life support. Climate change investment funds will soon become gold mines, creating a flood of new billionaires. The future is rosy as hell.

Mining corporations are slobbering with anticipation as Greenland's ice melts, providing access to billions of dollars' worth of zinc, gold, diamonds, and uranium. A defunct zinc mine, which operated from 1973 to 1990, provides a sneak preview of the nightmares to come. The Black Angel mine dumped its tailings into a nearby fjord. The zinc and lead in the runoff was absorbed by the blue mussels, which were eaten by fish, which were eaten by seals. Investors won, the ecosystem lost.

Other entrepreneurs are anxious to turn the torrents of melt water into hydropower, providing cheap energy for new server farms and aluminum smelters. Meanwhile, the tourism industry is raking in big money serving the growing swarms of climate disaster tourists.

As the Arctic ice melts, sea levels could rise as much as 20 feet (6 m). A number of low-lying islands are already on death row — the Maldives, Tuvalu, Kiribati, the Marshall Islands, Seychelles, Bahamas, and the Carteret Islands. Islanders are pissed that faraway rich folks are destroying their home. Bath time is also predicted for large portions of Manila, Alexandria, Lagos, Karachi, Kolkata, Jakarta, Dakar, Rio, Miami, Ho Chi Minh City, and a fifth of Bangladesh. There may be a billion climate refugees by 2050.

Five nations have shorelines on the icy Arctic Ocean: Canada, Russia, Norway, Denmark (Greenland), and the United States (Alaska). Beneath the rapidly melting ice are billions of dollars' worth of oil, gas, and coal. We would be wise to leave this sequestered carbon in the ground but, of course, we won't. There will be abundant testosterone-powered discussion over borderlines in the region, and this might include blizzards of bombs and bullets. Both Canada and Denmark claim ownership of Hans Island. Russia has planted a flag on the North Pole.

A melted Arctic will also provide a new shipping lane, connecting the Atlantic and Pacific, providing a much shorter and much cheaper alternative to the Panama Canal. Both sides of the Northwest Passage are owned by Canada, but other nations, like the U.S. and China, disagree that Canada owns the waterway. They prefer it to be an international route of innocent passage, like Gibraltar. Funk took a cruise on the Montreal, a frigate of the Royal Canadian Navy. They were engaged in Arctic war games, which included an exercise that seized a naughty American ship.

The core driver of climate change is simple: "add carbon, get heat." As carbon emissions skyrocket, so does the temperature of the atmosphere. We can't undo what has already been done, damage that will persist for centuries, but it would be rather intelligent to quit throwing gasoline on the fire. Unfortunately, the titans of capitalism have a different plan. Renewable energy cannot power our nightmare. Governments are careful to ignore this prickly issue, because voters delight in living as wastefully as possible. Technology is our only hope.

Cutting emissions would blindside our way of life (and so will not cutting emissions). But cleverly exploiting climate change will greatly enrich the titans, temporarily. There's growing interest in seawalls, storm surge barriers, and floating cities. Israelis are making big money selling snowmaking and desalinization equipment. Biotech firms are working hard to produce expensive drought resistant seeds. India is building a 2,100 mile (3,380 km) fence along its border with Bangladesh, to block the flood of refugees that are expected when rising seas submerge low-lying regions.

Others dream of making big money creating monopolies on the supply of freshwater, which is diminishing as the torrents of melting ice rush into the salty oceans. There are two things that people will spend their remaining cash on, water and food. Crop yields are sure to drop in a warming climate. This will lead to rising prices, and create exciting opportunities for profiteering. A number of wealthy nations are ruthlessly acquiring cropland in third world regions.

Funk visited Nathan Myhrvold, a Microsoft billionaire, who now runs Intellectual Ventures. His plan is to keep economic growth on life support by creating a virtual volcano called StratoShield. Volcanoes spew ash into the atmosphere, which reduces incoming solar heat, and cools off the climate. StratoShield would spray 2 to 5 million metric tons of sulfur dioxide into the stratosphere every year. This would make the sunlight one percent dimmer, and enable life as we know it to continue, with reduced guilt, for a bit longer (maybe) — hooray!

Funk also visited Alan Robock, who opposes the plan. Volcanic ash is not harmless. The goal of StratoShield is to block heat. The catastrophic side effect is that it's likely to severely alter rain patterns in the southern hemisphere, spurring horrendous droughts, deluges, and storm systems. On the bright side, life in Microsoft country, the Pacific Northwest, would remain fairly normal, and the sulfur dioxide sunsets would be wonderfully colorful.

Funk didn't mention that the geoengineering, if it actually worked, would have to be done permanently. Beneath the shield, ongoing emissions would continue to increase the atmosphere's carbon load. If the shield was discontinued, and full sunlight resumed, the consequences would not be pleasant.

Myhrvold's former boss, Bill Gates, is running a foundation that's spending billions of dollars to eradicate disease. The mosquitoes of the world are nervous, fearing near term extinction. The foundation is dedicated to promoting the wellbeing of humankind. Oddly, it has spent nothing on research to cut carbon emissions. Folks will be spared from disease so they can enjoy drought and deluge. There is no brilliant win/win solution. The path to balance will be long and painful.

Funk finished his book in 2012, a very hot year for climate juju all around the world. He had spent six years hanging out with tycoons, "the smartest guys in the room." All were obsessed with conjuring highly complex ways of making even more money by keeping our insane civilization on life support, for as long as possible, by any means necessary.

Climate change is a manmade disaster, and those most responsible are the wealthy consumers of the north. Funk imagines that the poor folks of the south will be hammered, while the primary perpetrators remain fairly comfortable. It's a wicked problem because "we are not our own victims." We feel no obligation to reduce our emissions or consumption. We care little about misery in faraway places.

I am not convinced that the north will get off easy. Anyone who spends time studying the Earth Crisis will eventually conclude that humans are remarkably clever, but pathologically irrational. We've created a reality far too complex for our tropical primate brains. We've created a culture that burns every bridge it crosses. Funk says, "We should remember that there is also genius in simplicity." I agree.

Indian Summer

Thomas Jefferson Mayfield (1843–1928) was among the first Americans to move into California's San Joaquin Valley. He arrived in 1850, when he was six years old. His family had moved west to get rich quick in the Gold Rush, but the gold belonged to the land, and it cleverly hid from the loony looters. His father shifted to raising livestock, assisted by his two older sons. Young Thomas and his mother stayed at their small shanty, near Kings River.

The wild valley was a magnificent wonderland, millions of colorful flowers, with snow-covered mountains in the background. Neighbors included elk, deer, antelope, grizzly bears, black bears, raccoons, rabbits, gophers, ground squirrels. The sky swarmed with clouds of blackbirds. There were billions of geese, and flocks passing overhead might be four square miles in size (10 km^2). Huge flights of pigeons would block out the sun. Wetlands were loaded with tules (bulrushes) that grew 20 feet tall (6 m). Along the streams were unbroken forests of ancient oak trees. Nearby was Tulare Lake, which was filled with fish and waterfowl. The region around the lake was home to a fantastic abundance of wildlife.

The Yokut Indians who lived across the river from the Mayfield's shanty were friendly. They generously brought food to the family (...so the strangers wouldn't shoot their guns and disturb the wildlife). Within a year of their arrival, Mayfield's mother died. The Yokuts offered to take care of the young fellow, and his father agreed. The boy spent almost ten years among the Indians. He fluently spoke their language, dressed like them, ate their food, and had almost no contact with white society. He helped them hunt and fish, and spent lots of time playing with the other boys.

The Indians were warm people. They rarely quarreled, often laughed, shunned gossip, respected their elders, and only spoke when something meaningful needed to be said. Honesty was the norm, and theft was unknown. Mornings began with a bath in the river. In the hot summer months, much time was spent in the cool water.

The Indians built houses made with tule mats, and some lodges were 100 feet long (30 m). Acorns were stored in elevated cylindrical granaries. Mostly, the Yokuts lived outdoors. Homes were only used for sleeping, and for shelter from bad weather. Cooking, eating, and other activities were done outside. Food was cooked in watertight baskets heated with hot rocks. They stored dried fish, dried meat, dried grasses, acorns, and many kinds of seeds. Tule roots were a staple food.

Around 1855, the Americans began rounding up Indians and moving them into concentration camps, known as reservations. Prior to the roundup, many had already died from the diseases of civilization. In captivity, living indoors made them miserable, and many died from tuberculosis and measles. Whiskey led to painful social breakdown. In 1850, at the beginning of Mayfield's stay, there were over 300 in the tribe, but ten years later only 40 survived. In 1862, his father was killed in an Indian war, and the young man said goodbye to the Yokuts and drifted away into white society.

Mayfield almost took his story to the grave. He spent much of his life in the valley, but never told anyone about his childhood. White folks hated Indians, and he would have been stigmatized by revealing his story. But in 1928, Frank Latta was working on an oral history of the San Joaquin Valley, heard about the 85-year old Mayfield, and went to visit him. For the first time, Mayfield had an eager listener, and he gushed stories for several months, until he died.

Indian Summer is the story of his time among the Yokuts. It's just 123 pages long, with large type. The writing is simple, just the facts. His story is the only eyewitness account of a colonist who knew California Indians when they were still wild and free, living in their traditional manner. It provides a wealth of details about how the Indians lived.

Even after Mayfield was a teen, old enough to take care of himself, his father left him with the Indians. "He said that I was in better company with the Indians than I would be staying around the white towns with him. There I would be in contact with saloons, gamblers, drunks, bums, and many other undesirables that I would not know at the rancheria." Whites were notoriously untrustworthy, and masters in the fine arts of vulgarity and profanity.

When he was in his eighties, Mayfield said, "There is no use trying to deny that the Indians I knew were, for the most part, naked savages. But I have found that in the sixty-six or more years since I left them that just wearing a lot of clothes does not make people decent. Neither does going around naked necessarily make people indecent." He added, "I knew the Indians in their natural state and I know that they were the finest people that I have ever met."

In the good old days, Tulare Lake covered Kings County, and portions of Tulare and Kern counties. It was the biggest freshwater lake west of the Mississippi, and it sometimes swelled to cover 760 square miles (1,968 km^2). A thriving fish mining industry was established by the Americans. Four rivers once emptied into the lake, but water-mining farmers and land speculators diverted their flows, and the lake disappeared by 1910. Tulare Lake is now called the Tulare Lakebed, flat dry land, mostly cotton fields. In extremely wet El Niño years, like 1997, the former lake temporarily holds some water. Now the Americans are pumping out the groundwater, and the land is sinking. Some locations are falling two inches per month. Roads are cracking, and pipelines are breaking.

There were 16 subcultures of the Yokut people, and there may have been up to 50,000 of them in the San Joaquin Valley 200 years ago. Abundant wildlife and plant foods allowed them to live in high density for hunter-gatherers — in good health, usually peaceful, with a leisurely lifestyle. By 2010, the valley was home to 3,971,659 Americans, and it had air pollution comparable to Los Angeles and Houston. The current way of life does not have a long-term future.

Thomas Jefferson Mayfield was born in 1843, the same year as my great-grandfather, Richard Edward Rees. Richard's granddaughter Martha lived until 2009, and she remembered him well. The Yokut people had lived in balance for several thousand years, but civilization furiously obliterated the wild paradise in less than three generations. Bambi was splattered by a runaway freight train, and nobody lived happily ever after. There may be important lessons here.

A huge and glaring omission from the book is California's wars of extermination on the Indians. The Tule River War was waged against the Kings River Yokuts at the time Mayfield was staying with them. In the first 20 years of the American occupation of California, 90 percent of the Indians died. Bounties were paid for the scalps and heads of Indians. This bloody genocide was omitted from the story.

The Destruction of California

Raymond Dasmann was a professor of conservation biology, and the author of many books. The poor fellow suffered from a devastating mental disturbance known as rationality, a condition that affects dozens of people in the civilized world. He frequently experienced painful attacks of foresight and common sense. Living in California, he was on the front line of the world war against the planet, an ecological blitzkrieg. "When this war is finally won, the consequences will be as severe and irreversible as though we had fought a nuclear war," he said.

Dasmann was born in San Francisco, in an era when there were few cars, the neighborhoods were pleasant, and men, women, and children felt perfectly safe, day or night, almost everywhere. He was cursed to be born whilst the fossil energy blip was skyrocketing toward its climax, creating a bewildering whirlwind of immense change. Young folks perceived the whirlwind to be normal, while older folks remembered better times, and were sickened by the senseless destruction, and the profound decay of society.

He wrote *The Destruction of California* when he was 45. During those 45 years, the state's population had grown six-fold, spurred by a tsunami of immigration. This was not good. In the book, he described the various crises that were propelling the state toward disaster. He wanted people to better understand the consequences of perpetual growth. The book was published in 1965, 50 years ago.

Before colonization, California had been a cool scene for thousands of years. Over time, the native hunter-gatherers learned how to live in a careful and respectful manner, and the ecosystem enjoyed jubilant health. Their children were lucky to receive superb educations, which inspired them to live mindfully, in balance with the land. The lasting marks that tribes left on the land were mostly mounds of discarded shells.

Later, the Spanish arrived, built missions, enslaved the Indians, introduced contagious diseases, and forced the natives to accept a foreign religion. With the invaders came livestock and shipments of hay, which included the seeds of Spanish weeds. The weeds were mostly annuals, and they were well adapted to thriving in a Mediterranean climate similar to California. The grasses indigenous to California were primarily robust perennials that provided an excellent source of nutrition.

During drought times, there was less vegetation for the Spanish livestock to eat, leading to overgrazing. The weed seeds sat patiently in the dust, waiting for a year when the rains returned. Sadly, the weeds won. The indigenous grasses are nearly extinct now. Decade by decade, the quality of rangeland declined. "In some places all that was left was worthless tarweed, star thistle, or cheat grass." Today, few people cruising through ranch country are capable of perceiving this glaring ecological train wreck.

Eighty years after the Spanish settled, a swarm of Americans rumbled into California, and they were out of their minds with Gold Fever. They didn't enslave Indians; they shot them. Indians had been known to trade gold for glass beads, because gold was not super-big juju in their culture. But gold made white folks crazy. They would kill for it. Gold was a magical rock that gave crazy people enormous illusions of grandeur. With hydraulic mining, they channeled flowing streams through high-pressure nozzles and washed away entire mountains to extract the shiny rocks.

Early visitors to California were overwhelmed by the incredible abundance of wildlife. Portions of the Central Valley looked like the Serengeti — herds of tule elk, pronghorn antelope, and black-tailed deer. There were many wetlands. "Here were birds in the tens of millions that darkened the sky when migrations sent them winging northward." In 1852, a man in Humboldt sat on a hill and observed 40 grizzly bears below. The swarm of gold digging crazy people inspired other crazy people to get into the meat business via full-scale industrial hunting. By 1910, the wildlife was in tatters.

Crazy people also became giddy with greed at the sight of 4,000-year-old redwoods, 27 feet (8m) in diameter. They sharpened their axes and went wacko. Profits were invested in technology that enabled them to cut more and more. There was no plan to leave anything for future generations. The plan was to make as much money as possible, as fast as possible. Floods washed away highways, bridges, and entire communities. Fish perished in the silt-choked streams. When Dasmann was writing, it looked like the old growth would be gone in 16 years. At the same time, the community of Arcata was fiercely resisting the proposed creation of Redwood National Park.

Hordes of well-educated elites, who did not suffer from rationality, were delighted to get rich quick promoting the rapid growth of ghastly megacities in arid regions having minimal freshwater resources. As the consumer mobs swelled in size, more streams were dammed, new aqueducts were built, rivers were pumped over mountains, and ancient water was removed from aquifers. Nobody questioned this. "Since growth is by definition progress, and progress is by definition good, this is deemed to be answer enough for any but a fool."

Dasmann was driven out of his wits by this highly contagious pandemic of Get Rich Quick Fever. Yet he was not an eco-revolutionary who recommended turning the clock back 400 years. He didn't preach the gospel of ecological sustainability. His dream was quite modest; stop making things worse — think! He worried about environmental destruction, the growing populations of people and automobiles, and the ongoing threat of water shortages. Today, we can add to this list climate change, economic collapse, and growing limits on energy and other resources. It's 50 years later, and the crazy growth has not stopped.

The Indians lived in the same land for thousands of years without destroying it. This is called "primitive." If whites had never arrived, the land would still be incredibly healthy. But the blitzkrieg arrived in 1769, and the destruction has been accelerating at an exponential rate. This is called "progress." The root problem here is not genes, but culture. During the pilgrimage from womb to grave, every human floats in the currents of culture, like fish swim in water.

Indian children received superb educations because they lived in rational cultures that were mindful about not rocking the ecological boat. Today's kids are taught to work hard, shop like there's no tomorrow, and leave the bill for their descendants. Those who rock the boat the hardest earn the highest social status. This screwy ritual is reinforced by teachers, preachers, peers, parents, the media — everywhere, all the time.

It's difficult to question the madness. We have a hard time comprehending how destructive and irrational our society is. It's nearly impossible to wrap our heads around the notion that the Indians enjoyed a way of life that had a long future. It's very hard for us to understand ecological intelligence, and desire it. Thinking outside the box requires us to summon our inner power and leap into the unknown. We have little to lose.

Across Arctic America

One hundred years ago, the expansion of the white world into the Arctic was disrupting the traditional culture of the Eskimo people. Into the far north came guns, traders, missionaries, educators, gold miners, and industrial hunting and fishing. Also, the diseases of civilization slammed the wild people who had no resistance to them. Eskimos seemed to be getting close to extinction.

Knud Rasmussen organized a scientific expedition to learn more about the Eskimos before they disappeared forever. From 1921 to 1924, they traveled by dogsled from Greenland, across Canada and Alaska, to Siberia, covering about 20,000 miles (32,000 km). Rasmussen was born in Greenland, and Kalaallisut was the first language he learned. He was surprised to discover that the Eskimos of Alaska spoke a similar dialect, and told similar stories, despite many centuries with no contact.

Rasmussen was not an arrogant bigot. He respected the natives, while also imagining that modern science, religion, and technology made life better. At every opportunity, he sought out the elders, won their trust, and learned their stories, songs, and beliefs. Rasmussen published ten volumes of notes, and then summarized his grand adventure in *Across Arctic America.*

I've read several books about the Eskimos of Greenland, learning of the endless challenges of Arctic survival. But the Greenlanders had it easy, compared to the Eskimos of northern Canada who had no access to the sea, and a less dependable food supply. These inland people had neither blubber nor wood to use for fuel. They spent the long, terrifically cold winters in unheated huts, dining on frozen meat. They lived primarily on caribou and salmon.

In the old days, their settlements were located along the caribou migration routes. Men hunted with bows and arrows, which required extreme patience, waiting for an animal to (maybe) wander within range. Later, they got guns, which could kill from a greater distance, making it much easier to fill the freezer. In response, the caribou abandoned their old routes, and went elsewhere. The hunters starved, and their settlements became Arctic ruins. While one group starved, another group several miles away might be feasting on abundant meat.

In Eskimo society, when daughters grew up, they married, and joined their husband's family. Sons, on the other hand, had obligations to their parents. Sons were the hunters and fishers, and more sons meant more security. "It is a general custom that old folks no longer able to provide for themselves commit suicide by hanging." Nobody wanted to be a burden on others.

Male infants were usually kept, and most females were killed, except for those who were spoken for. With the gift of a harpoon or pot, a marriage could be arranged for an infant daughter. One family had 20 children — ten girls were killed, four sons died of disease, one son drowned, leaving four sons and a daughter. The mother was happy to have four sons, which would not have been the case if the daughters had been kept. She had no regrets. This was normal in their culture.

Unfortunately, when the sons grew up, they discovered a grievous shortage of potential brides. Polyandry was common (marriages with multiple husbands), but these often generated friction, resulting in an unlucky husband dying violently. No matter what a group did, overpopulation was impossible, because the supply of food was finite. Starvation was very common, and there was no shame in cannibalism.

The carrying capacity of the Arctic ecosystem was small, and it varied from month to month. Each group needed a huge territory. Warfare was common in some places, even massacres. Sometimes the expedition came across piles of human bones. Eskimos fought both Indians and other Eskimos. It seems to me that the root cause of violence is crowding; humans do not tend to be violent when they have adequate space and food.

Modern consumers, who forage in vast climate controlled shopping centers, might perceive the Eskimo way of life as being unpleasant and undesirable. But, according to Rasmussen, "they were not only cheerful, but healthy, knowing nothing of any disease beyond the colds that come as a regular epidemic in spring and autumn."

"A notable feature was their lively good humor and careless, high-spirited manner." The women worked very hard, but "they were always happy and contended, with a ready laugh in return for any jest or kindly word." Eskimos perceived whites to be uptight and coldly impersonal.

Rasmussen's book contains many photographs of the wild people he met along the way. I was spellbound by some of the faces, which were gentle, radiant, and relaxed. Reading, writing, and arithmetic were unknown to them. They had no roads, clocks, or knowledge of the outside world. I imagine that the knowledge they possessed was mostly real, practical, and sane — like a deep, clear stream. My mind feels more like an enormous landfill.

As the expedition got into its homestretch, they passed through gold mining communities, bubbles of prosperity for the lucky ones. Eskimos were drawn into the cash economy, where they sold handicrafts and acquired sewing machines, kerosene lamps, and cameras. Hunters were paid high prices for skins, and they hunted "without any consideration for the future or their old age." Civilization makes people crazy.

Rasmussen and his two Eskimo companions sailed to Seattle, and then travelled to the skyscraper world of New York City. The book concludes with an exclamation by Anarulunguaq, his girlfriend for the journey: "Nature is great; but man is greater still." Would she have a different opinion today, as man's great imbalances are destabilizing the Arctic ecosystems, and the rest of the planet, too?

Before sailing from Alaska, Rasmussen spent a few hours with an angakoq (shaman) named Najagneq. He spoke about the great spirit called Sila. When Sila is happy, life is good. But when men abuse life, and feel no reverence for their daily food, Sila communicates to man "by storm and snow and rain and the fury of the sea; all the forces of nature that men fear."

Where the Wild Things Were

For the first billion years of life on Earth, all of our ancestors were single celled. One day, we aren't sure why, a hungry organism ate a delicious bystander, and became the first predator. Predation inspired evolution to become very creative. Some organisms became mobile by developing cilia or tails. Others shape shifted into multi-celled life forms. Critters developed scales, spikes, shells, fangs, and many other clever defenses. Thus, one group survived by dining on the unlucky, and the bigger group survived by evolving every imaginable trick for cancelling lunch dates with predators.

When predators became too powerful, they would wipe out their food supply, blush with embarrassment, and starve. Prey that managed to survive evolved stronger defensive capabilities. But if they got too good at this, their population would explode, deplete the available nutrients, and the vast mob would perish in an undignified manner.

Thus, evolution is an elegant balancing act. If the prey gets one percent faster, the predator gets one percent faster, not two. This balancing act is the subject of William Stolzenburg's book, *Where the Wild Things Were*. More specifically, the book focuses on how humankind uses its brilliant technological innovations to bypass the limits of our current state of genetic evolution, upset healthy balancing acts, and devastate ecosystems, often unintentionally.

In the early 1970s, zoologist James Estes travelled to the Aleutian Islands of Alaska to do research on sea otters. Sea otters can grow up to four feet long (1.2 m), and they have incredibly soft fur. Stylish women with too much money loved wearing fur coats, and for 150 years, from Alaska to Baja, otter hunting was a serious business, and very profitable. Somewhere between 500,000 and 900,000 otters lost their hides to the fashionable dames of high society.

The island of Amchitka had a healthy population of otters, and this is where Estes began his study, scuba diving in frigid water. Beneath the waves were thriving jungles of kelp, a popular hangout for a number of aquatic herbivores. Kelp can grow up to 200 feet tall (61 m). Urchins enjoy dining on kelp, and sea otters enjoy dining on urchins. What Estes observed was a healthy balance between the kelp, urchins, and otters.

Later, he spent some time on the island of Shemya, where the great extermination had wiped out the otters. Only a few had since recolonized there. The ecosystem here was stunningly different from Amchitka. In the absence of otters, the urchins exploded in numbers, and many were huge in size. The sea floor was wall-to-wall urchins, and there was no kelp at all.

So, when the keystone predators (otters) live in peace, the ecosystem is healthy and balanced. When they are eliminated, the ecosystem becomes a train wreck — a chain reaction known as a *trophic cascade*. Predators are essential.

A similar scenario occurred when Zion National Park was established in Utah. To make the park safe for tourists, the cougars (mountain lions) were exterminated. In their absence, the population of mule deer exploded, and the land was stripped of vegetation. The forests were dying, because young seedlings were devoured by deer. Meanwhile, over the hill in North Creek Canyon, the cougars had been left alone, and the land was remarkably alive and healthy.

The Kaibab Plateau in Arizona became a game preserve in 1906. Deer hunters were kept out, and 6,000 large carnivores were deleted. The deer population skyrocketed from 4,000 to 100,000, and the vegetation was promptly vacuumed up. In the winters of 1924 and 1925, 80,000 deer starved to death. Ecosystems pay an enormous price for the stunning ecological blunders conjured by experts who spent years in bleak classrooms tediously memorizing screw-brained theories.

Wolves and grizzlies had been absent in the Tetons for quite a while. Then, a few began drifting in from Yellowstone. At first, the moose and elk had no fear of them. Wolves calmly strolled into the herd and snatched their young. Before long, they learned that fearing predators was beneficial. Something similar to this innocent fearlessness likely existed in every ecosystem when humans first arrived with their state-of-the-art killing technology.

In the 1950s, Paul Martin connected some archaeological dots. The megafauna of the world, that had survived almost two million years of ice ages, often blinked out whenever armed humans arrived in a new region. This realization gave birth to his Pleistocene Overkill hypothesis, "that man, and man alone, was responsible for the unique wave of Late Pleistocene extinction." Despite many loud objections, it has generally been accepted, but it fails to explain the large numbers of mammoths and rhinos found in Siberia and Alaska that did not die from hunting.

The whites that first explored America were stunned by the abundance of wildlife they observed. But what they experienced was a bruised and battered ecosystem from which many key species were long gone. In 2005, a group of biologists published a paper on rewilding in the journal *Nature*. It recommended the reintroduction of missing species like cheetahs, camels, lions, and elephants. The mainstream crowd howled hysterically. It was groovy to reintroduce pretty butterflies, but the huge backlash boiled down to "no lions in my backyard!"

The elimination of millions of large predators over the millennia certainly contributed to the current population explosion. When climate change forced our ancestors onto the savannah, evolution had not prepared us for living amidst fast, powerful, heavyweight carnivores. We developed a highly unusual dependence on technology in order to survive. "They would eventually wield the power to level mountains, to dam the biggest rivers, to coat entire continents in concrete and crops, to alter the climate as it had once altered them." The chapter on how we morphed into apex predators is fascinating.

Today, we almost never encounter man-eating predators running lose. We no longer have to pay careful attention to reality, ready to react at any moment. The world has become safe for pudgy consumers — a dull and lonely place. This is seen as normal. I disagree.

The Abstract Wild

In 1964, plans were being discussed for the creation of the Canyonlands National Park, near Moab, Utah. Some wanted to include the Maze in the park. The Maze is a stunning network of desert canyons, and it was extremely inaccessible at that time. Few living people had ever seen it.

Jack Turner and his buddy were young rock-climbing adventure hogs. Their plan was to fly into the Maze, land the plane on a long-abandoned bulldozer scrape, take some cool photos, and sell them to *National Geographic*. Both survived the botched landing. While wandering around in the Maze, they found ancient pictographs of life-sized human images. The paintings had a striking presence, and the lads were mesmerized. They had walked into a different dimension, a place alive with a strong aura of spirit power.

Today, the aura has faded. The Maze is mapped and tamed. Visitors can drive in and hike around on happy trails. The pictographs have become photo opportunities for intrepid ecotourists. The sacred wildness of the place has become banal, like a museum exhibit. For the wild painters, who lived several thousand years ago, this place "was their home in a sense we can no longer imagine," said Turner. "Whoever they were, they knew how to express and present something we have lost."

Later, Turner worked as a philosophy professor in Chicago, a soul-killing bad trip. One day, he read a deep ecology essay by Arne Naess, and had a great awakening. He suddenly realized that he was on the wrong path. He escaped from the nightmare, and spent many years travelling around the world climbing mountains. This included at least 16 years as a guide at Grand Teton National Park.

Deep ecology helped him understand the crucial difference between ecocentric thinking (the ecosystem is not ours to trash) and anthropocentric thinking (yes it is). This echoes the huge gap between the wild Maze painters and the pudgy tourists. It's essentially the difference between sustainable and unsustainable cultures.

Wandering around the world taught him another vital lesson. He visited cultures that were something like the Maze painters, cultures with a profound spiritual connection to the past, the future, their community, and their sacred home. All of their needs were provided by the place they inhabited. Consequently, they lived with great care, striving to remain in balance with the land.

Today, Earth is being hammered. Typically, the designated villains include capitalism, greedy corporations, corrupt politicians, the evil enemy-of-the-day, and so on. Turner rejected this. The planet is being pummeled by a culture that is infested with absurd abstract ideas —

more is better, get rich quick, grow or die. This culture has reduced the natural world to an abstraction, a machine that must be controlled, a jumbo cookie jar for the amusement of infantile organisms.

So, Turner's enemies are not the designated villains. His enemies are abstractions, like the hallucinations that perceive a sacred old growth forest to be a calculable quantity of board feet, worth a calculable quantity of dollars. Abstractions are the foundation of the madness, and they are formidable opponents. They can make clear thinking impossible, and inspire remarkable achievements in foolishness.

In his book, *The Abstract Wild*, Turner describes why he has become a "belligerent ecological fundamentalist," and why he stands on the side of the grizzly bears and mountain lions. "Abstraction" is a word meaning mental separation, not a concrete object. Wildness is "the relation of free, self-willed, and self-determinate 'things' with the harmonious order of the cosmos."

There are eight essays in the book. One examines wilderness management, a hotbed of professional control freaks. This work is done under the banner of science, a way of knowing that can understand processes and predict their activities. What a joke! We don't understand friends or lovers. We don't understand ourselves. Ecosystems are vastly more complex and chaotic.

Wildlife biologists have a history of making wildly incorrect predictions, often leading to embarrassing disasters. Their clumsy conjuring is no more "science" than astrology is. Humans should always avoid fooling around with DNA, atoms, or wilderness management. "We are not that wise, nor can we be." Instead of trying to control nature by using a strategy based on hope, wishes, incomplete data, and misunderstanding, Turner recommends that we should get out of the way and leave the job to Big Mama Nature, who has a billion years of experience. (The experts hiss!)

Another essay snaps, snarls, and spits with rage. Civilization has been brutally molesting the planet for 10,000 years, at an ever-increasing rate. Over the centuries, we have responded to these assaults on wildness by forgiving and forgetting. We're now moving into the end game. Despite being blasted by a fire hose of depressing news, we remain pathetically timid helpless victims. We accept a wrecked planet as normal, and refuse to utter a peep of protest.

Turner screams. Enough forgiving and forgetting! It's time for some healthy rage. It's time to raise hell against the senseless destruction. This is spiritual business, so it takes precedence over society's laws. Nature is sacred, and must be defended. Destroying the planet is evil and unacceptable, even if it's perfectly legal and great for the economy.

Turner has lived much of his life out of doors, and he feels a profound reverence and respect for wildness. His book is rare for presenting this perspective, which is getting dimmer with every decade. This perspective can help us move toward healing. "We only value what we know and love, and we no longer know and love the wild," he says. "What we need now is a culture that deeply loves the wild earth." But the inmates of modernity have little intimate experience with wild nature, and almost no comprehension of what has been lost. Wildness is something seen on TV.

We must rejoin the natural world. This is still possible. Turner succeeded. Cool books, nature documentaries, and tourism cannot provide us with all we need to recover our wildness. What's needed is direct experience with a place, over time, complete immersion — observing the bird migrations, animal mating, leafing of trees, climate patterns, and so on. A week in the mountains is never enough.

In the end, Turner presents us with a tantalizing bittersweet enigma. He reveals to us the one and only silver bullet solution that can actually heal us, and guide us back home to the family of life. But this solution is impossible, as long as there are so many people, living so hard. The shamans have much work to do, to redirect our hearts toward healthy paths. It's time for the clans of creative folks to seize their power, work to exorcise our culture's terrible demons, and rekindle forgotten love.

A Sideways Look at Time

In the realm of wild nature, there are countless cycles of change. Geese arrive at winter's end, build nests, raise goslings, and depart in autumn. Apple trees leaf, blossom, fruit, and drop their leaves. The sunlight has daily cycles and annual cycles. The moon and women flow through their monthly rituals. This is circular time, round and round and round. This is wild time.

Once upon a time, the whole world was wilderness, and every creature was free. The planet danced in wild time, and all was well. Wild people caught salmon when the fish came home. They killed reindeer when the herds passed through. They ate blackberries when the fruit was ripe, and gathered nuts as they fell.

Wild people clustered in flourishing nutrient-rich ecosystems that were scattered here and there across the planetary wilderness. All was well... until the accidents. In a few of these clusters, clever smarty-pants, with wonderful intentions, devised strategies for forcing their land to produce more food. Why be content with paradise? Let's fix it.

We are finally starting to realize that some incredibly brilliant ideas should be flushed down the loo immediately (probably all of them). Here we are in the twenty-first century, and the world is the opposite of a vast wilderness. It has been reduced to a bruised and beaten land-scape by an ever-growing swarm of hungry two-legs. Wildness strug-gles to survive in scattered shrinking pockets. Wild tribes are nearly extinct.

As civilization metastasized, clock time gradually pushed wild time into the background. Clock time is linear, not circular — a straight path with a starting line (paradise) and a finish line (apocalypse). It's a furious dance of endless growth, which inevitably jitterbugs into a minefield of bleached skeletons.

The incredibly brilliant notion of endless growth should have been flushed down the loo immediately. Endless growth is insane, fantasti-cally irrational, and always ends in tragedy. But it's a lot of fun at first. Take a deep toke. The endless growth jitterbug is a soaring mania with no off switch. It stops when it dies. Any society that mindfully choos-es to quit jitterbugging becomes a helpless sitting duck for its jitterbug-ging neighbors, who are always hungry for more and more and more.

Jay Griffiths wrote *A Sideways Look at Time*, which discusses the mutation of time that followed in the wake of domestication, and rap-idly accelerated with the emergence of the industrial era. She thinks very highly of wild time, because it is normal, natural, and good. With

195

regard to linear time, she offers this sensible recommendation: "Drown your watch."

The multinational, patriarchal, monotheistic religions run on linear time. Their myths begin in a golden age of innocence and harmony, and go downhill from there, on a dead end road. Griffiths was raised in a Christian home, but she lacked the blind faith gene. The church taught that God's creation was a place of evil. The kinky male clergy denounced lust, joyful sex, and women of power. Their icon was a dying man nailed to a dead tree. Wild time, wild people, and wild places were the realm of the devil.

As civilizations grew, years were assigned ID numbers. In Rome, year #1 was the date of the city's founding. Numbering enabled better record keeping, and provided time markers for historians. Calendars enclosed days and years, and sundials enclosed hours. Later came mechanical clocks, and clanging church bells, factory bells, and school bells. The sweet freedom of childhood was enclosed by rigid schedules, as kids were herded into education factories to have their minds filled.

To keep large restless mobs under control, law and order is essential — police and clocks. Industrial civilization is impossible without synchronizing the mob to march in lockstep to the steady beat of the time machines. All around the world now, the current hour will conclude at the same moment.

Today, the wristwatch people are isolated from nature. They spend their lives in rectangular climate-controlled compartments with artificial lighting. Blackberries, nuts, and salmon are available every day of the year. Clocks and wristwatches were fabulous ideas, if the objective was to elevate stress and anxiety. The Lakota have no word for "late," and the Micmac have no word for "time." Native Americans were astonished by the wacky behavior of the colonists, who robotically followed the demands of ridiculous schedules.

In stable wild societies, older people became respected elders, folks with long memories who provided wise counsel. They could foresee problems, and recommend solutions. But in the lands of the wristwatch people, speed is of the essence, and the rate of change is dizzying. In modern times, much of the knowledge that older people possess is obsolete and useless. So, the elder's role is waning, at the same time that people are living longer. Progress has left them sitting in the ditch.

In a culture obsessed with youth, women with gray hair become invisible. Cosmetic surgery is very expensive, and its results are temporary. Tightly stretched facial skin is spooky looking, like "linoleum with lipstick." Hormone treatments promise the appearance of perpetual springtime. Griffiths laments that many women avoid the elder's path of wisdom and power. The era of patriarchy has not been kind to the ladies.

In the minds of the wristwatch people, the notion of progress is as real as the Grand Canyon. They have no doubt that the world is always getting better and better, because experts are tireless in their pursuit of continuous improvement. We are so lucky to live in an age of endless miracles.

Actually, progress is a smiley-face mask that disguises a parasite. Progress isn't kind to the salt of the Earth. The lands of the U'wa people of Colombia are being destroyed to extract the precious oil needed to fuel the insatiable excesses of the world's elite. Chinese women are dying from the solvents used to make cell phones, and women in Bangladesh are crushed when their garment factory collapses.

The parasite devours anything in its path, and never rests. The single thought on its mind is more now, more now, more now. Only the present matters, a mindset that Griffiths calls "chronocentric." Bleep the future. The grandchildren will simply have to adapt to living with radioactive wastes that remain highly toxic for a million years. It's not our problem.

Of course, it's heresy to voice doubts about progress. Doing so transforms you into a knuckle-dragging mouth-breathing dolt. The sacrifices needed to radically reduce the harm we cause are just too great. It is our God-given right to indulge in every imaginable excess to the best of our ability. It says so in the constitution. Well, it's time for gifted shamans to perform a magic act on our worldview — swap the dunce cap to progress, and the halo to sustainability. It's OK to be respectful to unborn generations of all species. It's normal.

So, that's a little peek into where this fascinating book takes us. Griffiths helps us remember what has been lost. Unlike the predicaments of peak cheap energy, peak food, and climate change, our time problems are nothing but ideas, and ideas can be flushed down the loo. A healthy life does not require seconds, minutes, and hours. We can do just fine with sunrise and sunset, full moon and new moon, solstice and equinox, wildness and freedom.

Hark! The bell has rung. This review is over. It's a cool book.

Encounters With Nature

Paul Shepard was a pioneer in human ecology, a young field that studies the relationship between humans and their habitats. The decades of his career were an exciting time. New research was challenging myths about low impact ("primitive") cultures, and scholars were starting to contemplate environmental ethics. He hoped that growing awareness might end humankind's war on the planet, but as his hair got grayer, his disillusionment grew. Enlightenment takes time.

Encounters With Nature is a collection of Shepard's essays, some of which reveal his thinking near the end of his days. It was compiled, edited, and published by his wife, Florence, after he died. She summed up the book in one wonderful sentence: "At the heart of our identity is a fundamentally wild being, one who finds in the whole of wild nature all that is true and beautiful in this world." The essays spin around two themes that shaped human development: animals and place.

Our early pre-human ancestors lived in the trees of tropical rainforests. Leaping quickly from limb to limb through the canopy required far more brainpower than herbivores needed to manufacture manure on the wide-open savannah. Our time in the trees provided us with sharp minds, grasping hands, stereoscopic vision, and the ability to see in color.

Later, our ancestors moved to the ground, and became larger and stronger. To defend themselves against predators, they became socially organized. By and by, they came to walk erect. They were hunters, but lacked speed, fangs, and claws. Instead, they became long-distance runners. Many herbivores were capable of amazing bursts of speed, but they couldn't outrun hunters who doggedly pursued them for hours. Some think that we lost our body hair to stay cooler while chasing lunch. Our ancestors also evolved arms and shoulders that were well suited for throwing sticks and stones.

Modern culture takes great pride in the Industrial Revolution and the Agricultural Revolution, but the most important revolution was the Hunting Revolution. We moved onto the savannah, and learned how to hunt in packs. Our ancestors were hunters long before *Homo sapiens* first appeared. If you look in the mirror, you will observe the body of a tropical omnivore, fine-tuned for running and throwing — a hunter. Species that eat only plant foods generally walk on four legs, so their mouths can be closer to the buffet. Imagine what you would look like if your ancestors had spent the last two million years staring at glowing screens.

When civilized folks look in the mirror, they don't see a hunter; they see the crown of creation, God's masterpiece. We are taught that every other species is inferior and non-essential. Only humans matter. A chimp looking in the mirror sees a wild chimpanzee. They have not lost their identity. Coyotes have never forgotten how to be coyotes.

Shepard described three phases in the "identity formation" of each individual. In the first phase, we bond to our mother. In the second phase, between learning to speak and puberty, we have about a decade to bond with the living place we inhabit.

Wild children are fascinated by other wild animals, which are far more interesting than rubber ducks and teddy bears. Kids observe the others, learn their names, categorize them, imitate them, and study their anatomy when butchered. They learn the daily and seasonal patterns of the others. They watch the others transform from youngsters to oldsters, and a strong feeling of kinship develops. "It is a family tie and carries responsibility."

Shepard has little to say about the realm of plants, which is equally alive and fascinating. Plants also play a major role in our bonding to nature. By puberty, wild children are well rooted in place, feeling at-one with the flora and fauna of the family of life. They have a profound sense of belonging that most modern tumbleweeds cannot begin to imagine, and will never experience.

Our bodies are those of hunters. Likewise, our minds were formed and perfected by two million years of hunting and foraging.

We do not thrive in McMansions, malls, or cubicle farms. We're like zoo animals with injured souls, enduring a dreary existence so far from home. Condors are at home soaring with great joy above the mountains. When imprisoned by humans, they become sad biological specimens. A writer once concluded that condorness consisted of 10 percent condor and 90 percent place. The same is true for us.

The third phase is initiation, the transition into adulthood. "The youth is ushered into adult status by ceremonies that include separation from family, instruction by elders, tests of endurance and pain, trials of solitude, visions, dreams, and rituals of rebirth."

What happens if the bond to mother is flawed? In her book, *The Continuum Concept*, Jean Liedloff described how wild people raised happy children, and how civilized folks often fail to.

What happens if we do not form a healthy bond to the family of life? We become space aliens, and see the natural world as static scenery, or something to plunder. Jay Griffiths described how wild children bond, and modern kids suffer, in her book, *A Country Called Childhood*.

What happens when adolescents aren't initiated into adulthood? They can remain immature and alienated, whirling in infantile anxieties, often for the rest of their lives. The natural identity-forming process fails, and they assume a synthetic identity appropriate for the industrial culture.

For wild people, life was generous and giving. Food was acquired without regular hard work. The fruit, nuts, roots, and meat they got were gifts, for which they regularly expressed thanks and gratitude. Meat was always shared.

For farmers, food was not a gift, but a wage received for months of backbreaking work. If everything went well, there would be food to harvest at summer's end. Food could be stored and traded. It became private property, and a source of wealth and power. For modern consumers, food is not a gift, it's a product sold at stores. Many do not comprehend the link between pizza and the natural world.

The bottom line here is that we were normal and healthy at birth. Evolution did not design us to be Earth-wrecking savages. What turned us into freaks was our homocentric culture, which elevates us above all other animals, and proudly celebrates our intelligence and technology. This illusion is certain to take a beating as we move into the age of collapses, driven by peak energy, peak food, peak humans, and peak everything else. Our crazy way of life is running out of time.

Our descendants are not going to hold homocentric culture in high regard, because its amazing bursts of cleverness could never out-run its tireless dark shadow. New and healthier modes of thinking are emerging, but have yet to go viral. Mainstream academia seems determined to cling to the cult of perpetual growth as it swirls around the drain, lost in pipedreams of techno-utopia.

Shepard has sketched out suggestions of what needs to be nurtured, and what needs to be dumped. This is precious information for people with imagination. Creative minds understand that other cultures are possible, and that it's time to envision them. There is much to do before the lights go out.

Grizzly Years

Doug Peacock grew up in rural northern Michigan. As a boy, he spent a lot of time alone outdoors, exploring the woods, swamps, and streams. Later, he fell in love with the West, especially the Rockies. He enjoyed fishing and rock climbing. His plan was to become a geologist, so he could wander around in the great outdoors and get paid for it. But one day he realized that his dream career would likely involve working for oil and mining companies, "whose rape of wild country repelled me." Sadly, he abandoned the plan, and volunteered for an exciting job with the U.S. government.

Peacock loved the central highlands of Vietnam. It was a gorgeous region, inhabited by good people. Then, the war spread there. He was employed as a medic in the Green Berets, an elite combat unit. His job was to provide first aid to injured soldiers and villagers, and the fighting kept him very busy. He witnessed far too much senseless death, destruction, and suffering, far too many dead children.

By and by, he came down with a devastating case of war rage, which he has been struggling with for most of his life. Back in American society, it was no longer possible to blend into the crowd, and feel at home. He couldn't talk to his family. He spent a lot of time in the woods, trying to pickle his demons with cheap wine. Finally, he bought a jeep, and headed west, to pursue two powerful medicines: solitude and wildness.

For American soldiers, Vietnam was not as safe and secure as strolling through a mall. There were tigers, vipers, snipers, booby traps, and Vietcong. The odds for survival were boosted by good luck, common sense, being with experienced warriors, remaining as silent and invisible as possible, and maintaining a state of heightened awareness. Survivors slept lightly, easily awakened by snapping twigs and other irregular sounds. Survivors developed an acute sense of smell, because an odd whiff could warn of danger. Survivors frequently stopped, looked, and listened.

Similar skills were useful when moving through grizzly bear country, where Peacock spent many post-war years. Near the beginning of his wilderness quest, he hiked around a corner and discovered that a large brown grizzly was approaching, and it was not at all happy to see him. The bear's head was swinging back and forth, jaws gnashing, ears flattened, hair standing up on his hump — the ritual that precedes charging, mauling, and a bloody hot lunch.

Peacock slowly pulled out his large caliber handgun, had second thoughts, and lowered it. His shooting days were over. He was ready to die. Something happened, the energy changed. "The grizzly slowly turned away from me with grace and dignity and swung into the timber at the end of the meadow." It was a life-changing experience. He became a grizzly tracker. He acquired a movie camera and began filming them. He did winter lecture tours, wrote about bears, and told his story in *Grizzly Years*.

Importantly, the book reminds us of a forgotten reality, living in wild country amidst man-eating predators — the normal everyday reality for our wild ancestors, whose genes we inherited. Outside my window each morning, the blue jays stop by for a pumpkin seed breakfast. Before they glide down from branch to porch, they look in every direction for winged predators and pussy cats. They don't live in a constant state of fear and paranoia, they simply live with prudent caution, look before leaping, and never do stupid things.

In grizzly country, Peacock stayed away from animal trails, and slept in concealed locations. He tried to remain invisible and silent. He tried to approach bears from downwind, so his scent would not alert them. He spent years studying bear behavior, and the quirks of individual animals. He was charged many times, but never mauled. He learned how to behave properly during close encounters. Never run, climb trees, make loud noises, move suddenly, or look weak and fearful. Instead, act dignified, and display peaceful intentions without appearing docile. Calmly talk to the bear, while keeping your head turned to the side.

Peacock's tales are intriguing, because they encourage readers to imagine wilderness as their true home, and to contemplate the normal everyday tactics used by our wild ancestors to avoid being eaten. Grizzly country was one place where humans were not the dominant critter. The bears could kill you and eat you whenever they wished. This ongoing possibility freed Peacock from wasting hour after hour in self-indulgence — thinking, analyzing, daydreaming. It demanded that he always be fully present in the here and now.

Americans expect wilderness to be as safe as a mall. We don't want to be killed and eaten when visiting a national park, yet parks foolishly build trails and campgrounds in high-risk locations. If a hiker is mauled, bears are killed. Now, if a cat kills a blue jay, we don't kill the cat. Why are government bureaucrats so uptight about what God-fearing American bears choose to have for dinner in the privacy of their own homes? Why do delicious primates from Chicago expect to be safe in grizzly country?

I've never seen a "Save the Grizzlies" bumper sticker. To maintain a pleasant Disneyland experience, and avoid lawsuits, the Park Service kills aggressive bears, and bears that beg for snacks. Backcountry outfitters kill them. Ranchers kill them. Violators get light punishment from judges in redneck country. Bear numbers are in decline, and this infuriates Peacock.

In Vietnam, he had a ringside seat at a contest between a full-blown industrial civilization and a society that practiced muscle-powered subsistence farming. He witnessed the indiscriminant massacre of countless innocent villagers and children. Back in the U.S., he saw that the same monster was obliterating western ecosystems, from mines in the Rockies, to developers in Tucson. He had escaped from the Vietnam War, but there was no escape from the American war on

America, where "greedy scumsuckers" were raping and desecrating "the last refuge of sanity on the planet."

Peacock wasn't the only Vietnam vet with war rage who found sanctuary in the mountains. Other vets were equally pissed at the scumsuckers. They had lost many friends while defending the freedom and democracy of God's most cherished nation. And so, in those mountains, angry American vets defended the sacred American ecosystem against the atrocities of the "syphilization" they had been trained to serve. When loggers built bridges that had not been authorized by the angry vets, the bridges were mysteriously demolished. So were helicopters used for oil exploration.

Peacock did not become a corporate geologist, and spend the rest of his life living with the herd. It was a great gift to live so many years outside the walls. He was able to observe the insane monster that lurks behind the cartoonish façade of the American Dream, and he was able to explain the horrors that so many folks inside the walls were unable to see, feel, or imagine. In wild country, Peacock was careful to never be seen, or reveal his plans. "If I got into serious trouble, I didn't want to be rescued. My considerable carcass could feed the bears."

Braiding Sweetgrass

Science is a painfully tight pair of shoes. It perceives the family of life to be little more than a complex biochemical machine. It has created powerful tools for ravaging the planet's ecosystems, creating a hard path for our descendants. It gives us knowing, but not caring. It's not about wisdom. It's about pursuing the wants and needs of humans, with little or no concern for the more-than-human world.

Robin Kimmerer is a biology professor. After being trained in the rigid beliefs of science, she heard a Navajo woman talk about the realm of plants from the perspective of indigenous knowledge. For that woman, plants were not subjects, but teachers. In a flash, Kimmerer realized the shallowness of her scientific training. It only provides a pinhole view of reality. Science is not enough.

Her grandfather was Potawatomi. When he was a boy, the government sent him away to the Indian Industrial School in Carlisle, Pennsylvania, where he was trained to become an English-speaking wageworker. He forgot his language and culture, and drifted away from his people. He never felt at home in either world.

Kimmerer has worked hard to reconnect with her Native American roots, because traditional indigenous cultures are blessed with a far more holistic relationship with the family of life. All people on Earth have tribal ancestors who once lived close to the land, but so much has been lost with the passage of centuries. Her book, *Braiding Sweetgrass*, is a collection of stories that focus on living with respect and reverence for the land.

She once asked a city lad where his sense of place felt strongest. He immediately responded, "My car." Her book is especially important for the impoverished millions, who have grown up indoors, in a ghoulish netherworld of glowing screens. She has a strong and respectful relationship with the land, and she describes it beautifully. It's a perspective that is almost absent in our culture. We must remember.

While explaining the culture of sharing, respect, and gratitude, she does not conceal her scientist badge. So, readers are less tempted to automatically dismiss her stories as daffy rainbows of New Age woo-woo. Science is not worthless. In the centuries of restoration that lie ahead, it can offer some useful ideas, if we keep it on a short leash. Nature will play a primary role in healing the land as much as possible — it knows what to do. The far bigger challenge is dealing with the monsters that inhabit the goop between our ears.

In the native world, when a patch of ripe strawberries is discovered, the plants are warmly greeted. The people ask permission to take some berries. If the response is yes, they take only what they need, never more than half of the fruit. The strawberry people are thanked for their gift, and the pickers leave an offering of tobacco.

Gifts and responsibilities are two sides of the same coin. The berry pickers now have an obligation to promote the wellbeing of the strawberry people, by depositing their seeds in good locations (not a toilet). This is a relationship of reciprocity. The berry eaters need the strawberry people, and the strawberry people need the berry eaters.

On the other hand, the relationship between mainstream people and nonrenewable resources is not reciprocal. The oil, coal, and iron people do not need the miners, nor is their wellbeing improved by the mining. The planet's atmosphere does not appreciate our toxic offerings of carbon emissions. The ecosystem does not benefit from being treated like an open pit mine.

Cultures that enjoy a direct and intimate relationship with their ecosystem have far more respect for it than those that forage at malls and supermarkets. Consumer culture receives enormous gifts from the land, but gives almost none in return. Kimmerer's students clearly understand that the relationship between consumers and nature is abusive. It's difficult for them to imagine what a healthy relationship would look like.

Kimmerer lives in the Onondaga Nation. At the school, the Haudenosaunee flag blows in the breeze, not the stars and stripes. There is no pledge of allegiance to a political system that claims to provide "liberty and justice for all." Instead, each day begins with the Thanksgiving Address, in which the students express gratitude for all of creation. It helps them remember that, "everything needed to sustain life is already here." We are wealthy.

I had one issue with the book. Natives from corn-growing cultures see corn as sacred. Corn was a recent arrival to the region of the eastern U.S. Its expansion spurred population growth and conflict. We know that hunter-gatherers could succeed in achieving genuine sustainability when they lived with the wisdom of voluntary self-restraint. But environmental history has not documented a culture achieving sustainability via intensive agriculture.

Potawatomi legends describe a dangerous spirit called the Windigo. It wanders across the land in the lean months of winter. It is always hungry, and never stops hunting. It's a selfish spirit that is obsessed with its own survival, by any means necessary. The Windigo is notorious for having an insatiable appetite. The moral of the story is to share, to take care of one another. Don't be a greedy butthead.

Much to the horror of the natives, the colonists imported a diabolical spirit of incredible overindulgence — Super Windigo. In white society, maniacal obsession with insatiable consumption was seen as an admirable mark of *success!* Kimmerer winces. "We spend our beautiful, utterly singular lives on making more money, to buy more things that feed but never satisfy. It is the Windigo way that tricks us into believing that belongings will fill our hunger, when it is belonging that we crave."

After a lifetime of working and consuming, we don't return our bodies to nature. The dead are placed in heavy caskets and buried deep in the ground, where nature will struggle for centuries to retrieve the nutrients. I've always hoped that my corpse would be eaten by mountain lions in a wild location, an offering to the ecosystem upon which I have lived far too hard.

From other books, I have learned about cultures that did something like this. Carl Jung noted that the Maasai tribe did not bury their dead. Corpses were left outdoors for the hyenas to eat. John Gunther wrote that the Bakutu people of the Congo recycled corpses by laying them on a termite hill. In sky burial, corpses are fed to the vultures. This is done in Tibet, and in Zoroastrian communities in India. Evan Pritchard noted that the Western Algonquin people also practiced it.

Over the years, Kimmerer has heard the Thanksgiving Address recited countless times. It is so inspiring to listen to people express gratitude for all of creation. She longs for the day "when we can hear the land give thanks for the people in return." So do I.

Lone Survivors

A million years ago, our *Homo erectus* ancestors consisted of maybe 20,000 breeding individuals, according to wizards who speculate on the hidden secrets of DNA. This is similar to the current population of chimpanzees or gorillas. The ancestors lived in scattered pockets of Africa, at a time when Earth was a paradise of abundant life. From these ancient roots, a number of hominid species evolved, but only *Homo sapiens* still survives, at seven-point-something billion and growing. The chimps and gorillas continue to live in a manner similar to their ancestors of a million years ago. What happened to us?

Chris Stringer is one of the venerable grandfathers in the study of human evolution. He's read the papers, attended the conferences, examined the skulls, and had a ringside seat at the noisy academic catfights. This field of knowledge is far from finished. New specimens continue to be found, and new technology provides deeper insights. Stringer's book, *Lone Survivors*, discusses some primary issues, and the scholarly disputes surrounding them, as they stood in 2012. He does a good job of providing an overview to a huge and complex subject, but readers with little background are advised to wear life preservers.

I learned a lot about Neanderthals. They survived 400,000 years on a climate change roller coaster. They hung out with hippos in warm forests near Rome, and they chased wooly mammoths on frigid treeless tundra. They had short, stocky bodies that were good for preserving heat, but which required more calories. Males and females were about the same size, suggesting little division of labor, everyone joined in the hunt.

The Neanderthal diet majored in the flesh of large game. Readers who have hunted hippos with wooden thrusting spears know that this is very dangerous. One site in Croatia contained the remains of 75 Neanderthals, and none were older than 35. In their clans, there were probably many orphans and few grandparents. The scarcity of elders, and the small size of their groups, sharply restricted the flow of cultural information from one generation to the next, and from clan to clan.

Some say that Neanderthals lacked shoes and close-fitting clothing. When Darwin visited chilly Tierra del Fuego, at the bottom of South America, he was shocked to see natives wearing little or no clothing and sleeping naked in the open. Stringer noted that modern Europeans seem to be poorly adapted to the cold, physiologically.

Cro-Magnons were the *Homo sapiens* that moved into Europe maybe 45,000 years ago. European Neanderthals disappeared around 30,000 years ago. Neanderthals went extinct in the Middle East, Siberia, Gibraltar, and Britain at different times, probably for different reasons. This was an era of frequent climate zigzags. When temperatures plummeted, habitable territories shrank, and fewer folks could be fed.

Cro-Magnons apparently had footwear and warm, fitted clothing. They had better tools for hunting, so their diet was more diverse and dependable. They were able to extract more nutrients from an ecosystem, so they could survive in places where Neanderthals could not. They lived in larger groups, and more of them survived to middle age or old age, so more cultural information could be passed to the young.

Large populations are better at preserving cultural knowledge, acquiring new information from outsiders, and generating innovations. More busy minds interact, exchange ideas, compete, and imagine cool ways for living even farther out of balance. Witness the city of Los

Angeles, where 14 million animals with hunter-gatherer DNA are temporarily able to endure a stressful existence because of a highly complex system of innovative technology. Note that this innovation is rarely guided by foresight or wisdom. Time is running out on Los Angeles.

On the other hand, less innovation occurs in smaller simpler groups, and that's often a blessing. Innovators can be dangerous loose cannons, introducing risky new ideas that result in horrid unintended consequences — like cell phones, automobiles, or agriculture. Nothing is more precious than a stable, sustainable, time-proven way of living, where the secret to success is simply imitating your ancestors, conforming to the norm, and enjoying life, like the chimps and gorillas do.

When the planet heated up 14,000 years ago, rising sea levels submerged the land link between Australia and Tasmania, terminating the exchange of people, ideas, and gadgets. Tasmania's traditional way of life was also squeezed as the warmer climate spurred the expansion of heavy forest. The natives experienced a cultural meltdown. "Tasmanians appear to have led an increasingly simplified life, forgoing apparently valuable skills and technologies, such as bone and hafted tools, nets and spears used to catch fish and small game, spear throwers and boomerangs, and anything but the simplest of skin clothing."

Will climate change have a similar effect on industrial civilization in the coming decades? Will it slash food production, sharply reduce population, eliminate travel between regions, pull the plug on modern technology, and erase lots of obsolete and unsustainable cultural information? Could collapse have a silver lining?

Climate change can derail any culture, and drive species to extinction. It can also produce beneficial conditions, like the unusually favorable climate of the last 10,000 years. Natural selection rewards species that can adapt to change, and it deletes those that fail. Another important variable is often overlooked: genetic drift — mutations that happen all the time when slight boo-boos occur during cell division. These tiny defects can provide a barrel of surprises.

We are repeatedly taught that humans are nature's flawless masterpiece, the glorious conclusion of three billion years of evolution. But, if Big Mama Nature had experienced slightly different moods over the eons, we might be Neanderthals or Denisovans today (or maybe slime mold). The fact that *Homo sapiens* is the lone survivor among the hominid species may be the result of nothing more than a temporary streak of good luck.

Homo heidelbergensis was an ancestor that lived 500,000 years ago. They had brains ranging in size from 1100 to 1400 cc (modern brains average 1350 cc). The average Neanderthal brain was 1600 cc — much larger than ours. Stringer noted that our brains today are ten percent smaller than our *Homo sapiens* ancestors of 20,000 years ago. What might that suggest?

Without words, chimps and gorillas can express contentment, affection, irritation, excitement. But without complex language, they are more trapped within themselves. Language took us "into new and shared worlds that were unknown to our ancestors." We can talk about the here and now, the past, the future, abstract concepts, feelings, imaginary worlds, and so on.

Later, innovative geniuses invented the use of symbols. Now we can convert words into patterns of squiggly lines, for example: "computer." Writing enables us to communicate with folks in faraway places. I can read words written by Julius Caesar, and so might the generations yet-to-be-born. Industrial civilization cannot exist without symbols — numbers, graphs, pictures, status symbols. Progress abounds with powerful and dangerous juju.

Stringer is a mild mannered humanist. And so, he portrays the human journey as one of admirable advancement (the chimps fall down laughing). On the last page, he confesses a profound doubt. "Sometimes the difference between failure and success in evolution is a narrow one, and we are certainly on a knife edge now as we confront an overpopulated planet and the prospect of global climate change on a scale that humans have never faced before. Let's hope our species is up to the challenge."

The Humans Who Went Extinct

Clive Finlayson is an evolutionary ecologist and a champion skeptic. He routinely questions theories based on no evidence, even if they are totally trendy, like the widely held belief in the inferiority of Neanderthals. What science now knows about human evolution is something like finding 10 pieces of a 100,000-piece puzzle.

Experts have a strong urge to fill in the blanks with their opinionated imaginations, an approach that is far from trusty. The peculiar mindset of mainstream science worships *Homo sapiens*, whilst the holy species rips the planet to shreds right before their eyes. For 300,000 years, Neanderthals had the good manners to remain in balance with life, as did most of our ancestors. Good manners are important.

The whims of Ice Age climate patterns are the primary reason why, today, you and I are not gorgeous, sexy, brilliant Neanderthals, admiring a passing group of wooly rhinos, in a healthy world where bison far outnumber people. Finlayson's book, *The Humans Who Went Extinct*, convinced me to reconsider my perception of the human journey. Not many books do that anymore.

The era we live in, the 10,000 years of civilization, human domination, and ecocide, is a sudden spasm in the long human journey. Our era is a freak, because the climate has remained relatively warm and stable for an amazingly long time. But the pattern of the last 70,000 years has been a roller coaster of surprising climate shifts, from milder and wetter, to colder and drier.

When the glaciers grew, sea levels plunged, forests shrank, countless animals died, and some went extinct. The deer and hippos fled or died, and were replaced by wooly mammoths, wooly rhinos, musk ox, and reindeer. Sea levels 30,000 years ago were 120 meters (400 feet) lower than today. You could walk from England to Holland.

The Younger Dryas cold snap lasted a thousand years, and ended 11,600 years ago. Then, warm weather melted the glaciers, life migrated northward, forests returned, and the land was filled with abundant megafauna. This was the last waltz for some cold-tolerant megafauna. The breezes were filled with the yummy aroma of sizzling mammoth meat.

In the Middle East, the Natufian culture was developing a sedentary way of life that majored in harvesting the abundant wild cereal seeds. Within a thousand years, folks were experimenting with the dangerous juju of cultivation. Tragically, they could never begin to imagine the enormous unintended consequences of their cleverness.

Many have pointed to agriculture as the father of our disaster. Lately, I've been more inclined to point to tool addiction. Hominids were able to move out of the forests and survive. The savannah offered immense amounts of meat, but acquiring it with bare hands was not easy.

Once you get started with innovation, is it possible to stop? Yes. The macaques of south Asia break open shellfish with stone axes — they have been tool addicts for ages, but their excellent manners and beautiful small brains protected them from being flushed down the toilet by the Technology Fairy.

The ancestors of the chimps evolved large canine teeth for dining on meat, whilst early hominids developed meat-processing tools instead. Baboons hunt small animals without weapons. Tool-free small-brained monkeys of the American tropics eat a wide variety of jungle critters.

Could large-brained humans ever comprehend the healthy consequences of living tool-free, like the monkeys? There is something wonderfully appealing about the notion of living in harmony for millions of years without psych meds, cell phones, and nuclear waste.

And now, the plot thickens. The ice ages did not hammer Africa, Australia, or India. These southern folks continued living in the traditional human manner, as low density, low impact hunter-gatherers. Northerners, on the other hand, stumbled onto a new and dangerous path.

Almost everyone has seen an image of the Venus of Willendorf, a female figurine. She was carved by a member of the Gravettian culture of early humans, which thrived across the chilly treeless plains of Europe, from 30,000 to 22,000 years ago. They were clever folks who loved reindeer stew. They lived in huts with frames made of mammoth bones, covered with hides. They made textiles, baskets, kilns, jewelry, and figurines. They painted the caves at Chauvet and Les Garennes.

Finlayson laments that we modern civilized folks suffer to this very day from the curse of the Gravettians, "who lost their own way and all sense of their Pleistocene heritage." It was these far-too-clever white folks who created the most diabolical invention of all time — (gasp!) the storage pit.

Southern folks enjoyed a warm climate, and a year-round food supply. Most foods could not be stored, because they would soon spoil. But the crazy Gravettians lived in a frigid climate, where all you could see in any direction was endless empty steppe-tundra. Food appeared occasionally, like when migrating herds of reindeer passed through. When they did, the Gravettians hunted like crazy, and stored surplus meat in the pits they had dug in the permafrost.

Finlayson referred to these pits as dangerous toys. "They had found ways of producing surplus, something almost impossible in warm climates, and with it emerged an unstoppable drive to increase rapidly in numbers." If some surplus was good, then more was better, and you could never have too much. Abundant food led to growing numbers. He emphasizes that our downfall actually began 30,000 years ago, and agriculture was merely its hideous grandchild.

Later, the weather warmed, and the megafauna were largely gone. Descendants of the Gravettians tried hunting small game for a while. They learned how to enslave herbivores, which led to domestication. Instead of storing meat in frosty storage pits, they stored living critters in grassy prisons. Others began growing plants for food, and storing the harvest in granaries. By and by, ecosystems fell under human control. Agriculture opened the floodgates to explosive population growth.

Multitudes of living beings were blown off the stage by climate shifts. Finlayson insists that luck may be the most important factor in the evolutionary process. Oddly, if luck had made Neanderthals the winners, and the world of today was an incredible paradise, we'd still be long overdue for a turbulent climate shift — a new ice age.

Reading this book, I was impressed by the incredible resilience of life. Over and over again, forest ecosystems were wiped out and replaced with treeless ecosystems that later changed back to forest ecosystems. Countless species disappeared in this exciting tilt-a-whirl ride of climate shifts, and countless species adapted and evolved. Our ancestors nearly died out 73,500 years ago, following the Mount Toba eruption. Only a few thousand survived. Today we're at seven-point-something billion.

This is a small book, but it is jammed with information. We really can't know who we are, and where we came from, if we don't understand the turbulent sagas of the ice ages. The end of our entire way of life is just a climate shift away. In the past, it was a zigzag between cold and warm. Future zigzags seem likely to be between warm and roasting.

Cro-Magnon

Once upon a time, long, long ago, musicians Stephen Stills and Judy Collins enjoyed a romance. Then, Judy sailed away and broke his heart. Stephen wrote a sweet song. One line made my head spin: "Don't let the past remind us of what we are not now." Why not? Remembering the past sounds like an excellent idea. What we are not now is wild and free human beings.

I just finished Brian Fagan's book, *Cro-Magnon*, which describes my European ancestors. There have been three studies of the mitochondrial DNA of today's Europeans, and their genes are primarily indigenous. The invading farmers from the Fertile Crescent did not exterminate the natives and replace them. The DNA of modern Europeans contains between 15 and 28 percent of the genes of the eastern immigrants.

It staggers the imagination to contemplate the astonishing wildness, beauty, and vitality of Ice Age Europe. It's heartbreaking — and illuminating — when these grand memories remind us of what we are not now. After reading the book, I feel a much stronger connection to the ancient cave paintings. Those artists were my ancestors, and their images belong in the family album. My people once lived in lands inhabited by wooly mammoths, aurochs, bison, and vast herds of reindeer. They lived beside streams that thundered during salmon runs. This gave me a sense of homecoming, a powerful remembering.

Fagan does a nice job of describing the world of the Ice Age, and the wild swings of the climate — growing glaciers and melting glaciers. When the climate warmed, the hunters and their game moved north, and when frigid times returned, they moved south. The hunters followed the meat, and the meat followed the grass.

"There were at least fifteen to twenty short-term events when temperatures were up to 44.5 degrees Fahrenheit (7°C) warmer than during the intervening colder intervals." The climate could swing from pleasant to freezing over the course of a lifetime. Siberia was once a tropical forest, the Sahara once had lakes and grasslands, and there was a time when you could walk from France to England.

The sad news is that the hunting tribes of Europe were eventually reduced to the drudgery of farming. This transition may have been similar to the spread of corn from Mexico to the tribes of the north — a tempting innovation that had enormous unintended consequences. Fagan helped me to better understand the transition to agriculture. It came in the wake of new hunting technology that allowed folks to take more and more game, which diminished the abundance, and created a bottleneck.

All hominids have African ancestors. Some of them migrated to Asia, where Neanderthals first walked onto the stage. Some Neanderthals moved to Europe maybe 300,000 years ago, where they hung out in cool temperate forests. Their primary weapon was a heavy thrusting spear with a sharp fire-hardened tip. These spears were capable of killing large slow-moving animals.

Fagan believes that the Neanderthals were luckless dullards, because they displayed almost no innovative cleverness over vast spans of time. They were simple and stable, and their dance on this planet may have been far longer than ours will turn out to be — yet they didn't destroy paradise. What dreary boors! Is it possible that their spears were perfectly adequate for a stable way of life?

"Cro-Magnon" refers only to *Homo sapiens* that inhabited Europe, but our species originated in Africa, maybe 170,000 years ago. Some of them moved to Europe around 45,000 years ago, and within 5,000 years, they lightly inhabited much of the continent. Cro-Magnons left us the gorgeous painted caves, magic peepholes into fairyland. Neanderthals went extinct about 30,000 years ago, for uncertain reasons.

The trademark weapon of Cro-Magnons was the lightweight throwing spear, tipped with stone or antler. It was excellent for hunting on open land, and it could kill from a distance. It made it easier to kill a wider variety of prey, like deer and reindeer. Thus, there was more meat on the table, more bambinos in the nursery, and more spear-chuckers running around the bloody countryside. Even during warm eras, European summers were short, and plant foods were limited, so meat was a core source of nourishment. *Homo sapiens* have been hunters since day one in Africa.

Later, the bow and arrow arrived. Bows may have been used 18,000 years ago, based on circumstantial evidence, but the oldest bow found so far was from 10,800 B.C. The bow was an awesomely powerful weapon. It could be fired from any angle, and quickly reloaded. It could kill critters large and small from a long distance. It was great for forest hunting. Nets, traps, and barbed fish spears also came into use. Rabbits, birds, and rodents now appeared on the menu — more meat, bambinos, and hunters — and less and less wildlife. Our consumption of plant foods and shellfish increased.

Around 12,900 years ago, the Younger Dryas period brought frigid weather back again, for a thousand years. It brought severe droughts to the Near East, and the humans adapted by harvesting and planting grass seeds. And the rest, as they say, is history. The combination of excess cleverness, deficient family planning, and climate change put us on a path to global catastrophe. The Near East and portions of Turkey quickly became dependent on agriculture. By 8,000 years ago, when warmer and wetter weather returned, farming spread into southeastern Europe.

What we know about Ice Age Europe is quite fragmentary. Time, glaciers, rising sea levels, and civilization have taken a big toll on the meager evidence. The timeline is full of holes, the dates are controversial, the theories are controversial, and research continues to discover new surprises.

Fagan inserted some opinions unsupported by hard evidence. For example, Neanderthals probably didn't have complex language because they persisted in living in a simple manner. Their primitive brains may have lacked the advanced neural circuits necessary for feverish innovation and pathological ecocide.

Fagan is the captain of the *Homo sapiens* cheerleading squad. He gushes with praise for our unbelievably clever species. "Effective technology, an acute self-awareness, and an intimate relationship with the environment made the Cro-Magnon personality practically invincible." In frigid regions of Europe, they "adapted effortlessly to the ever-colder conditions."

I'm glad that I read this book, because I learned a lot from it, and I will not forget it. The entire era of civilization has existed during an unusually long period of warm and stable weather. Our food production system is fine-tuned for this climate, and it's going to have tremendous problems as the planet gets hotter. Fagan helps us remember the scary patterns of climate history, and how it mercilessly thrashed the unlucky ones, over and over, big brains and all.

Given the fact that we're currently beating the stuffing out Big Mama Nature, the gushing praise for human intelligence and innovation emits a cloud of stinky funk. Where is the line between brilliant innovation and idiotic self-destruction? Are they the same? Is it possible that simple and stable does not mean stupid? These questions should not be swept under the rug. We really, really need to remember what we are not now. We need to discover the long lost treasure.

The Food Crisis in Prehistory

For several million years — almost the entire hominid journey — our ancestors survived by hunting and gathering. Until 10,000 years ago, everything on our menu was wild food. By 2,000 years ago, most of our food came from farms, a rapid and radical change. In his book *The Food Crisis in Prehistory*, archaeologist and anthropologist Mark Nathan Cohen explored two questions. Why did we switch to agriculture? Why did this shift occur, around the world, almost simultaneously?

His answer to both questions was population pressure. Our preferred foods decreased as our numbers increased. In the good old days, the preferred food for hunter-gatherers everywhere was large game. It took far less time to kill a two-ton wooly mammoth than it took to kill two tons of rabbits, rats, or snails. As long as large game was available, we were delighted to put the forks to them.

When large game became scarce, adventurous souls migrated into uninhabited regions, in search of nourishing four-legged banquets. Because we were so clever with tool making, we learned how to survive in almost any type of ecosystem, wet or dry, roasting or frozen. Eventually, we ran out of uninhabited regions, and large game became scarce everywhere. Before long, less-preferred foods began to look like a delicious alternative to starvation.

When large game was our primary preferred food, the planet's carrying capacity was maybe 15 million people, Cohen estimated. He believed that the transition to agriculture had three phases: (1) large game, (2) small game, aquatic resources, more plant foods, and (3) domesticated foods. The archaeological record in most regions generally supports this.

Climate change also played a role. As the ice ages passed, the weather warmed up, and tundra ecosystems were replaced by forests. Large tundra critters became hungry homeless ruffians, and many of them staggered toward the exit. Forest critters like aurochs, deer, and boars were not animals that lived in vast herds. Hunting them required more effort. By and by, we zipped past Peak Large Game.

Cohen found plenty of evidence that the trend throughout the long human journey had been one of population growth, slow but fairly steady. Some societies did a good job of voluntarily limiting their numbers, and others did not. Some surely lived in balance for multiple generations. Joseph Birdsell estimated that during the Pleistocene, 15 to 50 percent of all live births were eliminated via infanticide. Deliberate stability was better than growth-driven starvation, but stability was a slippery ideal. In an ever-changing world, stability can only be temporary.

The notion of carrying capacity sets a limit on how many deer an ecosystem can support long term. For humans, carrying capacity limits were more flexible, because we could digest a wide variety of plant and animal parts. When rhinoceros steaks were no longer available, we began eating more plant foods, smaller game, marine mammals, salmon, shellfish, birds, seeds, nuts, snails, reptiles, insects, and so on. It was more work, but it kept us fed, and our numbers slowly kept growing.

This transition from a Class A diet to a Class B diet occurred in all societies, in various forms, and it increased the carrying capacity for humans. You can guess what happened next. We eventually thumped against the ceiling once again, despite our new high-tech nets, bows and arrows, traps, weirs, fishhooks, harpoons, and so on. What now? Our options included die-off, bloody conflict, effective family planning, and/or a Class C diet.

We shifted toward a lower quality diet. Agriculture was not a brilliant invention. A million years ago, everyone knew what happened when seeds were planted. Everyone knew that tending plants was laborious. In a world of abundant animal food, most plant foods were held in low regard. "People worldwide eat meat and various fruits when they can, and eat cereals and tubers only when they must," said Cohen. A cereal-based diet had many nutritional drawbacks, and nothing was more excruciatingly dull than a diet that majors in hot porridge.

We routinely fail to appreciate the elegant time-proven culture of wild foragers. They ate a wide variety of nutritious wild plants that evolution had fine-tuned to survive in the local ecosystem. Because they weren't dependent on just two or three domesticated plant foods, Bushmen could easily survive a three-year drought that hammered nearby ranchers. Foragers were healthier people, because wild foods were more nutritious, and the nomadic lifestyle discouraged disease.

Farming was backbreaking work. It required tilling, planting, weeding, and watering — months of effort invested before the payoff, if any. The threats of drought, deluge, frost, insects, disease, fire, hail, and winds could zap a thriving crop at any time. When the grain was ripe, there was a window of opportunity for harvesting it, which sometimes only lasted a few days. If you missed it, you were doomed. The stalks had to be cut and then threshed. If the grains were not loose enough, some roasting was needed.

Storage pits or granaries had to be built, and constantly defended against assorted moochers and thugs. Before storing it, the grain had to be parched to prevent germination, and to discourage molds and fungi. Prior to cooking, grain had to be pulverized by pounding or grinding. In the New World, living on corn (maize) required even more work.

Population pressure encouraged the spread of agriculture to every suitable habitat. Small clans of hunter-gatherers were helpless to oppose the growing mobs of bread heads. In recent times, petroleum-based inputs have become core components of modern industrial agriculture. Today we've munched our way deeply into the realm of Class D processed foods, loaded with highly refined carbs, oceans of cheap empty calories.

We've succeeded in temporarily stretching our carrying capacity to seven billion, but little stretch remains before the inevitable snapback. Even ghastly Class D foods will slam into firm limits — cheap energy, synthetic fertilizer, cropland destruction, water shortages, salinization, desertification. Industrial agriculture has an expiration date. Somewhere down the road, climate change is likely to seriously affect most or all forms of farming. The unusually stable climate of the last 10,000 years is a freak.

Observing the human journey from Cohen's mountaintop, we can see above the fog of myths, and the big picture comes into better focus. Even the hunter-gatherer way of life, as it occurred, was not sustainable over the long run. Voluntary self-restraint was not the universal norm, and innovations presented new threats to stability. If we had remained in balance, agriculture and civilization would have never happened.

On a misty morning, a group of chimps sits at the edge of the forest, gazing at us. They are our closest relatives, and for millions of years they have not blundered into tool addiction, domestication, or population explosions. Predators are always free to invite the less alert to lunch. Wild chimps are still healthy, happy, and sustainable. They wonder how we became so lost and confused. What happened? Get a grip! We miss you! Come home!

Europe Between the Oceans

I've long been interested in learning more about my wild ancestors, the indigenous hunter-gatherers of Europe, to better understand who I am. Descriptions of them recorded by the ancient Greeks and Romans were too meager to satisfy my curiosity. Recently, I came across Barry Cunliffe's book, *Europe Between the Oceans: 9000 BC – AD 1000*. Cunliffe is an archaeologist, and ongoing research is discovering many new pieces for the puzzle. His book serves readers a staggering amount of information.

Cave paintings have preserved beautiful memories of the wild paradise of Ice Age Europe, and the lucky people who enjoyed the continent in the days of its undiminished vitality. The party began breaking up around 9600 B.C., when a warmer climate returned. Glaciers melted and forests expanded northward into tundra country. Tundra critters like the reindeer and elk were forced to migrate further north. Others, like the mammoth and wooly rhino, walked off the stage.

The recovering forests provided habitat for smaller animals, like deer, elk, boars, and aurochs. Here's a surprising notion: "This forest fauna amounted to only about 20-30 percent of the total biomass of herbivores that had roamed the tundra before them." In a land of trees, there was far less meat nibbling on the foliage. Folks were forced to live in smaller and fewer groups. Their population "drastically declined." They preferred locations close to coastlines, lakes, rivers, and wetlands, where a year round supply of food could be gathered with little effort.

Meanwhile, over the border in Asia, dark juju was swirling in the Fertile Crescent. Between 12000 and 9600 B.C., the number of permanent settlements was growing, based on hunting and foraging the (temporarily) abundant wild foods. This was followed by the ominous Aceramic Neolithic period (9600 to 6900 B.C.). By its end, people were growing fully domesticated cereals, and dining on domesticated sheep, goats, pigs, and cattle. Cunliffe blames population pressure for this shift to domestication.

The laborious new way of life worked for a while in Asia, but turned into a nightmare when supersized — large-scale irrigation-based agriculture, reckless forest mining, explosive population growth, bloody warfare, and full-blown civilizations run by power-crazy tyrants awash in testosterone. Few civilizations, if any, recognized their huge mistake, and deliberately returned to low impact living. Most simply hoped for the best, followed their traditions, and collapsed. It was easier.

Geography has played a starring role in European history. The continent is a lumpy peninsula protruding from the posterior of Asia. It is largely surrounded by navigable seas, and interlaced with navigable rivers. Even in the days before roads, it was fairly easy to journey back and forth across it. The continent had immense forests, fertile soils, a nurturing climate, plenty of water, thriving wildlife and marine life, and large deposits of industrial minerals and precious minerals.

The Fertile Crescent, on the other hand, was an arid region that was poorly suited for supporting large complex societies. But the region to the west, Europe, was a vast yet-to-be-raped paradise. Consequently, the wild hunter-gatherers of Europe were among the unluckiest people in the world, similar to the Native Americans in 1492. Their valuable assets were irresistible to the growing mobs of hungry dirty farmers.

Cunliffe rejected the myth of the Neolithic Revolution, which said that the Asian farmers swept across Europe in a blitzkrieg, nearly exterminating the indigenous folk, as the white folks did in America. New evidence suggests that diffusion played a significant role in the spread of agriculture, similar to the spread of maize in the eastern U.S. Whenever the folks down the river start growing lots of calories, and feeding swarms of bambinos, your options are: exterminate them, take up the dirty habit, flee, or be overrun. Since farmers outbreed hunters, agriculture tends to spread like a steamroller.

Recent studies of mitochondrial DNA conclude that about 80 percent of European females are genetically indigenous, not related to Asian immigrants. In France, Germany, and northeast Spain, only 15 to 30 percent of males have Asian genes.

In a nutshell, Europe was essentially a continent of hunter-gatherers in 7000 B.C., and by 4000 B.C. it was reduced to a gulag of farmers and herders. "The rapidity of the spread of the Neolithic way of life was remarkable." According to Cunliffe, wild Europe disintegrated in the face of increased mobility, connectivity, innovation, and imbalance.

Mobility was stimulated by factors such as growing population, depleted soils, overgrazing, and bloodthirsty invaders. Connectivity was increased as trading networks expanded, often leading to tribal alliances led by cocky warlords. Innovation was the clever process of devising new ways for living farther out of balance with nature, a tireless war on the future. The Neolithic path was a devastating hurricane of imbalances — population growth, inequality, warfare, technological innovation, ecological destruction.

Friendly traders who made it through the gauntlet of pirates and highwaymen delivered wine, weapons, jewelry, furs, smallpox, and the bubonic plague. Diseases delighted in paying regular visits to the filthy, malnourished communities, and providing much needed assistance in resolving family planning imbalances. Slave trading was a major industry.

In central Asia and southern Russia, ancestors of the Aryans hunted the fierce wild horses of the grassy steppes and ate them. Over time, they succeeded in reducing them to submissive beasts, and used them for hunting, herding, trading, and raiding. Before long, Europeans on the plains were periodically being raped, pillaged, and slaughtered by scruffy hordes of horse-mounted Cimmerians, Scythians, Sarmatians, Alans, Huns, Avars, Bulgars, Magyars, and Turks.

Equally catastrophic was the dark art of metalworking, another diabolical gift from the Middle East. The Bronze Age began around 3300 B.C., and the Iron Age arrived around 1200 B.C. The awesome new technology resulted in the deaths of millions of trees and people, and the permanent destruction of many mining regions.

Conflict was the core of the story. Every page I turned unleashed a thousand screams, as jets of hot blood squirted out of the book, forming a sticky puddle around my desk, page after page. They never tired of killing each other. This psychic epidemic — "grow or die" — has now driven us deep into the valley of the shadow of extinction. It's a game we can neither win nor deliberately abandon. Everyone loses.

Native Americans have always been appalled by the immense craziness of the Europeans who washed up on their shores. Ward Churchill says that we suffer from a profound sense of identity confusion, having lost all connection to our tribal roots. John Trudell says we have become disconnected from spiritual reality. We have lost our identity and need to remember who we are. The cave paintings are the strongest medicine we have — wild white folks celebrating the perfection of creation.

Cunliffe's 10,000-year tour tells us almost nothing about tribal Europeans living in relative harmony with the ecosystem, but it exhaustively describes the birth of disharmony, which is useful to understand. Many of the important lessons in life are learned from teachers who demonstrate the wrong way to do something, and the Neolithic Europeans excelled at this, as did their descendants around the world.

They weren't stupid or evil. It's nearly impossible to intentionally stop or turn a complex society that's in motion. They were born in the wrong place at the wrong time, and had little choice but to be swept away by the roaring currents of their era, as we have been. But calmer waters lie downstream, when overshoot passes, and some folks may survive the journey. May they learn well from our mistakes, let the planet heal, and remember who they are.

Megafauna

Baz Edmeades ("ed-meedz") grew up in South Africa. His grandfather, Thomas F. Dreyer, was the paleontologist who discovered an unknown species, *Homo helmei*. The new species was an immediate predecessor of *Homo sapiens*, and it lived 239,000 years ago — in Africa! Europeans, the self-elected master race, naturally assumed that humankind emerged somewhere closer to London. White folks were shocked to realize that they were Africans.

South Africa's Kruger National Park is home to megafauna (large animals) that once inhabited vast regions of the world. Sadly, poachers have been pushing a number of species close to extinction. This drove Edmeades crazy. It inspired him to begin research on a book that became *Megafauna — First Victims of the Human-caused Extinction*.

During the project, he became friends with Paul Martin, who strongly influenced his thinking. Martin was the father of the Pleistocene Overkill hypothesis, which asserted that overhunting was the sole cause for the megafauna extinctions.

Other scholars disagreed. They blamed climate change, and its effects on vegetation. But the extinct species had previously survived a number of big climate swings. Still others blamed disease, a comet strike, or a combination of factors. The issue is highly complex, and there is currently insufficient evidence to confirm a theory, unify the experts, and drive the controversy extinct.

On every continent except Antarctica, there were spasms of megafauna extinctions. They occurred in different regions, at different times, not in synch with climate swings. There is real evidence that humans were not innocent bystanders in these murder mysteries. They likely played a primary role.

In Australia, some say that the species driven to extinction 50,000 years ago were victims of the newly arrived humans. On the islands of New Zealand, Tasmania, Hawaii, Tonga, Madagascar, the Caribbean, and the Mediterranean, extinctions occurred at different times, following the appearance of humans.

Much earlier, Africa suffered a severe spasm of extinctions, long before *Homo sapiens*. The continent was loaded with megafauna 1.8 million years ago, but many were gone by 1.4 million years ago. There used to be nine species of big cats (three today), nine types of elephants (one today), four hippos (one today). There were giant antelopes, giant hyenas, giant pigs, giant monkeys, and giant baboons, all gone.

Some, including Edmeades, blame overhunting for the African extinctions. At the time, our ancestor *Homo erectus* had been busy, inventing a new and improved toolbox — knives, saws, axes, cleavers. This was the Acheulian Revolution. They knew how to use fire, and they may have been the first to use the wooden spear.

In North America, when humans arrived, there were at least nine species of big cats, and seven species of elephants. The biodiversity was incredible — beavers as big as bears, two-ton buffaloes, armadillos the size of VW Beetles. Until 14,000 years ago, mammoth country ranged from Western Europe, across Asia, to Mexico. Aurochs ranged from England to Korea, and south to India and North Africa. Rhinos ranged from Europe to Sumatra. Under downtown London are the remains of hippos, elephants, giant deer, aurochs, and lions, residents of the thriving rainforests of England.

Prior to the spear, our ancestors had been similar to baboons and chimps, scavenging lunch from carnivore kills, and bludgeoning small critters like monkeys and lizards. Over many thousands of years, evolution had gradually made us better hunters. Changes to our bones and muscles improved our ability to accurately hurl projectiles, and kill from a distance. Evolution also improved our long distance running skills. Our ancestors were much slower than antelopes, but we could chase them for hours, until they collapsed from exhaustion.

Before the spear, we acquired new abilities very slowly, *by evolving*. At the same time, other species were also busy evolving new abilities for countering our advances, and maintaining the balance. With our transition to tool making, we began gaining new abilities *by inventing* them, a far quicker process. Spears enabled our ancestors to kill or repel the man-eating predators who kept them from exploding in numbers. This defied the laws of nature. Imagine rabbits inventing tools that allowed them to overpower foxes. With spears, we could also kill large game, acquire abundant meat, and feed more bambinos.

Like the trend of population growth, the trend of techno innovation proceeded slowly for ages, until exploding in recent times. Innovation allowed us to sneak around the checks and balances of evolution, and discover the painful consequences of violating the laws of nature. We invented the ability to dominate and exploit the ecosystem.

All wild animals live in the here and now, paying acute attention to the immediate vicinity. If they get food, they eat; if not, they starve. Amazingly, some tool-making societies eventually developed a sense of foresight. They practiced enlightened self-restraint, which included taboos on overhunting and overbreeding — never-ending responsibilities. Foresight was a slippery path, and some groups slid off into domestication. Unfortunately, societies that master self-restraint are helpless sitting ducks when discovered by unbalanced societies — a serious and perplexing predicament.

What really captured my attention while reading, was realizing the incredible abundance of huge, beautiful, powerful forms of life that once thrived on Earth. It's almost impossible to imagine how spectacularly alive and healthy this planet was in the days before the toolmakers. Today, it feels like we're living in desolate ghost towns, nothing but humans. I can walk alone all night without fear of being eaten. Our soundtrack is the rumbling, roaring, screeching noise of planet-eating machinery — not wolves, hyenas, elephants, elk — the wild music of a wild land.

And so, here we are. We have unluckily inherited a treasure chest of nasty predicaments, all getting worse. Do you think we can somehow find a way to return to ecological harmony by continuing down the path of technology — solar panels, wind turbines, nanotechnology, space exploration, computer-driven cars?

Cultures die. The culture of endless growth and insatiable consumption is moving into its twilight years, as resource limits draw the curtains closed. A muscle-powered future will require a muscle-powered culture. We could resurrect the unsustainable cultures of centuries past, and repeat their blunders. Or, we could learn from their mistakes and try something different and better — like rejoining the family of life, and obeying the laws of nature. Imagine that. What can we do to move in that direction?

Anyway, Edmeades provides a long and fascinating discourse on megafauna extinctions. *Megafauna* is an unfinished work in progress (as of February 2015). The manuscript has not been copyedited, but the text is well written, easy for general readers to understand. Edmeades' deep knowledge of paleontology is obvious, but he lacks credentials in that field. He's a lawyer. Publishers aren't interested in paleontology books written by lawyers, so we can read it for free (www.megafauna.com).

In the Shadow of the Sabertooth

Doug Peacock, the grizzly bear expert, lives near the Yellowstone River in Montana. In 1968, the largest collection of Clovis artifacts was found not far from his home, on the Anzick ranch. The Clovis culture of Native Americans existed for about 300 years, from 13,100 to 12,800 to years ago — during the era of megafauna extinctions. Of the 35 genera of large mammals that went extinct in America, half of them vanished in a 500-year period, from 13,200 to 12,700 years ago.

The Clovis culture developed a new and improved design for the flaked stone points used as spearheads. The long broad sharp points made it much easier to kill large animals, like mammoths and mastodons. Amazingly, this new technology spread to every corner of North America within just 200 years. Clovis points are sometimes found close to the remains of extinct animals. Clovis technology appeared suddenly, and vanished suddenly.

Today, the waters of the Bering Strait separate Siberia from Alaska. During ice ages, sea levels dropped, and the strait became dry land, called Beringia. Around 20,000 years ago, the last era of glaciation peaked. The glaciers made it impossible to travel from Beringia to warmer regions in the south. Few, if any, humans migrated into America prior to 15,000 years ago.

About 14,700 years ago, the climate changed when the Bøling-Allerød warming period began. At that time, sea levels were 450 feet (137 m) lower than today. During the warm period, thawing opened up a corridor to the south, vegetation recovered, and by 13,100 years ago, it became possible to migrate from Beringia to Alberta and northern Montana.

The human immigrants from Siberia did not live at the top of the food chain. They often had lunch dates with hungry sabertooth cats, lions, dire wolves, American cheetahs, grizzlies, and short-faced bears. Short-faced bears weighed a ton, and when they stood on their hind legs, were 15 feet tall (4.5 m). Maybe Clovis points were invented to reduce losses to predators. Better weapons also made it easier to hunt large animals.

After 1492, the early European explorers were astounded by the incredible abundance of wildlife in the Americas, compared to the battered ecosystems back home. But what they saw in America was actually a biosphere that was missing many important pieces. The zenith of American wildlife was prior to 13,000 years ago.

So, the Clovis period began, existed for 300 years, and vanished. It ended when the frigid Younger Dryas period began, 12,800 years ago. The Younger Dryas lasted 1,300 years. When warmer times returned, some clever societies began fooling around with plant and animal domestication, which blew the lid off Pandora's Box. We're still living in this warm phase, an unusually long period of climate stability. We're long overdue for another ice age, but industrial civilization has seriously botched the planet's atmosphere, and we're sliding sideways into an era of ecological helter-skelter.

There are four theories about the megafauna extinctions, and this subject is the source of decades of loud shouting and hair-pulling. One theory asserts that a comet or asteroid strike filled the atmosphere with dust, causing a very long winter. Where's the crater? There is none, because the impact hit a glacier. Why did the short-faced bears vanish, but not the other bears? How did moose, bison, elk, and humans manage to survive?

The disease theory notes that some viral pathogens, like influenza or cowpox, are sometimes able to transfer from one species to another. Maybe species that migrated from Asia smuggled in some virulent viruses. But species-to-species transfers are more likely to happen in confined conditions, like barnyards and livestock herds. During the extinctions, a variety of browsers, grazers, and carnivores disappeared, from an entire continent, in a short stretch of time.

The climate change theory notes that when the Younger Dryas blast freezer moved in 12,800 years ago, the Clovis culture suddenly vanished. Eventually, "nearly every animal over 220 pounds (100 kg) died off and only animals weighing less than that survived this extinction. A notable exception was the grizzly, along with modern bison,

228

moose, elk, caribou, musk ox, polar bear, and chunky humans." Why hadn't numerous earlier ice ages caused similar mass extinctions?

Paul Martin was the father of the Pleistocene overkill theory, which asserts that man, and man alone, was responsible for the unique wave of Late Pleistocene extinctions. He believed that the American extinctions occurred rapidly, in a "blitzkrieg" of overhunting. He argued that across many thousands of years, extinction events corresponded to human colonization — in Australia, the Americas, Tasmania, New Zealand, the Caribbean, and so on.

Hunting clearly played a role, but it's hard to believe that all of the horses and dire wolves living in America were driven to extinction by hunters with spears. Blitzkrieg seems like too strong a word. Unlike mice and bunnies, large mammals have low rates of reproduction. "If hunters remove just 4 or 5 percent of a population of slow-reproducing wildlife, those animals are on a road headed toward extinction." The megafauna extinctions could have occurred gradually, over decades and generations, too slowly to raise alarm.

Climate shifts can spur extinctions. The hills near Peacock's home are red, because pine beetles are killing the whitebark pines. The beetles are thriving because warmer winters enable more to survive. For grizzlies, pine nuts are a dietary staple. He worries that the bears might be driven to extinction by tiny beetles that benefit from the carbon emissions of consumer society.

Let's zoom back to the Clovis site discovered near Peacock's home in 1968. He didn't learn about the site until the mid-1990s. Scientists had hauled away a bunch of artifacts, but didn't return to perform a thorough excavation. Peacock was able to encourage additional work at the site, which began in 1999. This inspired a years-long adventure in learning, which eventually resulted in a book, *In the Shadow of the Sabertooth*.

The Anzick site was the richest discovery of Clovis artifacts. Among the findings was the skeleton of a boy, about 18 months old, the only remains of a Clovis human ever found. It is also the oldest human skeleton found in the Americas. The results of DNA sequencing were published in 2014. "The Montana Clovis people are direct ancestors to some 80 percent of all Native North and South Americans living today." This line came from Northeastern Asia. The boy's genes strongly resemble those of a 24,000-year-old skeleton from Lake Baikal in Central Siberia.

"The one unmistakable lesson of the Late Pleistocene extinction is that human activity combined with global warming is a potential, ageless, deadly blueprint for ecological disaster." Today, the disaster we're creating will be of far greater magnitude, and technology will not be able to rescue us. It's time to rise up and defend this planet.

Coming Home to the Pleistocene

Paul Shepard was a human ecologist and a turbocharged original thinker who spent his life trying to understand (a) how ordinary animals like us managed to evolve into a highly destructive swarm, and (b) what we could do to correct this. Genetic evolution is the primary engine of change for all forms of life, except humans. With humans, cultural evolution has changed us far more, and much faster.

Shepard's research came to conclusions that did not thrill the professors of mainstream academia. He was more or less dismissed as a nutjob. Most of his fame came after he died, when a new generation of fresh minds discovered an underappreciated genius. His masterpiece, *Coming Home to the Pleistocene*, summed up the scholarly pilgrimage of his life. He wrote it as cancer was drawing the curtains on his journey.

The Pleistocene epoch was the era of ice ages. It began somewhere between 2.6 and 1.6 million years ago (definitions vary), and concluded about 11,700 years ago. It was during this time that the hominid line slowly evolved into *Homo sapiens*. Shepard believed that the zenith of the human journey was the Upper (or Late) Pleistocene, 126,000 to 11,700 years ago.

When it ended, the climate had warmed up and stabilized, farmers and herders fell out of the sky, and all hell broke loose. The frantic 10,000-year whirlwind that transformed healthy wild foragers into insatiable consumers is a mere eye blink in the long human voyage. Our genome is mostly unchanged from the Pleistocene, but the cultures of civilization have mutated into a snowballing catastrophe.

Back in the Pleistocene, our wild ancestors lived in a sacred world where everything, both animate and inanimate, was spiritually alive. They were healthy, strong, and had a nutritious diet. They lived in small groups, and were skilled at cooperation, conflict resolution, and sharing. Women were not second-class. Folks spent their entire lives in Big Mama Nature's magnificent wonderland.

Wild people were highly attuned to their ecosystem. They paid acute attention to every scent, sound, and flicker. Because they were both predators and prey, survival required them to pay complete attention to reality, all the time. Unlike the human livestock in corporate cubicle farms, our wild ancestors were intensely alive, and they lived authentically, in the manner for which evolution had fine-tuned them. Even today, all newborns are wild animals, expecting to spend their lives in a wild world. Sadly, while all critters in the cubicle farms have the time-proven genes of Pleistocene hunter-gatherers, they have lost the far wiser cultures of their wild ancestors.

Shepard increasingly comprehended the tragedy of what had been lost: "Through writing and contemplation over the years, I have somehow bonded firmly to those ancient ancestors, their society and ecology, and this kinship has guided my writing and thinking." He spent his boyhood hunting and fishing in rural Missouri. Later he spent two decades in Los Angeles, and this experience undoubtedly sharpened his perceptions of modernity's pathology.

With the arrival of agriculture, folks shifted from *being* nature, to *controlling* nature. We became dependent on the products of domestication, and population clusters swelled and spread. Domestication created "a catastrophic biology of nutritional deficiencies, alternating feast and famine, health and epidemic, peace and social conflict, all set in millennial rhythms of slowly collapsing ecosystems."

Most animals have numerous offspring that mature rapidly, with few surviving to adulthood. Humans have few offspring, we mature slowly, and our lives pass through many phases. Wild cultures guided people through these phases, so that they could smoothly move down the path, living in balance from birth to death. Today, eight-year olds spend much of their time surrounded by other eight-year olds. In wild communities, they normally lived amidst people of all ages. Every day was lived in the presence of the extended family. Grandma and grandpa were never far away, nor were aunties and uncles.

Shepard believed that modern cultures do an especially terrible job at guiding newborns through their first two years, and through the crucial transition from adolescence to adulthood. When a phase is not successfully completed, this failure can permanently arrest the development process. "We slide into adult infantility and its neurotic symptoms," a widespread problem today. Many never develop a mature sense of social responsibility or emotional stability.

Shepard's tour visited a wide variety of other topics. His analysis of pastoralism gave me quite a thump. Domestication replaced intelligent and powerful elk and deer with "total potato-heads" like cattle and sheep. Potato-heads were not sacred wild beings worthy of respect; they were just personal property. The more potato-heads you owned, the bigger man you were. Nothing was more important than status, and it was impossible to have too much.

The enslavement of horses provided a big boost to the careers of ambitious status seekers. It became far easier for mounted warriors to raid other camps, swipe their livestock, and kill anyone who objected. Eventually, the lords of the cavalry joined up with the lords of civilization to conquer vast empires. Few settlements were safe from the raids of mounted warriors. With the growth of civilization, conquered humans were reduced helpless flocks of slaves and serfs that required the surveillance of vigilant shepherds.

When the Navajo acquired potato-heads from the Spanish, their traditional hunting and foraging culture was destroyed, according to James Mischke, a social scientist at Diné College. They became herders of sheep and goats. Horses provided high mobility, and the raiding game led to an era of devastating tribal warfare. "The rise at that time of the hero/warrior was far more disastrous for Navajo society than the advent of colonial militarism two centuries later."

This book is juicy because it presents us with ideas that challenge our glorious heroic myths — at a time when our crazy culture is ravaging the planet. Shepard rips our worldview inside out, and the shocking result presents a reasonable imitation of coherence. Is it possible that our modern consumer wonderland is not, in fact, paradise? Could there really be better ways to live? Are we mentally capable of wrapping our heads around other modes of perception?

Shepard clearly understood that it was impossible for us to march out of our freak show malls and promptly return to a Pleistocene way of life, but he did have powerful dreams that we could heal over time.

Right now, we could begin recovering forgotten social principles and spiritual insights. Right now, we could begin weaning ourselves from addictions and illusions.

He knew that all humans share the same Pleistocene genome, and that our genetic memories all trace back to a common ancestral culture in Africa. Long-term human survival requires that our cultures reintegrate with nature. It's important to understand how we got lost, and where we came from. Shepard tosses us a lump of hopium: "We humans are instinctive culture makers; given the pieces, the culture will reshape itself." That would be nice!

Bonobo: The Forgotten Ape

In the family of life, humankind's two closest living relatives are bonobos and chimpanzees, two apes with strikingly different approaches to living. Ninety-eight percent of our DNA is the same as theirs. With them, we share a common ancestor that lived five to seven million years ago. In his book, *Bonobo: The Forgotten Ape*, primatologist Frans de Waal does a superb job of comparing the three cousins. The photos of Frans Lanting are fantastic.

In Africa, chimps far outnumber bonobos, and inhabit a larger territory. The two never meet in the wild, because apes cannot swim, and the Zaire River keeps them apart. Both reside in dense tropical rainforests, and both sleep in the trees. They are similar in appearance. It wasn't until 1929 that scientists realized that bonobos and chimps were different species.

Bonobos are lucky to live in a dense and rugged rainforest that is difficult for humans to get to, explore, and destroy. Researchers can spend many days thrashing around in the foliage, completely unaware that a group of bonobos is silently looking down at them from the thick canopy above. Bonobos were not studied in the wild until the mid-1970s, and research was interrupted from 1994 to 2003, by a civil war that claimed three million lives. Chimps, on the other hand, have been known and studied for a long time.

During the twentieth century, industrial warfare brutally exterminated millions of humans. For some reason, it became trendy to perceive humans as inherently violent. Chimps were seen in a similar light, because of their resemblance to industrial humans. Once, when two chimp groups came into contact, researchers observed the brutal massacre of the weaker group.

De Waal offered this insight on male chimps: "Their cooperative, action-packed existence resembles that of the human males who, in modern society, team up with other males in corporations within which they compete while collectively fighting other corporations."

Chimps and civilized humans typically live in groups dominated by alpha males who actively subdue their rivals. Females are second-class. When an alpha male chimp reaches retirement age, and is clobbered by a vigorous young upstart, the new alpha often kills the old fellow's youngsters, so their mothers can promptly begin producing offspring with his genes. Because of this, females with young tend to go off and forage alone, avoiding contact with the bloody stud and his buddies.

Bonobos look a lot like chimps, but live very differently. Bonobo groups are matriarchal, and males are second-class. Females determine how food is shared, and they eat while the males wait. Chimps only have sex when a female is fertile. Bonobos have sex almost anytime, several times a day, with anyone interested, young or old, in every imaginable way.

The genitals of female bonobos become enormously swollen when they are receptive to sexual delights. They are receptive almost half of the time, whilst being fertile for just a few days. Non-reproductive sex is an excellent way to defuse conflicts, keep everyone relaxed, and have a pleasant day. Because everyone has sex with everyone, paternity is impossible to determine. Therefore, male bonobos do not kill infants, because any infant might be their offspring.

Hominids have taken a third path, the nuclear family. Long ago, with the arrival of a chilly glacial era, the rainforests we evolved in came close to disappearing. Our ancestors shifted outside the forest. The nuclear family was an adaptation for surviving on the open savannah. Hominid offspring benefitted when their mothers and fathers lived together and cooperated. Tightly knit groups of aggressive hominids could successfully kill game and fend off predators. The strongest, fiercest males were more likely to survive and reproduce, so natural selection favored these traits.

Promiscuity was discouraged, because males did not want to spend their lives raising a rival's offspring. Thus, the nuclear family reduced the reproductive freedom of females, via moral constraints. Hominid societies have probably been male-dominated from the start. Male control further increased with the shift to sedentary living, and the accumulation of property. Males wanted their life savings to be inherited by their own offspring. This led to an obsession with virginity and chastity, and the prickly patriarchal mindset.

Civilized societies have developed patriarchal cultures. "With a few notable exceptions, such as spotted hyenas and the lemurs of Madagascar, male dominance is the standard mammalian pattern." Chimps follow this pattern but, to the great delight of feminists, the discovery of female-dominant bonobo society has presented a less macho alternative. So, who are humans? De Waal says that humans are in the middle, between the two poles — both aggressive and empathetic.

Why are chimps and bonobos so different? Both have low birth rates, and nurse their young for four or five years. But bonobos live in a habitat with abundant food, and no serious competitors in their ecological niche, an ideal situation. Chimps live in leaner lands, and compete for food with gorillas and baboons. They feel the squeeze of crowding, and they reduce this pressure by infanticide, and by killing competitors. Infanticide is common in many species, including lions, prairie dogs, mice, chimps, and gorillas.

We live in an era of extinctions, and the numbers of chimps and bonobos are in sharp decline, as their human cousins relentlessly overbreed and expand. Diamond miners, loggers, bush meat hunters, and war refugees continue pushing into their habitat.

De Waal appeared in a fascinating documentary, *The Last Great Ape* (released in the U.K. as *Bonobo: Missing in Action*). It includes many scenes of bonobos living in the wild. We see them enjoying a pleasant life — eating fruit, having sex, climbing trees, playing, having sex, grooming each other, nursing. In one scene, viewers look down from a plane zooming over the jungle, and the narrator says, "This part of the forest is like a time capsule; bonobos may have existed here in much the same way for two million years." Wow!

Viewers see animals that look like our ancestors, live like our ancestors, and still inhabit the region where our species originated. The bonobos have obviously remained far more stable over two million years than humans have, because they enjoy good luck and exactly enough intelligence to live well in their niche. When I contemplate the era of my 63-year life, and the skyrocketing destruction caused by humankind, it breaks my heart — and mindlessly killing the planet doesn't even make us happy. Big brains do not guarantee long-term stability and ecological sustainability.

Patriarchal chimps have also succeeded in living for two million years, in the same region, in a stable manner. While they rudely offend our humanist and feminist sensibilities, they have evolved a way of living that is thousand times less destructive than that of the humanists and feminists in our insane society.

Clearly, bonobos were dealt an unbeatable hand and won the jackpot. If humans had been dealt a similar hand of luxurious abundance, we'd probably be running around naked in an African paradise, having sex ten times a day. Instead, we got a crap hand — the queen of technology, the joker of excess cleverness, and the ace of self-destruction.

This raises an embarrassing question. Exactly how did we benefit from complex language, literacy, technology, domestication, agriculture, civilization, and industrialization?

Psychic Epidemics

I read the news today, oh boy… we seem to be living in an age of craziness, all around the world. I am reminded of the famous psychologist, Carl Jung, and his notion of psychic epidemics. He was born in 1875, as the Industrial Revolution was turning many societies inside out. It was a gold rush for psychologists, because mental illness was soaring in advanced societies.

Urbanization led to the "insectification" of city dwellers, which fueled the emergence of mental imbalances. The human mind evolved to function nicely in small groups, not large crowds. The neurotic urban hordes bore no resemblance to the Pueblo Indians that Jung had met in New Mexico. He was fascinated by his encounter with these shockingly sane and content humans, and he spoke fondly about them throughout his life.

Three issues spooked Jung. The world wars, with their new and improved technology, took death and destruction to unimaginable new levels. Nuclear war was a big threat, but it was avoidable, in theory. What scared him most was population growth, a runaway train with no brakes. World population nearly doubled in his lifetime. It had soared to almost three billion when he died in 1961.

Jung was horrified by the rise of Hitler. Danger grows when large crowds are manipulated by a few people. Germany suffered from an inferiority complex following its defeat in the First World War. The collective unconscious of the Germans begged for a savior, a Messiah. Hitler helped them compensate for their shame by leading them on a heroic adventure in megalomania. He had a remarkable ability for bringing the nation's unconscious into his conscious awareness. He told the people exactly what they wanted to hear.

After Hitler's defeat, Jung concluded, "The phenomenon we have witnessed in Germany was nothing less than the first outbreak of epidemic insanity, an eruption of the unconscious into what seemed to be a tolerably well-ordered world." I don't believe that this was "the first" such epidemic. Many, like the Inquisition, preceded the Nazis.

Jung died 55 years ago, before the first Earth Day. Since his death, population has more than doubled again, and continues to soar. Climate change is getting warmed up for unleashing centuries of big surprises. The sixth mass extinction is now officially recognized. The list of ongoing catastrophes is long and growing.

Consumer society's lack of response to numerous devastating predicaments is incomprehensible. We generally ignore it all, and live as if we were the last generation. Our social status and trendy lifestyle habits must be fully preserved at any cost. The Earth Crisis feels like the mother of all psychic epidemics, making the Nazis look like naughty peewee league delinquents.

Jung was perplexed by the notion of consciousness, a slippery concept. Consciousness includes being aware of what our senses are telling us about the here and now. It allows us to think about people and events in different times and places, and share this knowledge with others. We are very self aware, and know that we will die. We can think in words, and use words to assemble reasoned concepts and abstract ideas.

Among our wild ancestors, the development of consciousness was minimal. They had what Jung called the "original mind." A wild lad could put on a lion mask and literally become a lion, in his mind. Modern insurance salespeople can't do this, because they have been trained in the differentiated consciousness of civilization, which makes the original mind unconscious.

Jung believed that consciousness in humans developed slowly over a very long time. By 4000 B.C., consciousness in civilized societies was approaching its modern form. He noted that primitive people were less conscious than we are. At the same time, even in its advanced form, consciousness remains highly unstable, far from finished. Consciousness is merely the mind's thin surface, floating on an unconscious ocean. Throughout every day, our minds flutter in and out of consciousness, frequently drifting off into daydreams and fantasies. Conscious thought is tiresome, requiring deliberate effort, while fantasyland is effortless.

Education factories indoctrinate students with the notion that reason is the guiding force in our nation's affairs. But our ability to reason is flimsy. Like the Germans of the 1930s, we are always vulnerable to slick talking advertisers, politicians, and woo-woo hucksters. Those with skills for prodding unconscious fears, doubts, and desires will find many sitting ducks to corral and exploit. Here's my favorite Jung line: "Our present lives are dominated by the goddess Reason, who is our greatest and most tragic illusion."

Jung was an important pioneer in exploring the unconscious, home of the ancestral soul, which stores content that is millions of years old. We drift into the unconscious whenever we dream, or daydream. When we remember dreams, we can bring unconscious content into the realm of our consciousness. This content can provide important guidance, or solutions to inner conflicts. Instinct can often see the elephant that the conscious mind blocks out. Instinct is our ally.

Jung believed that our loss of instinct created many huge problems in modern society. We are cut off from our roots, making us childish and infantile. Some primitive people remain connected to their ancient instincts, and are therefore more stable. Their dreams guide them through life. They inhabit a reality that is sacred, beautiful, and alive with wonder.

Non-human animals obviously have some degree of consciousness, but a form far different from that of the glowing screen people. Unlike many domesticated critters, wild animals are not neurotic basket cases. Nor are primitive people, who do not suffer from advanced stages of consciousness. People with advanced consciousness have conquered the Earth, but Jung could not escape the painful paradox that consciousness is "both the highest good and the greatest evil."

Sometimes, Jung wondered if the solution was to deliberately pursue the further development of consciousness, complete our unfinished quest, and become perfectly reasonable. But based on his long experience with many damaged souls, this notion seemed to be ridiculous and impossible. At the same time, returning to animal unconsciousness was not an option.

But we are, in fact, animals. When we squirted out of the womb, our standard issue equipment included an animal mind, with an excellent instinct collection. This mind was fully capable of spending its entire existence operating without words, tools, fire, or clothing, like all other animal minds.

In both wild kids, and kids born in captivity, rudimentary self-aware consciousness (ego) emerges when a child is about four. Kids born in civilization go on to absorb a highly unstable civilization-grade form of consciousness.

For Jung, the magic word was *individuation*, which means becoming who you are, like a unique acorn develops into a unique oak tree. Every newborn is a unique being, not a blank slate. The mass mind of industrial society could care less about that unique being. The mass mind expects everyone to become robo-consumers. But the ancient original mind expects us to use our gifts, and pursue our calling. Individuation allows us to develop a strong and healthy relationship with the rest of the family of life, so we can avoid being swept away by psychic epidemics.

Individuation does not happen automatically, it requires effort to set foot on your own path. Our ancestors benefitted from initiation ceremonies, in which adolescents received important visions that revealed their identities and destinies. Modern society provides no such assistance, hence the mobs of robo-consumers.

People will go to ridiculous extremes to avoid facing their own souls. The path to healing requires looking inward. Deliberately move away from the torrents of distractions that bombard our society. Seek solitude, nature, imagination, and intuition. Intuition is perception via the unconscious. It opens channels to the unconscious, and draws up the life. Humankind has enormous conflicts to resolve. The experts of our society are largely out to lunch, still lost in toxic hallucinations of perpetual growth and material wealth.

So, Jung does not give us the secret formula for mass enlightenment and a heavenly utopia. Instead, he gives us a mirror. Humankind can only heal individual by individual. There are mountains of books describing the ecological damage we cause. Far less attention has been given to the psychological twists and turns that have brought us to the brink. Maybe we don't need to study Mars.

Epilogue

So, here we are in the twenty-first century. We are not a generation born wild and free, running around naked in lush tropical rainforests, nibbling on fruit, nuts, and grubs. We inherited an age of challenges, the result of a long string of risky experiments. Negative consequences have piled up over the centuries, and we now stand in the dark shadow of a mountain of predicaments.

Humans are not cursed with defective genes, but we have succeeded in creating a highly unsustainable way of living and thinking — a defective culture. The clock is running out on this troublesome experiment. It would be wise to acknowledge this, and mindfully explore saner ways of living and thinking.

Like all other animals, humans focus their attention on the here and now, the immediate vicinity. Many animals are capable of foresight. Some know that panthers hunt at night, so they sleep in the trees. With regard to the manmade realm of techno-innovation, foresight is largely impossible. Nobody could have imagined the enormous consequences of metal making, fossil energy, or the domestication of plants and animals. A few wild cultures still live sustainably with barely any technology.

Low impact cultures do not believe in human superiority. They do not suffer from a persistent itch to hoard personal property. They have exactly what they need. They do not control and exploit the ecosystem, they adapt to it. They have time-proven cultures in which everyone practices voluntary self-restraint. In this manner, they could enjoy extended periods of real sustainability, living in a healthy wild ecosystem.

High impact cultures, by definition, cannot have a long-term future. In their spooky fantasies, the primary goal is to pursue economic growth, by any means necessary, for as long as possible, without regard for the generations yet to come. Nothing is more important than perpetual growth, at any cost. This is the dominant paradigm in consumer societies, where it is perceived to be perfectly normal and intelligent.

But deviants on the fringe, who enjoy an amazing ability to recognize the obvious, warn us that normal is insane. For revealing this inconvenient truth, they are called doomers. But the consumer hordes, who are enthusiastic lifelong participants in the most destructive culture in human history, are the true champions of doom.

Consumers are annoyed by the truth tellers, and denounce them for their negativity, but it's actually the other way around. Sending tons and tons of waste to landfills, via a lifetime of recreational shopping, in an effort to gain social status, is a heartbreaking tragedy. It's a path of ferocious negativity.

The truth-telling deviants are not doomers; they are simply more present in reality. For them, the foolishness in our culture becomes less invisible. Being present in reality, in the fullness of the darkness, puts them in a far better position to think clearly and make wise decisions. They become less vulnerable to peer pressure. They become less willing to mindlessly do what a mindless society expects of them.

In the process of healing from acute ignorance, you cross a painful threshold. One day, you realize that the consumer fantasyland has little relationship with reality. Big storms are coming, and the future will not be a prosperous and pleasurable joyride — a painful realization.

When this occurs, despair is an appropriate response. It's OK to grieve for the loss of a major long-held illusion. At the same time, it's also appropriate to celebrate your mind-expanding awakening, your successful escape from the realm of the living dead. Despair is like a hangover, a painful headache resulting from an unhealthy binge. It's a normal temporary experience on the long journey to growth and healing.

The consumers scream, "We can't go back," and that's true. We also cannot indefinitely remain on our current dead-end path. John Trudell, the Santee Sioux activist, summed it up nicely. "There is no old way, no new way. There is a way of life. We must live in balance with the Earth. We must do it. We have no choice."

Eight words precisely describe the one and only sustainable destination, "We must live in balance with the Earth." This sacred destination has never been farther from where we now stand. So, what should animals with legendary big brains be doing? Obviously, we need to change how we think and live.

At the moment, consumer society feels little or no desire to critically question its mode of living and thinking. Many have chugged the Kool-Aid of the techno-wizards, and have a blind faith in the wondrous solutions promised by clever experts. Many others have little or no understanding of reality, because they suffer from ignorance, or a limited ability to think. Still others can sense the growing darkness, but are paralyzed with fear and powerlessness, and block out the yucky feelings with false hope.

Nothing can stop the coming storms of change, all paths lead to turbulence. Because collapse will bring the death machine to its knees, it's a necessary phase in the healing process, but it won't be fun. You can't save the world. You can't fix everything, but you can use your gifts, and do what you can to confront ignorance, protect your ecosystem, and lessen the long-term damage. There are infinite opportunities for doing beneficial work.

It's time for unlearning, identifying the silly nonsense we've absorbed over the years, and hurling it overboard. It's time for learning, continuing our exploration of reality. It's time for communicating, helping each other learn. It's time to get outdoors, without electronic distractions, and develop an intimate relationship with the planet of our birth. It's time to grow and heal.

We are living in the most momentous century in the entire human experience. It will be a time of immense learning and awakening. As our glorious house of cards disintegrates, we will experience a beautiful die-off — countless idiotic myths, fantasies, and illusions will lose their hypnotic power, tumble into the tar pits, and never again entrance us.

It will be a century of huge lessons, an era of tremendous enlightenment. No, climate change was not a hoax! Yes, there really are limits! Concepts like carrying capacity and overshoot will become well understood by any who survive. The powerful storms of the Great Healing will inspire a rising tide of questioning, critical thinking, and clear understanding.

No matter what we do, the Great Healing will eliminate a number of key predicaments, even if we don't change our ways. Whether or not we get serious about rapid population reduction, the current population bubble will become an ex-predicament. Finite resources will certainly strangle the mass hysteria of consumer mania. As we move beyond the era of climate stability, every ecosystem will be hammered by big changes. The consumer lifestyle will no longer be an option.

Big Mama Nature has little tolerance for overshoot. One way or another, sooner or later, some form of balance will be restored, with or without us. But if we summon our power, and strive to live with responsibility, we may be able to prevent some destruction. It's essential to understand the mistakes that got us into this mess, so we will not be tempted to repeat them. Learn! Think! Heal!

Bibliography

Abbey, Edward, *Desert Solitaire*, Simon & Shuster, New York, 1990.

Alley, William M. and Alley, Rosemarie, *Too Hot to Touch*, Cambridge University Press, New York, 2013.

Anderson, M. Kat, *Tending the Wild*, University of California Press, Berkeley, 2005.

Armstrong, Jeanette and Hall, David E., *Native Perspectives on Sustainability: Jeanette Armstrong*, 2007. www.nativeperspectives.net

Bartlett, Albert A., The Essential Exponential, Center for Science, Mathematics & Computer Education, University of Nebraska, Lincoln, 2004. Similar essays at www.albartlett.org

Basalla, George, *The Evolution of Technology*, Cambridge University Press, New York, 1988.

Basso, Keith H., *Wisdom Sits in Places*, University of New Mexico Press, Albuquerque, 1996.

Bolster, W. Jeffrey, *The Mortal Sea*, The Belknap Press, Cambridge, Massachusetts, 2012.

Bourne, Joel K., *The End of Plenty*, W. W. Norton & Company, New York, 2015.

Brody, Hugh, *The Other Side of Eden*, North Point Press, New York, 2001.

Brown, Lester R., *Who Will Feed China?*, W. W. Norton & Company, New York, 1995.

Carson, Rachel, *Silent Spring*, Houghton Mifflin Company, New York, 2002.

Carter, Vernon Gill and Dale, Tom, *Topsoil and Civilization*, University of Oklahoma Press, Norman, 1974.

Catton, William R., *Overshoot*, University of Illinois Press, Urbana, 1980.

Childs, Craig, *Apocalyptic Planet*, Pantheon Books, New York, 2012.

Cohen, Mark Nathan, *The Food Crisis in Prehistory*, Yale University Press, New Haven, 1977.

Cribb, Julian, *The Coming Famine*, University of California Press, Berkeley, 2010.

Cronon, William, *Changes in the Land*, Hill and Wang, New York, 1983.

Cunliffe, Barry, *Europe Between the Oceans: 9000 BC – AD 1000*, Yale University Press, New Haven, 2008.

Dasmann, Raymond F., *The Destruction of California*, The MacMillan Company, New York, 1965.

Davis, Wade, *The Wayfinders*, Anansi Press, Toronto, 2009.

Edmeades, Baz, *Megafauna*, 2013, www.megafauna.com

Ehrlich, Gretel, *This Cold Heaven*, Pantheon Books, New York, 2001.

Ehrlich, Paul R., *The Population Bomb*, Ballantine, New York, 1968.

Ehrlich, Paul R. and Ehrlich, Anne H., *The Population Explosion*, Simon & Schuster, New York, 1990.

Fagan, Brian, *Cro-Magnon*, Bloomsbury Press, New York, 2010.

Fagan, Brian, *The Great Warming*, Bloomsbury Press, New York, 2008.

Finlayson, Clive, *The Humans Who Went Extinct*, Oxford University Press, New York, 2009.

Flannery, Tim, *The Future Eaters*, George Braziller, New York, 1995.

Funk, McKenzie, *Windfall*, Penguin Press, New York, 2014.

Gore, Albert, *The Future*, Random House, New York, 2013.

Gray, John, *Straw Dogs*, Granta Books, London, 2003.

Griffiths, Jay, *A Country Called Childhood*, Counterpoint, Berkeley, 2014. Titled *Kith* in the U.K.

Griffiths, Jay, *A Sideways Look at Time*, Jeremy P. Tarcher, New York, 1999.

Griffiths, Jay, *Savage Grace*, Counterpoint, Berkeley, 2015. Titled *Wild* in the U.K.

Gunther, John, *Inside Africa*, Harper & Brothers, New York, 1953.

Hardin, Garrett, "Extension of the Tragedy of the Commons," *Science*, 1 May 1998, Vol. 280, no. 5364, pp. 682-683.

Hardin, Garrett, *Living Within Limits*, Oxford University Press, New York, 1993.

Hardin, Garrett, *The Ostrich Factor*, Oxford University Press, New York, 1998.

Heinberg, Richard, *Afterburn*, New Society Publishers, Gabriola Island, British Columbia, 2015.

Heinberg, Richard, *Snake Oil*, Post Carbon Institute, Santa Rosa, California, 2013.

Hopkins, Rob, *The Transition Handbook*, Chelsea Green, White River Junction, Vermont, 2008.

Huesemann, Michael and Huesemann, Joyce, *Techno-Fix*, New Society Publishers, Gabriola Island, B.C., Canada, 2011.

Jung, C. G., ed., *Man and His Symbols*, Doubleday & Company, New York, 1979.

Jung, C. G., *Memories, Dreams, Reflections*, Vintage Books, New York, 1965.

Jung, C. G., Sabini, Meredith, ed., *The Earth Has a Soul*, North Atlantic Books, Berkeley, 2008.

Kimmerer, Robin Wall, *Braiding Sweetgrass*, Milkweed Editions, Minneapolis, 2013.

Kolbert, Elizabeth, *The Sixth Extinction*, Henry Holt and Company, New York, 2014.

Korn, Larry, *One-Straw Revolutionary*, Chelsea Green, White River Junction, Vermont, 2015.

Leopold, Aldo, *A Sand County Almanac*, Oxford University Press, New York, 1989.

Leslie, Jacques, *Deep Water*, Farrar, Straus and Giroux, New York, 2005.

Liedloff, Jean, *The Continuum Concept*, Addison-Wesley, New York, 1977.

Little, Charles E., *The Dying of the Trees*, Viking, New York, 1995.

Lockwood, Jeffrey A., *Locust*, Basic Books, New York, 2004.

Lowdermilk, Walter, *Conquest of the Land Through Seven Thousand Years*, Soil Conservation Service, Washington D.C., 1948. (Free download)

MacKinnon, J. B., *The Once and Future World*, Houghton Mifflin Harcourt, New York, 2013.

Marsh, George Perkins, *Man and Nature*, Harvard University Press, Cambridge, 1965. (Free download)

Mayfield, Thomas Jefferson, *Indian Summer*, Heyday Books, Berkeley, 1993 (1929).

McGuire, William and Hull, R. F. C., eds., *C. G. Jung Speaking*, Princeton University Press, Princeton, 1977.

McKibben, Bill, *The End of Nature*, Random House, New York, 2006.

McNeill, J. R., *Something New Under the Sun*, W. W. Norton & Company, New York, 2000.

McNeill, J. R. and McNeill, William H., *The Human Web*, W. W. Norton & Company, New York, 2003.

McNeill, William H., *Plagues and Peoples*, Anchor Books, New York, 1998.

Meadows, Donella; Randers, Jorgen; and Meadows, Dennis, *Limits to Growth — The 30-Year Update*, Chelsea Green, White River Junction, Vermont, 2004.

Monbiot, George, *Feral*, Allen Lane, London, 2013.

Nelson, Richard K., *Make Prayers to the Raven*, University of Chicago Press, Chicago, 1983.

Peacock, Doug, *Grizzly Years*, Henry Holt and Company, New York, 2011.

Peacock, Doug, *In the Shadow of the Sabertooth*, Counterpunch, Petrolia, California, 2014.

Perlin, John, *A Forest Journey*, Harvard University Press, Cambridge, 1993.

Plumwood, Val, edited by Shannon, Lorraine, *The Eye of the Crocodile*, Australian National University Press, Canberra, 2012. Free download: http://epress.anu.edu.au

Pritchard, Evan T., *No Word for Time*, Council Oak Books, San Francisco, 1997.

Rasmussen, Knud, *Across Arctic America*, G.P. Putnams Sons, New York, 1927.

Rasmussen, Knud, *The People of the Polar North*, Kegan Paul, Trench, Trübner & Co., London, 1908.

Reisner, Marc, *Cadillac Desert*, Penguin Books, New York, 1986.

Rubin, Jeff, *The Big Flatline*, Palgrave Macmillan, New York, 2012.

Shapiro, Judith, *Mao's War Against Nature*, Cambridge University Press, New York, 2001.

Shepard, Paul, *Coming Home to the Pleistocene*, Island Press, Covelo, California, 1998.

Shepard, Paul, *Encounters With Nature*, Island Press, Washington, D. C., 1999.

Shepard, Paul, *The Tender Carnivore*, University of Georgia Press, Athens, Georgia, 1998.

Shepard, Paul, *Thinking Animals*, University of Georgia Press, Atlanta, 1978.

Shepard, Paul, *Where We Belong*, University of Georgia Press, Atlanta, 2003.

Stolzenburg, William, *Where the Wild Things Were*, Bloomsbury, New York, 2008.

Stringer, Chris, *Lone Survivors*, Times Books, New York, 2012.

Thoreau, Henry David, *The Maine Woods*, Ticknor & Fields, Boston, 1864. (Free download)

Thoreau, Henry David, *Walden*, Ticknor & Fields, Boston, 1854. (Free download)

Trainer, Ted, *Renewable Energy Cannot Sustain a Consumer Society*, Springer, Dordrecht, The Netherlands, 2007. http://simplicityinstitute.org

Turner, Jack, *The Abstract Wild*, University of Arizona Press, Tucson, 1996.

Waal, Frans de, *Bonobo*, University of California Press, Berkeley, 1997.

Wilson, Richard Leland, "The Pleistocene Vertebrates of Michigan," *Papers of the Michigan Academy of Science, Arts, and Letters*, Vol. LII, 1967.

Wolff, Robert, *Original Wisdom*, Inner Traditions, Rochester, Vermont, 2001. http://wildwolff.com

Index